# Middle East Studies
## History, Politics, and Law

*Edited by*
Shahrough Akhavi
University of South Carolina

A Routledge Series

MIDDLE EAST STUDIES: HISTORY, POLITICS, AND LAW
SHAHROUGH AKHAVI, *General Editor*

NEW PYTHIAN VOICES
*Women Building Political Capital in NGOs in the Middle East*
Cathryn S. Magno

TURKEY IN GERMANY
*The Transnational Sphere of Deutschkei*
Betigül Ercan Argun

ISLAMIC LAW, EPISTEMOLOGY AND MODERNITY
*Legal Philosophy in Contemporary Iran*
Ashk P. Dahlén

# Gender, Literacy, and Empowerment in Morocco

Fatima Agnaou

Routledge
Taylor & Francis Group
NEW YORK AND LONDON

Published in 2004 by
Routledge
711 Third Avenue
New York, NY 10017
www.routledge-ny.com

Published in Great Britain by
Routledge
2 Park Square, Milton Park
Abingdon, Oxon OX14 4RN
www.routledge.co.uk

*Routledge is an imprint of the Taylor & Francis Group, an informa business*

First issued in paperback 2012



10 9 8 7 6 5 4 3 2

Library of Congress Cataloging-in-Publication Data

Agnaou, Fatima.
Gener, literacy, and empowerment in Morocco / Fatima Agnaou.
p. cm.
Includes bibliographical references (p. ) and index.
ISBN 0-415-94765-0 (alk. paper)
1. women—Education—Morocco. 2. Literacy—Morocco. 3. Women—Morocco—Social conditions. 4. Women—Morocco—Economic conditions. I. title. II. Series: Middle East studies (Routledge (Firm)).
LC2472.2.A36 2003
370'.82'0964—dc21 200203009731

ISBN13: 978-0-415-94765-7 (hbk)
ISBN13: 978-0-415-64793-9 (pbk)

# Contents

# Acknowledgments

The study this book reports on was PhD research financed by WOTRO, the Netherlands Foundation for the Advancement of Tropical Research, which I highly acknowledge. It was co-supervised by Professor Fatima Sadiqi from the University of Mohammed Ben Abdellah, Fès, Morocco and Professor Jan Jaap De Ruiter from the University of Tilburg, the Netherlands. Many thanks are due to both professors for their guidance and stimulating feedback.

I am also indebted to the personnel of the Adult Literacy Directorate and the office staff of the visited centers who provided me with a number of interesting official documents and who gave me permission to do field work. My thanks go also to the research group of the UFR: Langue, Culture et Education, directed by Professor Ahmed Boukous at the Faculté des Lettres, University Mohammed V, for their interesting comments and feedback.

Special appreciation is extended to the informants, both learners and teachers, who participated in the study for their gracious help and co-operation. In particular, I want to thank my mother who not only transgressed tradition and sent me to school but was my first informant as well.

I also wish to thank CODESRIA for awarding me a fellowship and affording me training in quantitative analyses in Senegal.

I am also grateful to Professor Linda Rashidi from Mansfield University of Pennsylvania and Professor Jilali Saib, formerly from Mohammed V University and currently Director at the Royal Institute of the Amazigh Culture, for their help with proofreading some chapters of this book.

# List of Tables and Figures

# Introduction

## Investigating Women's Literacy in Morocco

Women's literacy has become a priority target of many developing countries since WCEFA, the *World Conference on Education for All,* which was held in Jomtien, Thailand, in March 1990. The conference acknowledges the need to reduce the gender gap in illiteracy by encouraging and ensuring girls' and women's education. Accordingly, non-governmental and voluntary associations in Morocco joined the government's efforts to combat female illiteracy. It is to be noted, though, that ten years after WCEFA, two million Moroccan children were left out of primary school and female illiteracy has decreased only moderately, as it is still as high as 60 percent at the national level and 80 percent at the rural one.

In fact, although great, the effort to reduce female illiteracy in Morocco remains inefficient and this is, partly, due to high drop-out rates. By way of example, on the eve of the undertaking of this research, the drop out rate was as high as 72 percent (Proceedings of la Direction de la Lutte contre l'Analphabétisme, 1997). Evidently, the challenge is not only how to attract girls and women, who due to the gender gap in education constitute the majority of the participants in Moroccan adult literacy campaigns and programs, but how to retain them and sustain their motivations. Given this context, where retaining women in adult literacy classes is problematic, there is conjecture that the designed courses do not answer their needs. This creates a rationale for carrying a comprehensive needs analysis research that is centred on women by identifying their profiles, the causes of their illiteracy and dropping out of the literacy classes, assessing their literacy needs and attainments, and analyzing the teaching materials through which they are made literate.

Given the importance of the foregoing issues for the formulation of effective policies and the designing of appropriate programs, and hoping for some contribution, they are investigated inclusively in this book in the form of a set of four research questions, composed of diverse sub-questions:

*What are the characteristics of the female participants in adult literacy programs? And what are the causes of their illiteracy and dropping out of the literacy course?*

*What are their literacy needs and learning needs? And to what extent are these needs satisfied by the designed program?*

*To what extent do they master what they have learned? Are they able to apply what they have learned to deal with the everyday literacy tasks they seek to learn through their participation in the literacy course? And what are the variables that affect their literacy attainment?*

*To what extent is the ascribed content consonant with a perspective that seeks women's empowerment?*

One practical rationale for dealing with these research questions (RQs) is to see whether the female beneficiaries of the literacy courses under study are prepared to process printed information encountered in daily life through a training which answers their literacy needs and ensures their empowerment.

Data related to women's literacy needs and the causes of their illiteracy are drawn from a sample of 204 current participants in Moroccan adult literacy courses. 140 graduate learners and forty post-literate graduates are investigated to assess their literacy attainments through a basic test and a functional literacy test. Seventy-five former adult literacy beneficiaries are interviewed on the causes of their dropping-out of the literacy course and three textbooks are analyzed to gain insight into how much space is given to women and the way they are portrayed in the designed teaching materials. For more details on the adopted methodology and design, see chapter 4.

One theoretical rationale for the present work consists in its contribution to the major debate on the view and definition of literacy. Researchers such as Jones (1990) and Wagner (1992) claim that wastage and errors in adult literacy programming can be avoided if greater attention is paid to the definition of literacy. Eventually, the definition of literacy is at the heart of any policy decision related to adult literacy programming. Perhaps the most urgent need is to seek answers to the following complex but interesting questions: what is literacy? What are its functions and goals? How is literacy perceived by the target learner and the program designer? Is literacy seen as an end in itself, whereby the learner possesses the skills of reading, writing, and numeracy? Is literacy seen as a means of social and community improvement by the application of the new skills and knowledge acquired through literacy? Or is literacy something even more profound, such as consciousness-raising?

By dealing with adult literacy as basic, functional and empowering within a framework that considers female literacy as a necessary means to answer women's *practical* and *strategic* needs (Molyneux, 1987; cited in Stromquist, 1987) and by assessing the learners' perceived literacy needs and the literacy designers' ascribed target needs, it is hoped that the present book will contribute to an understanding of the concept of literacy and its relation to gender and empowerment. Investigation of the learners' characteristics, literacy obstacles and attainments bear relevance to other diverse but crucial issues related to literacy efforts directed to adults in general and women in particular, namely, the feminization of illiteracy, the diversity versus the uniformity of adult literacy courses, language and literacy, literacy acquisition, literacy materials, and obstacles to literacy. For a detailed relevance of the present work and the issues it addresses, see chapter 1.

The present book deals with women's literacy in Morocco in nine chapters. The first chapter gives a quick review of the research that has been carried out outside and inside Morocco and highlights the present study's contribution to the field of adult literacy in general and female literacy in particular. The second chapter presents the conceptual framework that is adopted. As already explained the research investigates female literacy as basic, functional and empowering. The aim of chapter 2 is to explain these concepts of literacy and present the ways they have been measured in previous research in general and in the present work in particular. The third chapter informs the reader on the planning and organization of the Moroccan adult literacy campaigns and programs since Independence in 1956. The fourth chapter describes the methodology and the research design used in the collection and analyses of data. More specifically, it explains the research design, measuring instruments, and statistical techniques used in the investigation of the issues addressed in this book. The fifth chapter consists of a description of the learners' profiles and literacy obstacles. It presents the characteristics of the informants of the present research, and analyzes the causes of their illiteracy and obstacles to their effective participation in the literacy courses as addressed by the first research question (RQ1) given above. The sixth chapter comprises data on the learners' literacy and learning needs. It reviews the theories of need in adult education and uses them as a background against which it surveys both the target and the learning needs of the present study's informants (RQ2). The seventh chapter provides quantitative and qualitative analyses of the learners' ability to handle in-school literacy and everyday literacy and investigates some predictor variables that significantly affect such ability (RQ3). The eighth chapter is devoted to an analysis of the learners' empowerment through the literacy content. In so doing, it investigates the textbooks used in literacy classes within gender-based theories, which deny any forms of sexism and discrimination (RQ4). The last chapter summarizes the objectives, the methodology and the findings of the research. It also considers the limitations of this work and discusses its theoretical and practical implications for the design of gender-based literacy programming in Morocco.

1

# Literacy, Gender, and Empowerment

## The State of the Art

The present chapter attempts to review studies on adult literacy. One aim is to gain cognizance of the main issues pertaining to literacy research and gender and insights from the findings made by previous scholars. Another is to provide the necessary theoretical and methodological background for the issues undertaken in this book. In so doing, this chapter highlights the present study's contribution to the field of adult literacy in general and female literacy in particular.

### ADULT LITERACY RESEARCH AND GENDER: A BRIEF OVERVIEW

The literature abounds with adult literacy studies that are of both a theoretical and a practical nature. Educationalists and psychologists investigate literacy in terms of the possession of the basic skills of reading, writing, and computing through standardized achievement testing (Lytle and Wolfe, 1989; Newman and Beverstock, 1990; Beder, 1991). Cognitive psychologists examine the power that has been ascribed to literacy as a skill in highlighting the importance of literacy in the building of the cognitive and psychological faculties of the illiterate (Vygotsky, 1962; Goody, 1968; Scribner and Cole, 1981). Anthropologists observe the cultural constructions of literacy and its practices among specific cultural groups (Heath, 1983; Reder, 1987). Comparative historians analyze conceptions of literacy as they change over time (Arnove and Graff, 1987; Stedman and Kaestle, 1991). Politicians of education and pedagogy address the question of literacy as a prerequisite for the changing of the stratified structure of society and as a liberating process for the oppressed masses (Freire, 1970a; Freire, 1970b; Mezirow, 1978; Dave, 1985). Linguists tackle the problem of language choice in terms of mother tongue versus national language in adult literacy programs (Bowers, 1968; Dumont, 1973; Bamgbose, 1976; Shrivastava, 1980; Shaw, 1983; Coulmas, 1984). Methodologists provide guidelines regarding the use of the instruments assessing literacy (Couvert, 1979). Socio-economists of education deal with the issue of literacy as a means of the socialisation of the individual and his or her integration in the labour market (Ehrighaus, 1990; Stercq, 1993; Al-Saadate, 1993). Assessment specialists assess literacy attainments in terms of the number of years spent in school, the number of enrolments, dropping outs, and graduates, and auto-evaluation (UNESCO reports, national census ) or in terms of effective application of the acquired skills (Kirsch and Jungleblut, 1986; Ziegahn, 1990). Other scholars within this perspective describe and assess the effectiveness of literacy campaign experiences across countries (Bhola, 1984; Arnove and Graff, 1987; De Clerck, 1993). Finally, gender scholarship address the question of literacy as a means of redressing women's condition and position and as a way of attaining justice, equity and gender equality (Molyneux, 1987; Stromquist, 1987; Kazemek, 1988; Ramdas, 1989; Carmack, 1992).

This brief overview of adult literacy studies highlights the diversity of the disciplines that have dealt with the subject of adult literacy outside Morocco. These include psychology, sociology, anthropology, history, linguistics, economics, education, politics and gender. A consideration of the publication dates of the studies presented above shows that interest in adult literacy evolved from the early seventies. In fact, special interest in adult literacy started with the publication of the works of Paulo Freire, who came up with critical theory and pedagogy in the field of adult literacy research. His studies '*Adult Literacy Process as a Cultural Action for Freedom*' (1970a) and '*The Pedagogy of the Oppressed*' (1970b) carry revolutionary perspectives in the direction of adult literacy. The author's conception of literacy consists of stimulating the adult learners' awareness of the conditions that perpetuate their oppression and providing them with new ways of transforming what is oppressive to gain full empowerment.

Empowerment as related to gender evolved from women's movements in the mid 1970s with the first world conference on women in 1975. This conference gave birth to CEFDAW, *the Convention on the Elimination of All Forms of Discrimination Against Women*, in 1979. The main article of the convention pleads for the promotion of equality between the sexes and claims women's rights. Interest in gender and literacy followed in the eighties when gender scholarship strongly advocated Freire's *emancipatory* conception of literacy and began to explore the place of women in society, question their oppression and marginalisation and fight for equity through literacy. In this vein, Molyneux (1987; cited in Stromquist, 1987) distinguishes between *practical gender inter-*

*ests* and *strategic gender interests*, where the former are linked to women's basic needs like employment and family. The latter, on the other hand, are linked to women's empowerment as they seek to redress their condition within and outside the family, to combat discrimination, oppression and violence against women, and promote their political participation. This distinction between women's condition (*practical interests)* and position (*strategic interests*) engendered the impetus for research on gender and literacy.

Drawing on Molyneux's *gender interests*, Stromquist (1987) claims that literacy instruction directed to women must undergo drastic changes so as to make them *emancipatory* and *empowering*. Likewise, Kazemek (1988) stresses the importance of rethinking and restructuring adult literacy instruction from a gender perspective. Convinced that the underlying causes of women's illiteracy and the gender lag in education find their origins in certain political and socioeconomic arrangements in society, Ramdas (1989) calls for heightening men's awareness to question the traditional values and attitudes toward women and criticizes male dominance in literacy policy making. In so doing, she questions the relevance of literacy campaigns addressed to women and suggests that they should draw on Molyneux's *gender strategic interests*. In the same vein, Carmack (1992) states that Freire's theory of change and social transformation should be adopted by gender studies to address women's issues in terms of oppression, discrimination and inequity and redress their position through the design of gender specific programming that are based on *emancipatory* learning.

## THE NEED FOR MORE RESEARCH

The emancipatory theorizing of women's literacy has not been accompanied by empirical research on the *feminization* of illiteracy. In fact, women constitute the undereducated majority worldwide. In the nineties, UNESCO, the United Nations Educational Scientific and Cultural Organization, sounded the alarm on women's illiteracy. The *World Education Report of UNESCO* (1993) explains that approximately 65 percent of the world's illiterates are women. Since then, their absolute number has certainly increased. Female illiteracy is still striking in many parts of the world, notably in South Asia, Sub-Saharan Africa, the Arab states and the Maghreb. By way of example, 67.5 per cent of women in Morocco are illiterate. Regional disparities indicate an alarming situation, as the illiteracy rate of Moroccan rural women is 89.1 percent (Direction de la Statistique, 1995).

Many studies stress the need for research in the field of adult female literacy. For instance, Kazemek (1988) deplores the fact that most prominent literacy theoreticians and researchers have depreciated the relationship between women and literacy. She states that this has significant implications for adult literacy teaching as explained by her saying that "[t]his omission of information, uses, and needs of literacy among women makes any theoretical or practical discussion of adult literacy incomplete, if not suspect" (Kazemek, 1988, 22). Likewise, Carmack (1992) suggests that literacy research should be undertaken to address the needs of women in terms of literacy and education.

Other researchers, namely Wagner (1992) and Ryan (1992) state that the lack of critical research studies on adult education development has resulted in repeated mistakes and wasted efforts. They explain that much of adult education resorts to child education as a model. Still, the difficulty of finding a common definition of literacy constitutes a stumbling block for the progress of research even in child literacy acquisition. Along this vein, Wagner (1992) claims that literacy research is hampered by the diversity of existing definitions; the scarcity of research on adult literacy acquisition, notably in developing countries; the lack of information on how literacy is acquired and retained, and how it affects both the individual and the society.

Ryan (1992) ascribes the difficulty of dealing with the issue of adult literacy to the broad gap existing between research, policy formulation and practice. The author states that this is mainly due to the nature of current research, which has not yet provided policy makers with common definitions and issues relevant to their broad perspective. He adds that in other contexts, namely developing nations, as is the case of Africa, it is the scarcity of studies on adult literacy rather than the quality or the irrelevance of research that affects the policy choices.

## ADULT LITERACY RESEARCH IN MOROCCO

In Morocco, interest in adult literacy is recent. The few research works available consist of an evaluation of the government's endeavor to combat illiteracy nationwide. This evaluation is based on official ministerial documents and/or the review of the literature on adult literacy. Examples of such research include the works of El Joundi, Eddabiali and Mahboub (1998), Essaknaoui (1998), Kabbaj (1998) and Maddi (2000).

El Joundi et al. (1998) is a monograph which gives a detailed review of past and current adult literacy campaigns in the Maghreb, namely Morocco, Algeria, Tunisia and Mauritania. The aim of the authors' study is to come up with a common strategy for combating illiteracy in the Maghreb. While stressing the important efforts the Maghreb governments have made to combat illiteracy in the region since their independence, the authors report that such efforts have been handicapped by general, pedagogical and financial obstacles.

The reported general obstacles pertain to the inability to attract and motivate the non-literate, insufficient volunteer participation, increasing drop-out rates, non-mobilization of religious institutions, politicians and intellectuals to encourage effective participation, unreliability of literacy census data and the non-availability of legislative texts that would govern literacy action at national and regional levels. Pedagogical problems, on the other hand, involve insufficient pedagogical training and equipment, lack of planning of follow-up and continuing education programs, non-availability of post-literacy materials such as books and libraries, lack of skilled and trained staff as regards literacy conceptualisation, designing, implementation and assessment, and finally scarcity of adult literacy research. Financial restrictions include insufficient premises, lack of schools, and limited funds and budgets.

Essaknaoui 's study (1998), which is an unpublished M.A thesis, deals with the subject of adult literacy through an analysis of literacy actions in both developed and developing nations with a focus on the Moroccan literacy policy. Based on a comparative and systemic approach, Essaknaoui states that Morocco's anti-illiteracy efforts are handicapped by a host of problems. The reported ones include the following: the lack of political will, the non-establishment of global planning actions with long term objectives, insufficient budgets, discontinuity, non-existence of legislative laws that would govern literacy action as is the case in Kuwait, Iraq, Syria and Egypt, the weakness and centralization of the institutional structure despite the creation of a local anti-illiteracy authority and lack of co-ordination between the involved sectors in opposition to what takes place in other countries, namely Brazil, Afghanistan, Mali, Algeria and Mauritania.

Kabbaj (1998) addresses the issue of illiteracy as a kind of disease that requires a quick treatment as it constitutes an obstacle to the attainment of sustainable development of more than half of the Moroccan population. Drawing on Western research, the author suggests some broad initiatives to combat illiteracy. These could be summed up as follows:

1. The political will of the leadership together with the institutional power of the state play an important role in the success of a literacy campaign. This endowment has to be clearly defined and based on convictions that motivate the entire population.
2. Governmental involvement alone is not enough. Both literate and non-literate people should also be mobilized for the literacy action.
3. Priority action should involve women and girls especially in remote villages.
4. The learner should play an important role in the determination of the literacy program and its course contents.

5. Teacher training and post literacy instruction should be an integral part of the literacy programs.

In the same vein, Maddi (2000) stresses the important role of the instructor in eradicating illiteracy and sustaining the learners' motivation. Based on his experience as a teacher-trainer, the author provides the adult learners' instructors with workable ways of designing course objectives and aims as well as testing techniques.

Field-work based research on Moroccan adult literacy encompasses two types of studies, namely census-based studies and learner-centred studies. The former include the works of EL Anzoule (1997), and Lavy and Spratt (1997); the latter comprise the study of Boukous and Agnaou (2001).

Both the studies of El Anzoule (1997) and Lavy and Spratt (1997) question the use of the census-based literacy assessment methods that have so far been used in Morocco. In so doing, they suggest new methods based on direct assessment rather than self-report. Their claim is that their subjects have a tendency to overestimate their literacy performance through the self-report as revealed by their low performance through the direct assessment method. Elaborate information on these methods is given in chapter 2 in the section dealing with the problem of measuring basic literacy

Based on testing tasks and questionnaires, Boukous and Agnaou's study (2001) is so far the first published empirical research that is centred on the adult learner. Convinced by the important role of literacy in contributing to social change and sustainable development, the authors seek to investigate the extent to which non-literate adults are prepared to operate functionally in the literate ecology in which they have so far been marginalized. Their findings come out with the following conclusion: instead of preparing the non-literate adult learners to have access to new resources and opportunities, Moroccan literacy instruction is rather used as a means of reproducing and perpetuating their position of dependence.

The Moroccan adult literacy studies reviewed above provide invaluable findings that bear relevance on the establishment of effective adult literacy campaigns as they describe the Moroccan government endeavors to eradicate illiteracy, show the causes of the little gain achieved in combating illiteracy; suggest new strategies for national literacy training and propose new methods for teaching and assessing literacy levels. Unfortunately almost none of these studies address the relationship between adult literacy and the learners in an empirical way. While Boukous and Agnaou (2001) have met these criteria, their study does not address illiteracy as a gender-based issue. Therefore, to obtain a general picture of adult literacy in Morocco, it is necessary to supplement these studies with others dealing with women in particular as they are the most affected members of the society by the scourge of illiteracy and constitute the majority of the beneficiaries of adult literacy courses.

In academic research, hints to female literacy versus illiteracy are often given in the form of observations in studies meant to deal with other questions. .Belarbi (1991), for instance, deals with the situation of the Moroccan rural girl. Specifically, the author investigates the rural girl's socialization within the family and the community, her health condition and nutrition, her work and delinquency, how she spends her leisure time and how she is perceived in the oral and written literature. Her education and illiteracy received scanty attention. Yet, the study reports alarming gender educational disparities, brings to light the most affected rural areas and highlights the most significant obstacles to female literacy in these areas.

The lack of studies that address the issue of women's literacy in Morocco is probably due to the fact that the subject of adult literacy is still a new area of investigation. Another reason may be the overall limited attention allotted to women in society. Of notable exception, however, are two articles: Spratt (1992) and Agnaou (1998).

Spratt's study (1992) investigates Moroccan women's literacy in terms of gender inequities and their implication for development issues such as employment, fertility, and family health. The study also presents the formal and informal institutions which grant child and adult literacy in Morocco, and makes an appeal for more effective literacy work. In regard to this, the author concludes with a set of recommendations. These include: the improvement of literacy data collection techniques, more consideration of societal expectations and the need for research investigating the language needs and aptitudes of female adult learners in a second-language setting.

Agnaou (1998) investigates the language needs, attitudes, and difficulties of female participants in Moroccan adult literacy programs. While the study contributes to the language choice question in adult literacy as it brings to light the languages that answer the literacy needs of the female learners, it is limited by the fact that it assesses the learners' reading difficulties on the basis of their opinions rather than on their real aptitude. To deal with this limitation, the present research tackles the language aptitude of the learners through an investigation of their literacy attainments (see chapter 7).

As regards unpublished work on women and literacy, Mekayssi's thesis (1999) is a case in point. While this research has some bearing on the effectiveness of functional literacy training in the agricultural sector, it is marked by some methodological limitations. First, it deals with a limited sample and case in Tadla, which is located in central Morocco. In so doing, it restricts its study to small-scale adult literacy programs. In addition, only forty-eight beneficiaries were asked to evaluate the quality of the literacy instruction they received and the equipment used for their training in ORMVA, *Office Régional de Mise en Valeure Agricole*. Third, it uses the questionnaire as the only means of assessing the learners' literacy attainments. Given the very likely subjectivity of the learners' answers, such an assessment may result in biased findings. In addition, the author investigates female literacy needs within a monolithic perspective, which limits the functions of literacy to the applicability of a set of academic skills in the job situation to increase productivity.

Given the limitations of this research, there are two possible ways of usefully extending it. First, one might consider the empowering aspects of literacy training among a larger sample by using other instruments, namely class observation and content analysis. Second, one might also investigate the respondents' needs in terms of their real performance to control biased opinions. This could be done within a research design that uses diverse assessment techniques. Indeed, such suggestions are taken into consideration in the present study, which investigates both the learning needs and the literacy attainments of a much bigger population within a holistic perspective that regards literacy as basic, functional and empowering. For a definition of these concepts, see chapter 2. Such an approach subscribes to the issue of human rights as it considers female literacy provision a democratic means through which knowledge and power are shared between men and women and among women themselves. Theoretically, the study draws its principles from Molyneux's (1987) practical *gender interests* and *strategic gender interests*. In the present research, *practical interests* refer to women's right to become literate and hence be able to process everyday literacy. On the other hand, *strategic interests* refer to their right to be made literate through an empowering content that is free of sexism, stereotyping and marginalisation. To attain its objectives, and as explained in the introduction of the book, the present work is carried out within a research design that addresses questions on:

1. the profiles of non-literate women and obstacles to their literacy,
2. women's literacy and learning needs,
3. women's literacy attainments,
4. women's representation in the designed textbooks.

Now the question is: How relevant are these issues to adult literacy research in general and in Morocco, in particular? The answer to this question is given in the next sections.

## DEALING WITH PROFILES AND LITERACY OBSTACLES

As already stated, one of the aims of the present research is to assess women's target *needs* and *learning needs* (Hutchinson and Waters, 1987) with respect to literacy training. To keep in line with the requirements of needs assessment research, which considers the question "who are the learners?" as one of the crucial questions that the needs analyst has to address in order to deal with any eventual motivational and learning differences, the present research investigates the issue by providing data on the learners' socio-economic and educational background such as their age, marital status, occupation, and schooling. It also describes the causes of women's illiteracy and dropping out of the courses during their childhood and adulthood as addressed in the introduction of the book and analyzed in chapter 5. The aim is to see to what extent the learners under study constitute a homogenous group and to draw implications as to how to improve female literacy rates and increase women's effective participation in the literacy courses. The relevance of dealing with the learners' literacy obstacles consists in investigating the feminization of illiteracy in an empirical way and contributing to the issue of the diversity versus the uniformity of adult literacy courses. As explained in chapter 4 and briefly presented in the introduction of the book, data on the learners' characteristics and illiteracy are drawn form 204 current female learners. Data related to the informants' dropping out reasons are collected from a sample of seventy-five subjects who dropped out of the literacy course.

## IDENTIFYING WOMEN'S LITERACY NEEDS

The research gap in adult literacy in Morocco is enormous, particularly with regard to how women perceive and acquire literacy. The adult learner, unlike the child, engages in a literacy course with a set of specific needs in mind. Therefore, needs assessment should be accepted as a crucial element of adult education programming. Indeed, one would support a position where one first determines the goals of literacy education and then designs a program that is consistent with these goals. However, this technique is ignored in most cases. Kowalski (1988) gives four reasons for the non-use or low use of needs assessment in adult education. The first reason pertains to the gap between theory and practice. The author explains this by the heavy reliance of education programs on intuition, tradition, and their consideration of political pressure and advantages of the use of available resources. The second relates to avoidance as a result of ignorance of how to use needs assessment as a planning instrument. The third concerns the consideration of needs assessment as a *luxury* rather than a necessary constituent of program designing. The last reason of discarding needs assessment in program planning is that it may be a *potential source of conflict* between the literacy designers and the literacy learners as their needs may vary depending on what they consider as a priority in acquiring literacy.

The issue of the learner's needs is an important question to be considered before the establishment of any adult literacy program, especially that participation in such courses is basically voluntary and open to different age groups, literacy levels, geographical settings and linguistic communities. In addition, as the offered instruction is of a curing nature, it must have practical meaning for the adult student; otherwise, all efforts are doomed to failure.

Many studies argue that literacy education will remain inefficient and ineffective unless it takes into consideration adult active participation in all aspects of the program including curriculum development, instruction, and management. Manzoor (1992) states that the issue of literacy should be considered in the context of the basic learning needs of children and adults and the specific circumstances for social and economic development involved. Hunter and Harman (1979) and Fingeret (1989) express the need for the involvement of the learner in the conception of literacy programs. In this respect, they judge current literacy efforts as being constrained by the program designers' underlying philosophy, which does not take into consideration the learner. In so doing, they suggest that adult basic education should be a bottom-up enterprise taking into consideration the participants' intervention rather than a top-down one. Chlebowska (1992) claims that the first step to undertake in preparing literacy materials for illiterate women should be an assessment of their learning needs. She adds that once needs assessment is completed, groups should be selected according to their needs priorities and assigned appropriate training.

In keeping with the importance of assessing the learners' needs, the present research analyzes women's *literacy needs*, namely their motivations and expectations, and *learning needs*, which refer to the conditions under which learning takes place and the constraints that affect it. It also investigates the extent to which the designed program is consonant with the learners' literacy needs. As explained in chapter 4, the learners' needs analysis draws its data from two structured interviews addressed to current participants in adult literacy programs (N=204) and their teachers (N=37). The analysis of the aims and objectives of the literacy programs under study is done through the use of official documents and an interview with the head of the teacher training department at *la Direction de la lutte contre L'analphabétisme*, henceforth, the Literacy Directorate, which is the body responsible for adult literacy campaigns and programs. Detailed information regarding this institution is given in chapter 3.

## ASSESSING WOMEN'S LITERACY ATTAINMENT

The effectiveness of adult literacy campaigns and programs is often assessed in terms of the number of enrolled participants and dropouts or self-assessment techniques (Wagner, 1992; Lavy, Spratt, and Leboucher, 1995). Notable exceptions are the works of Carron, Mwiria, and Righa (1989), and Boukous and Agnaou (2001).

Carron et al. deal with literacy retention among graduates of literacy programs in Kenya. Boukous and Agnaou investigate the use of literacy tasks among graduate participants in adult literacy programs in Morocco. Based on a proficiency test, both studies provide data on the learners' reading ability of everyday literacy documents. Given the nature of their perspective, which is development-oriented, the two studies do not address the reading strategies that the learners use when handling the literacy tasks they are assigned. Therefore, the studies deal with the learners' literacy attainment as an end product rather than a process. In so doing, they do not provide information on how the learners learn literacy and what language problems they encounter.

To fill in this gap, and to keep with the requirements of the needs analysis which considers the learners' knowledge, skills and learning strategies as important issues to be analyzed in addition to the learners' target needs, the learners' basic and functional literacy ability are dealt with in the present research both as a product and as a process. More specifically, this research seeks to investigate the extent to which the learners under study master the reading skills they have acquired during their training and their ability to perform the literacy tasks they sought after through their participation in the courses. At the same time, it describes the learners' reading strategies and analyzes a set of predictor variables that might affect their performance, namely age, motivation, literacy experience, grade level, mother tongue and area as presented in chapter 7. The aim is to shed light on the effectiveness of the learners' literacy training and identify the linguistic features or skills that are difficult to learn. Last but not least, it seeks to highlight the relationship between the learners' literacy attainment and the variables pertaining to individual, regional, linguistic and educational differences

The relevance of investigating the learners' literacy attainments lies in its contribution to some issues that are of theoretical nature such as the universal route of learning a second language. For more details, see chapter 7. Practical issues pertain to the efficiency of the designed program, the adopted language, the learners' environment and the fundamental question of the type of the program and the quantity of the training that a country needs to provide for its non-literate population to reach the levels of skill acquisition that are deemed necessary for people to operate as effective citizens.

The issue of how much schooling is necessary to acquire literacy yields contradictory results. While there is a general agreement among literacy providers in the Arab World, including Morocco, that four years of primary schooling represent the minimum threshold level for permanent literacy, research reveals that more than that is needed. Oxenham (1980) states that four to six years of primary education are necessary for the attainment of sustainable economic development. Wagner, Spratt and Ezzaki (1989) claim that fifth grade education completion in Morocco is necessary to prevent a relapse into illiteracy. On the other hand, Lavy, Spratt, and Leboucher (1995) found that Moroccan primary education completion guarantees its graduates only *rudimentary* competence in writing, reading and calculating. They predict that to achieve the highest level in literacy, fourteen years of secular schooling are needed particularly for rural girls who live in poor and illiterate settings.

During the fieldwork of the present study, which took place from 1998 to 1999, participation in Moroccan adult literacy courses lasted for two years after which a literacy degree is delivered to the successful graduates. Some non-governmental associations, however, initiated a follow up level for their graduates. This post-literacy level consists of three years of instruction, as was the case for the NGO's *Ribat al Fath* and *L'Action Féminine*. Others, namely *Illigh* association, in Casablanca, provide literacy instruction for five years. By comparing graduate and post-graduates samples, the present study helps to find out whether the designed literacy period, which consists of a two year course, prepares the subjects under study for the demands of the literate community they belong to. At the same time, it investigates whether such ability increases at the post-literacy level.

In dealing with literacy attainment, the ability to read is fundamental. Reading ability is often associated with the status and the inherent features of the language of literacy. In multilingual countries, the issue of language choice is a key ingredient in the success or the failure of a literacy project. As this issue is largely dealt with in chapter 2, this section limits itself to a quick review of the language policies that have been adopted in adult literacy programs. Shaw (1983) states that some nations, namely the Soviet Union's literacy campaign under Lenin and Papua New Guinea, developed a full mother tongue approach where over hundreds of languages were used for literacy. On the other hand, other nations launched literacy programs in a limited number of mother tongues as is the case in Mali, Senegal, Guinea, Niger, Ghana and Zambia. Still, others like Peru, Mexico, and Vietnam used the mother tongue for initial literacy instruction as a bridge to literacy in the official language or some other major language. While positive results have been reported in the foregoing language policies, mother tongue literacy teaching didn't succeed in other countries such as Gambia (British Council, 1978) due to the learners' preference for English literacy. Likewise, in Thailand an experiment using a combination of mother tongue literacy and the national language literacy failed because the government and the learners were reluctant to acquire mother tongue literacy. Other reported reasons relate to the lack of trained teachers in the bilingual approach. At the same time, the Ethiopian literacy campaign that sought to enhance literacy in the national language, Amharic, which is not known to the learners, reported an 87 percent drop out rate (UNESCO, 1976).

In Morocco, literacy instruction for non-literate adults is granted in *fusha* (Standard Arabic), the official language. It is to be noted that this language is not spoken at home and its use is limited to formal domains such as religion, administration, mass media and education where it is mainly used in reading and writing. Speaking in such institutions, however, is done in three languages depending on the individual's educational experience and language proficiency. These languages are: Moroccan Arabic, French and or Middle Arabic, which is a mixture of Standard Arabic and *ddarija* (Moroccan Arabic). *Amazigh* (Berber) is the mother tongue of an important segment of the Moroccan population as it is spoken by bilingual and monolingual Berbers, the majority of whom are women who live or come from rural areas in the north, the middle and the south of the country. It is also spoken among bilingual Berbers in urban areas where it is used in the family and the market domains. Mother tongue literacy, especially as concerns Amazigh, has gained attention since the late king Hassan the second's appeal for its teaching in 1994. But, it is only in October 2001, that its teaching has been officially acknowledged by His Majesty King Mohammed Sixth with the creation of the Royal Institute of the Amazigh Culture. The implementation of Amazigh in the educational system is programmed for the academic year 2003–2004.

Given the investigated language policy, which excludes the mother tongue of the learners and at the same time provides them with the *target symbolic capital* accruing from the learning of the languages of literacy (Boukous, 1995), it would be interesting to investigate the learners' attitude toward it and compare their reading competences based on their mother tongue. Language has certainly important implications for gender inequality and regional disparity in literacy attainment especially that many rural Amazigh women, whose social roles are restricted to the home, remain monolingual for the rest of their lives. Language acquisition in Moroccan adult literacy programs has yet to be investigated. While there is evidence on how Amazigh-speaking children attain literacy (Wagner, 1993; Ruiter, 1997, Saib, 1995) nothing is known on how non-literate Amazigh women learn the language of literacy. The present study is an attempt to fill this gap in research on adult females' acquisition of Standard Arabic in Morocco.

## INVESTIGATING EMPOWERMENT THROUGH LITERACY

Addressing female literacy provision in terms of *practical* or *strategic gender interests* begins from a deficit perspective. Advocates of *practical* gender needs consider women as victims of illiteracy and that their integration could be achieved within a framework that links their emancipation with economic growth and returns. As explained in chapter 2, this movement is headed by WID, *Women in Development* (Haider, 1996). This economic-development-oriented tendency aims at integrating women in society within their accepted social roles through concrete developmental processes such as literacy, education, and employment. In Morocco, this movement is headed by urban middle-class or bourgeois integrated Moroccan women, who are involved in voluntary associations or organs of government. Their movement aims at the improvement of the socio-economic conditions of women in both rural and urban areas through developmental processes such as literacy, education, professional training, agricultural cooperatives, health services, income generating activities, and bank loans. It obtains financial support from numerous national and international organizations. Despite the magnitude of the challenge, the Moroccan government is now leaving the responsibility of addressing women's *practical* needs to the leaders of this movement, who are confronted to many obstacles such as lack of infrastructure, limited resources, unqualified expertise, and the heavy weight of tradition.

Within this perspective, non-literate women are regarded as ignorant creatures that retard their countries' socio-economic development. Thus, they are cured through a "nutritionist" approach by learning the technical drills of reading and writing from texts that deal with good citizenship, patriotism, and family planning. Such literacy training reproduces and reinforces the traditional values of the society. While this movement should be credited for its voluntary endeavor, though this is not always the case as it hides many socio-economic and political stakes, it should be criticized for neglecting non-literate women's *strategic interests* and for their dealing with literacy within the patriarchal and traditional model.

Proponents of *gender strategic interests,* on the other hand, seek to design a new society, where relations between men and women are more democratic and equitable. The deficit perspective they start from considers women as victims of discrimination, marginalisation and oppression. Thus, their ideology is based on parity with men and sticks to the values of human rights. It calls for the participation of women as equal partners with men in all fields of work, education, training and politics. As stated in chapter 2, this trend is conveyed by GEA, the *Gender Empowerment Approach* (Haider, 1996). The contribution of this approach to female literacy research resides in its supporters' high interest in the literacy content (Michel, 1986; Ramdas, 1989; Carmack, 1992; Chlebowska, 1992; Stromquist, 1992). As already stated, these studies agree that women's position and condition can be changed through empowering teaching materials. Accordingly, they claim that literacy textbooks should convey female liberation and empowerment through an act of knowing, questioning and transforming. In so doing, the authors reject the society's perception of women's needs as being subordinate to family and society and claim that gender specific programming is a necessity if perspective transformation and empowerment are to take place.

In Morocco, GEA is headed by liberal and reformist feminists, usually university teachers or members of leftist political parties as explained in Sadiqi (2000) and Agnaou, 2001. Liberal feminists investigate the gender issue in terms of dominance and difference. In so doing, they refute the socio-political oppression exerted on women (Naamane-Guessous, 1988), deny violence and injustice against them (Mernissi, Laouedj, and Belarbi, 1993) and launch an appeal against all forms of discrimination and sex stereotypes (Sadiqi, 1995; Bourqia, Charrad, and Gallaghers, 1996).

While advocates of the strategic gender movement in Morocco have succeeded in sensitizing the elite and even some decision-makers to women' issues, notably the Personal Code issue, theoretically, it remains a top-down movement which the non-literate majority does not know of or misunderstands. The merit of the gender movement activists lies in addressing such a hot issue, which is in fact common to all women whether literate or non literate, urban or rural, rich or poor. Still, this movement should take an interest in the non-literate mass that suffers from additional inequalities due to illiteracy. To my knowledge, no study has ever addressed women's *strategic* interests in terms of literacy provision. Yet, literacy teaching can be used as a means to change the traditional values in society and as a promoter of gender equity among adults and children alike.

Thus, the effort to reach the grassroots and to design gender specific literacy programs within a wider strategy of economic development still represents an enormous challenge to the Moroccan feminist movement. Therefore, the struggle against women's subordination and discrimination cannot be effective unless female literacy programming operates within a wider strategy whose aim is to eradicate not only basic illiteracy, but underdevelopment, exclusion, dependence, and injustice as well. Accordingly, textbooks designed to teach adults should lay the foundations for the future equality between men and women, which constitutes one of the main goals of democratic societies all over the world. In fact, gender *strategic needs* can be attained in line with the practical ones, and the two constitute a theoretical basis for gender specific programming for women. In this respect, Ramdas (1989:529) redefines literacy and extends its meaning beyond the acquisition of the mechanical skills of reading, writing and numeracy to include the empowering of women as explained in her saying:

> Reading and writing skills would then truly become a weapon with which each woman could be empowered to read and write her world, analyze and understand it, and where necessary transform it. That alone is true justice.

Likewise, Chlebowska (1992:29) claims that in addition to the teaching of the 3R's "the empowerment of women should form the main focus of literacy and post-literacy materials." She explains that her point is not to develop negative attitudes toward men but rather to encourage women to develop critical thinking of their conditions, gain self-confidence and self-esteem, take part in decision-making, acquire independence, control their living conditions, and change their position in society. She adds that the empowering literacy content should aim at:

> Avoiding sexual stereotype and macho references; promoting task sharing between men and women both outside and within the home; projecting a proper image of women that does not err on the negative side; and highlighting the status of women, asserting their rights and stressing the importance of women's participation.

While condemning any forms of discrimination against women, the author claims that literacy programs should unveil the subordinate conditions of women's lives and provide them with ways of controlling and changing these conditions. This of course could be attained only within a favorable policy climate, which perceives literacy as a democratic distribution of knowledge, goods and power within society.

In Morocco, women undergo intra- and inter- discrimination. First, they are all equally discriminated against in comparison to men with respect to sexist legislative texts, namely *Al-mudawwana*, the Personal Code. Second, they are further discriminated against by class, language, area and level of education. Obviously, non-literate women are the most affected by discrimination. Female illiteracy finds its origins in traditional societies, communities, or families where women's primary role consists of procreating and lactating. In such settings, women's social life is confined to the house where they are *protected* from too much learning they may obtain from education or other channels of communication. Culture and tradition, which are mostly conveyed by women, reinforce their limited role in society and family and indirectly contribute to an internalization of a low self-image, which inhibits their incentive for learning and eventually that of their daughters. To compensate for their illiteracy, which is nowadays considered as an obstacle to socio-economic development, literacy programs have been developed to improve literacy rates, child care and immunization, and to decrease fertility rates. The question would be: what is the place of women's empowerment among such target national goals?

As explained earlier in this chapter, the present study considers literacy as an educational project that seeks to satisfy women's right to learn how to handle everyday literacy through an emancipatory and empowering content. In so doing, the primary objective of investigating the learners' empowerment is to see whether the textbooks that are assigned in the Moroccan adult literacy programs convey an empowering culture where women are represented in plural, balanced and non-discriminatory social roles. Theoretically, the relevance of such analysis, the results of which are presented in chapter 8, lies in its contribution to the major debates on women' literacy, namely how non-literate women should be taught and for what purpose. Practically, it contributes to gender-based program contents. Last but not least, the learners' empowerment analysis, in particular, fills in the research gap on gender and literacy.

## CONCLUSION

The literature, which is briefly reviewed above, shows that the subject of adult literacy received a considerable attention among researchers from diverse academic backgrounds. The discussion reveals that there is still much to be done, especially with respect to the adult female as a learner. The present study attempts to contribute to this issue by addressing questions on: who are the learners? What caused their illiteracy? Why do they enrol in adult literacy courses? Are they satisfied with the courses? Do they learn what they are supposed to learn? Do they use what they have learned to handle everyday literacy? How are they represented in the textbooks? And what are the obstacles to their effective participation in the courses?

The assumption underlying this research is that the investigations of these questions, though limited as they are, would come up with findings that contribute to promoting female literacy in general and in Morocco in particular. This research also bears relevance on the relationship between gender, literacy and empowerment and also importantly on the definition of literacy. But what is literacy? How is it defined and measured in previous research and in the present one? These questions are investigated in the next chapter.

# 2
# Conceptions of Literacy and Related Issues

The present research draws on Molyneux's (1987) model of women's *practical* needs and *strategic* needs. Therefore, it investigates women's literacy within a global approach which considers literacy as basic, functional and empowering. In the present chapter, each concept is analyzed in relation to its definition, accessible literature, and the ways it is measured in previous studies and in the present book.

## DEFINING LITERACY

As agreed upon, literacy is by no means a unanimous concept as it means different things to different people within and across societies. Literacy is, thus, a relative and complex phenomenon with varying interpretations in different societal, national and cultural contexts. As a context-specific phenomenon, literacy varies in accordance with the values, perspectives, cultural practices, social position, and gender roles of the individuals or groups who use it (Heath, 1983; Street, 1985; Auerbach, 1992; Stromquist, 1992; Wagner, 1993).

Understanding the term literacy often involves the idea that literacy is simply the ability to read and write. In this case, Bormuth (1975:72) defines it as 'the ability to exhibit all of the behaviors a person needs in order to respond appropriately to all possible reading tasks'. This quite simplistic view of literacy, however, involves other skills. The common definitions of a literate person as found in dictionaries refer to a well-educated person who is versed in literature. Scribner (1988) adds to this skill of great learning, the attributes of moral superiority and religious salvation. Today, many adjectives are attached to the concept of literacy, and thereby increasing its complexity. Thus, cultural literacy, political literacy, technological literacy, computer literacy, media literacy, etc. have come into use, each having a different meaning. Accordingly, the notion "literacies" has been developed (Ouane, 1992). The point is that, whatever their literacy benchmarks, literate people may not be able to read or write in all languages or even use many of the specialized functions of the language(s) in which they are made literate. For instance, they may not understand political jargon, notations of music, phonetic alphabets, engineering blueprints, or computer languages.

While accepting that literacy is a construct of *literacies*, this book deals with only conceptions that have relevance to the issues it addresses. Hence the following review is, of necessity, selective.

## CONCEPTIONS OF ADULT LITERACY

Various workable definitions of literacy have been adopted in the field of adult literacy. To gain a greater understanding of these definitions, it might be helpful to consider them chronologically. From 1946 to 1964, the definition of literacy was restricted to the acquisition of reading, writing and arithmetic usually referred to as the 3 R's. Thus, according to UNESCO (1958), a literate person would be the one who "is able to read, write and understand a brief and simple exposé of facts in relation to his or her daily life". This definition of literacy has been adopted by most countries including Morocco and used as a basis for designing adult literacy courses.

During the period 1965–1974 the concept of *functional literacy* and its link with economic growth and returns was developed. This concept emerged from the *World Conference of Ministers of Education on the Eradication of Illiteracy* which was held in Tehran in 1965. This new concept of literacy, which was basically work-oriented, was put into practice in the form of the EWLP, *Experimental World Literacy Program*, launched during the period 1966–1974. The *functionally illiterate* was then defined as being unable to perform all the reading, writing and calculating tasks for which literacy is necessary in the interest of the proper functioning of and development of the community. After the evaluation of the EWLP, literacy has gained another dimension where priority is given to the well being of the individual. Literacy has then come to be conceived of as a political, human and cultural process of consciousness-raising and liberation. Its aim is not only how to teach adults to read a set of letters and words but also how to read and understand the world. This is expressed in the following statement by Kassam (1989: 531):

> To be literate is to become liberated from the constraints of dependency. To be literate is to gain a voice and to participate meaningfully and assertively in

> decisions that affect one's life. To be literate is to gain self-confidence. To be literate is to become self-assertive. To be literate is to become politically conscious and critically aware, and to demystify social reality.

This new conception of literacy as an empowering skill came out as a reaction against the limited functions of literacy, which underscores the applicability of a set of neutral academic skills to the tasks of work and daily life. Such a traditional conception of literacy is increasingly understood as maintaining the learners' assimilation into the existing system where power is unfairly divided in terms of class and gender.

In consideration of the foregoing definitions, there are three broad views about literacy whose differences bear significance for planning and implementing literacy programs for women. First, there is the tendency to regard literacy as the learning of the basic skills of reading, writing and numeracy. This knowledge, usually referred to as *traditional literacy*, is necessary for both men and women, as it constitutes the basis for any further educational opportunities. Second, there is the idea to view literacy as a process of acquiring useful *functional* skills to improve production capacities, increase income, and ameliorate the learners' lives. For instance, when such an approach is adopted in teaching women, it would regard them as able to engage in productive activities that will allow some degree of financial independence. Third, there is the consideration of literacy as a *liberating* and *empowering* means through which the socially disadvantaged learners, particularly women, are made aware of their conditions of subordination and the factors that create such conditions. When such a definition is adopted in the teaching of adult non-literate women, it will help them develop a feeling that they can improve their condition in a successful way (Stromquist, 1992). In sum, such an approach would aim at women's social and political empowerment, as it would convince them of their own value and their ability to take part in public life and decision-making.

While these views of literacy as the means to acquire basic skills, functional skills and empowering skills are not completely exclusive of one another, they can constitute a workable conceptual framework for assessing women's literacy needs and attainments. In the following sections, I explain each definition, indicate its relevance for the present research, and show how it is measured.

## LITERACY AS A BASIC SKILL

Defined as a basic skill, literacy refers to the ability to read, write and count as measured through standardized and achievement tests. In addition, it is often related to the number of years of schooling (Lytle and Wolfe, 1989; Newman and Beverstock, 1990; Beder, 1991). Considering this definition, a literate person is someone who has been in school for a certain amount of time and who possesses a composite of discrete academic skills, which an illiterate lacks. In this regard, research into adult literacy as a basic skill involves two perspectives. The first addresses the issue of literacy as comparable to years of schooling and the problems of measurements accruing from this definition. The second investigates literacy as the mastery of basic academic skills in terms of language choice and language policy. The following sections explain each perspective with a focus on issues that have relevance to the present research.

### Measuring basic literacy: some problems

When literacy is defined in terms of a given grade level, it becomes country-specific. For example, in Brussels, people who have not attained a level of education equal to twelve years are designated as illiterate (Stercq, 1992). In Canada, the Canadian Association of Adult Education has defined literacy in terms of the completion of nine years of formal schooling. In the United States, passing high school equivalency exams is considered to equate the minimum literacy levels for adults. In Morocco and in many Arab countries, an individual is qualified as literate upon his or her completion of four years of primary schooling (Maamouri, 1998). World literacy reports are based on the nations' measurements of literacy through self-report as stated in UNESCO's statement: "As a rule, it is on the basis of a simple statement on the part of the individual concerned that the condition of literate or illiterate is determined" (UNESCO, 1991:6). This, however, may not accurately reflect the real literacy levels of the individuals as discussed below.

Measurements of literacy levels, as provided by UNESCO, use national census based information collected through self-assessment questionnaires and numbers of years of schooling. Literacy as attested by previous school attendance may be misleading, especially when school leaving is much distanced from present time with no use of previously acquired skills. Such a situation certainly leads to the attrition of those skills. In addition, the years of schooling do not automatically equate school grade levels due to possible repeated school year(s). In such cases, dropping-out may take place before the attainment of threshold levels beyond which permanent literacy is acquired. In Morocco, for instance, school enrolment especially in rural areas is seldom sustained due to limited transportation, low numbers of qualified teachers and widespread child labor. Hence, limited schooling and early dropping out may cause the erosion of previously learned skills and, thus, lead to a relapse into illiteracy (Wagner, 1993).

Likewise, the self-reported assessment technique which identifies literates and non-literates based on their answer to the question of whether they can read and/or write is unreliable, especially in cases where there is confusion between "reading as a decoding process" and "reading as a comprehension process". Furthermore, the self-reported information can be subjective when its source comes from informants who would not accept themselves as illiterate or from those who underestimate their competence in reading and writing. Usually, informants tend not to report accurate information about them. In such cases, they believe that investigators may reflect negatively on them and underestimate their competences. Hence, there is a good reason to doubt the reliability of their report as to their grade level and literacy ability.

In line with this argument, El Anzoule (1997) and Lavy and Spratt (1997) question the reliability of the self-reported information as it involves problems of definition and measurement and has many implications for anti-illiteracy action. Their argument is that self-assessment questionnaires may either overestimate or underestimate perceived literacy levels. In this regard, they designed an assessment approach, which uses a series of tests in both Standard Arabic and French. This new literacy assessment approach, financed by the World Bank for the Moroccan Ministry of Planning, consists of the administration of tests measuring the reading, writing and numeracy skills of 2, 240 households. In addition to these tests, the informants were asked to give self-reports on their literacy levels. When self-judgements of competency data were compared with achievement scores, Lavy and Spratt revealed that an important percentage of their informants overestimated their literacy skills. Of 45.6 percent of people who reported that they could read and write, 11.2 percent lack such skills and 17.2 percent had rudimentary reading and writing skills. Similar mismatching was reported when dealing with gender and urban versus rural settings. The direct-assessment technique reveals an overestimation in the traditional self-report technique. This overestimation is 5 percent for the non-literate male, 1.8 percent for the non-literate female, 8 percent for the non-literate rural male, 12 percent for the 9–14 age group, 5 percent for the 25–34 female age group and 10 percent for the 25–34 years-old urban adults.

Similar results were found by El Azoule (idem). In comparing census-based rates of literacy and direct-assessment based techniques, the author concludes that 10.9 percent of the investigated population who declared themselves literate were revealed illiterate by the direct assessment method. He adds that 17 percent of rural adults who dropped out of the primary school had no literacy skills.

These studies clearly indicate that literacy rates based on self-report may contain a high proportion of people with no or low literacy skills. The authors stress the risk of patterns of bias in self-assessment methods as they may mask important gender, age and rural versus urban disparities. These results also reveal that relapse into illiteracy is not to be taken into consideration by the self-assessment method.

This implies that the reported official national literacy rates may be very well overstated. This in turn suggests that even with regard to the optimistic calculations circulated as a result of national literacy campaigns; one has to be very careful, as they can be misleading. In fact, studies have shown that such campaigns have succeeded in teaching the illiterate only rudimentary skills, such as writing names and addresses (Bordia and Kaul, 1992). Due to this limited acquisition, relapse into illiteracy is certainly inevitable among neo-literates. Therefore, any objective and reliable assessment of literacy should not rely on the self-report and previous schooling as an assessment technique. Instead, it should assess the learners' real ability through the design of a series of tests that measure all literacy skills and levels. Aware of this, and gaining insight from Bowren and Zintz (1977), and Wagner (1993), the literacy levels of the informants of the present research are determined on the basis of their real competence and not of their perceived competence. Details related to this issue are presented in chapter 4.

## Measuring basic literacy: some solutions

Given the limitations of the self-reported assessment technique, the *United Nations National Household Survey Capability Program* (United Nations, 1989) designed a new assessment technique through which populations are directly assessed on their literacy skills. This assessment technique evaluates reading and writing proficiency through a measuring scale where skill ability ranges from simple word decoding and copying, to producing a new text and seeking information from documents. Four literacy skills are taken into consideration. These are: decoding, comprehension, writing, and information seeking. These literacy skills are assessed within three literacy domains: words and sentences; prose such as texts and stories; and documents like newspapers, drug instructions, bills, and so on. Decoding consists of reading words and making word picture matching. Comprehension refers to the learner's ability to understand words, sentences and prose. Writing competencies include signing one's name, recopying words or a written text, or producing a new text. Information seeking involves the ability to find specific information in texts and documents.

The United Nations' approach to measuring literacy classifies the tested populations in terms of four main categories depending on their achievement in the designed tests as non-literates, low literates, moderate literates or high literates. A non-literate is a person who has no command over the literacy skills and the literacy domains explained above. A low-literate is an individual who can decode and understand familiar words and sentences, write his or her name, or copy a text, but is unable to understand a brief text. A moderate literate is the one who, while mastering the skills of a low literate possesses, can with much difficulty understand and write a text, locate information from written texts, and identify information in authentic documents. Finally, a high literate is a learner who, while making little effort and few errors, can perform all the tasks acquired by low and moderate literates. These categories are further defined by Wagner (1993) as follows:

1. A "non-literate" is an individual who is not able to read, comprehend, produce, or recognize a piece of everyday written information, and who cannot sign his or her name or understand the meanings of public signs.
2. A "low-literate" is a person who is unable to read, comprehend, produce a piece of written information but who can recognize words, sign his or her name or understand the meanings of public signs.
3. A "moderate literate" is the one who can, with "some difficulty" and "making numerous errors", read, write and understand a text in "a significant national language".
4. A "high literate" can perform these tasks but with "little difficulty" and less errors.

This classification of learners according to their literacy levels gives a better understanding of the literacy levels of a nation. For example, rather than simply classifying people into literates versus non-literates, it shows the literacy levels they are functioning at. In addition, it can be very useful as an assessment means for literacy programs and teachers as these latter can use them in designing both placement and proficiency tests to determine the literacy levels of their target population both before and after the literacy course and assess its efficiency in examining the learners' progress from one category to another. This categorization also helps curriculum makers to develop materials that would fit the levels of the learners within each group. This technique can also be used in research studies that analyze their informants' literacy levels, as is the case in the present research. However, it should be supplemented by other methods especially when dealing with second or foreign language acquisition. For instance, the researcher should provide a qualitative analysis of his or her informants' interlanguage. Moreover, it should take into consideration the learners' scores as well, as this method permits the researcher to compare the learners' proficiency with respect to some predictor variables such as age, motivation, mother tongue, grade-level, and so on. In this way, the researcher will be able to evaluate literacy as a learning process and as a product.

## BASIC LITERACY AND LANGUAGE CHOICE

The mastery of basic literacy skills, namely reading and writing, requires a good knowledge of the language in which their teaching is implemented. Hence assessments of adult basic literacy should normally comprise information on the efficiency of the adopted language policy. However, most of the world's language policies in adult literacy programs and campaigns are either unreported or unanalyzed. In fact, many adult literacy programs, including the Moroccan ones, have failed to address the language issue in their reports. This ignorance, as Shaw (1983: 47) states, may be due to the fact that the official language is assumed to be the natural medium of adult literacy, or to "the result of an intentional vagueness regarding language policy in general". Shaw explains this *theory of vagueness* through Bamgbose's statements regarding language policies in Africa. Bamgbose (1976) contends that African language policies are hardly made explicit for fear of political repercussions; they tend to vary in response to transformation in attitudes and change in personnel, and frequently demonstrate a discrepancy between policy and practice due to implementation difficulties.

The paucity of information on the language approach used in many literacy campaigns and programs is also accompanied by a lack of research on the language choice in adult literacy. Hints to the issue are often in the form of observations in studies that are meant to evaluate other aspects of the campaigns and programs (UNESCO, 1953; Bhola, 1984; Arnove and Graff, 1987; Jones, 1990). So far, the only work which exclusively deals with the issue is Shaw (1983) who, while being essentially documentary in nature, provides decision makers with workable criteria for language choice in adult literacy programs within multilingual settings.

What follows is an overview of the world's language policy experience in adult literacy. The main sources of information used in this respect are Shaw (1983), UNESCO (1953) and Bhola (1984). For discussion purposes, insights have been drawn from Coulmas (Ed) (1984), which deals with problems relating to literacy acquisition among linguistic minorities. Related papers in Coulmas focus on issues such as centralization versus cultural diversity, literacy eradication and the protection of linguistic and cultural minorities, the contribution of literacy campaigns in overcoming domestic and intercultural communication, factors determining the choice of literate language for the linguistic minorities, and the impact of literacy on non-native languages.

The world's experience with language policies in adult literacy is far from being similar. While people were made literate in their mother tongues, as was the case in the first great mass literacy campaign in Russia and in Vietnam, others were asked to read and write in major indigenous languages, as in Mali,

Senegal, Guinea, Niger, Ghana, and Zambia; or in official languages, as in Korea, Cuba, Somalia and China, Ethiopia, and Tanzania. Other countries use the learner's mother tongue as a transitional stage to the learning of the official language, as in Peru, Mexico, and Vietnam.

**Mother tongue literacy experience**

The mother tongue approach was espoused by UNESCO language experts in 1953. In their final report, the *Use of Vernacular Languages in Education* (1953:11) they stated the following:

> It is axiomatic that the best medium for teaching a child is his mother tongue. Psychologically, it is the best system of meaningful signs that in his mind works automatically for expression and understanding. Sociologically, it is a means of identity among members of the community to which he belongs. Educationally, he learns more quickly through it than through an unfamiliar learning medium.

In view of this statement, many linguists and educators believe that language is not merely an instrument of communication but also an important part of a group's history, culture, and identity. They maintain that language is unquestionably the product of a culture and rejection of it means rejection of the culture it conveys, a threat to its expansion and existence. Moreover, they believe that learners who are made literate in languages other than theirs are put at a disadvantage from the beginning. In addition to learning the script, they have to learn the language. As a result, their economic and social chances are affected.

The use of the mother tongue in teaching adult literacy was adopted by the Russian literacy campaign. In the early years of the campaign under Lenin, over seventy languages in Russia were used and the learners were given the choice to become literate in their mother tongues and/or in the official language. When Stalin came to power, the literacy work was carried out in the Cyrillic alphabet and with fewer dialects (Bhola, 1984).

The pedagogical, social and psychological benefits that accrue from mother tongue literacy are undeniable. Such goals, however, have not always been heeded. According to Spencer (1963), the Soviet Union's promotion of minor languages was politically based as it aimed to repress and control the emergence of regional interest groups, particularly in the Muslim areas. In other cases, the learners' potential has been limited to the opportunities available in the mother tongue. In South Africa, for instance, the promotion of ethno-linguistic homelands and the teaching of indigenous languages prevented the indigenous people from benefitting from the socio-economic and political power associated with the acquisition of the national and international languages. In other situations, namely Papua New Guinea, the development of tribal languages lessened people's attachment to their nation and their assimilation into national culture (Shaw, 1983). In this respect, UNESCO (1953:55) encouraged the importance of the promotion of a national language for unity, communication, and socioeconomic purposes by stating that:

> If, however, a child is brought up in a community which speaks a language different from the official one of his country, or one which is not a world language with a well developed technological and cultural vocabulary and literature, he needs to be taught a second language; in order to feel at home in the language in which the affairs of his government are carried on; in order to have access to world history, news, art, sciences and technology.

Practically, this would mean that to remain literate and satisfy their economic, social and political needs, speakers of minor or minority languages have to learn one or perhaps two other languages. These mediums would be the official language of their nation and another language of wider-communication, namely English or French, as is the case in many independent African countries.

### Selected mother tongue experience

While recognizing the importance of using mother tongue for literacy, many African countries were faced with the impossibility of launching literacy programs in all existing mother tongues. Therefore, they established a set of criteria upon which they selected the dialect to be used in literacy teaching. The criteria based on for the development of a selected mother tongue policy include the size of the language group, the cultural values associated with the language, and the availability of written material in the language. Therefore, the number of the selected languages varied from one country to the other. For example, Mali conducted its literacy in four major mother tongues especially in rural areas where French was unknown to the population. Senegal used three languages in the literacy programs. Nigeria, where more than 200 languages are spoken, used at least forty-four languages in teaching literacy. After the 1974 revolution, Ethiopia switched from the use of one single language, Amharic, to the use of five languages in the 1979 campaign. In Afghanistan, the 1977 revolution resulted in the teaching of five languages.

Many problems associated with literacy in selected mother tongues have been reported (Shaw, 1983; Coulmas, 1984). The most important ones pertain to the development of orthographies and teaching materials, the training of teachers and the possible relapse into illiteracy due to limited written material, as was the case in Mali (Hoben, 1980). Other problems have been reported by the 1978 UNESCO's literacy recommendations which explain that while mother tongue literacy is effective, its teaching poses some problems in certain situations. Among the reported problems are: the lack of a writing system, the problem of the script, the difference between the written and spoken forms of the language, the plenitude of mother tongues, cost, the non-availability of instructors and textbooks, to name but a few. UNESCO recommends that these problems should be studied carefully in order to come up with the best choices for particular situations. Still other problems emanated from the learners. These include the feeling of resentment among the speakers of the non-selected languages, and the non-motivation of the target population to become literate in non-prestigious languages, as was the case in Nigeria (Okezie, 1975), and in Gambia (The British Council, 1978).

### The transitional stage experience

UNESCO's language experts encouraged the teaching of literacy in the mother tongue to adults, especially in cases where it is different from the official language, and suggested that once literacy is achieved in the mother tongue, the learners should be encouraged to read in a major language or in one that particularly interests them.

This transitional stage in acquiring literacy has been advocated by Cummins (1979) and was revealed to be efficient through the confirmation of his *developmental interdependence hypothesis* which holds that the level of second-language competence that a child acquires is partly dependent on the level of competence achieved in the first language, as a result of a *common underlying proficiency.* Accordingly, many linguists and educators maintain that first language literacy facilitates the acquisition of second language literacy. Research findings from educationalists in both developed and developing nations support the hypothesis (Wagner, Spratt and Ezzaki, 1989; Skutnabb-Kangas and Toukomaa, 1976; Tomori and Okedara, 1971). Although Wagner et al's. (1989) study does not deal with the transfer of mother tongue literacy (Moroccan Arabic and/or Amazigh as teaching in such languages is not yet applicable in Morocco) but rather the transfer of Classical Arabic reading skills to French, their findings still support the hypothesis as the transfer is mainly due to decoding skills based on the first-language literacy knowledge.

In keeping with Cummins' hypothesis, Bamgbose (1984) suggests that in cases where learners have to acquire literacy in a non-native language, it is absolutely necessary for them to go through a transitional period where they would acquire basic skills in their mother tongue. The concept of "mother tongue" has been defined as the initial or first language that is naturally acquired. In the same vein, Srivastava (1984) proposes a *Vernacular-cum transfer* approach to literacy acquisition. This approach claims that literacy in India should be initiated in the language that is most familiar to the learner and then transferred to the medium of formal instruction. The author explains that in so doing, the learner proceeds from the known to the unknown. S/he will, thus, be spared the burden of learning two skills at a time, namely literacy skills such as reading and writing and oral and aural skills like speaking and listening. The author adds that within this approach, the learner will be proud of his or her language and avoid stigmatising it.

While maintaining the importance of mother tongue literacy, Okedara and Okedara (1992) believe that mother tongue literacy in Nigeria would not be effective unless governmental efforts to develop indigenous language orthographies and literature are taken. In the same vein, Akinnaso (1993) reports that the mother tongue could be a facilitating factor in acquiring literacy only when other conditions are met with such as good quality instructional facilities. Likewise, Cowan (1983) argues that the hypothesis which states that the *indigenization* of the languages of instruction would pave the way for literacy in the official languages is not *self-implementing* in Sudan. Based on results from the *Bari* children who, after three years of instruction in the local language, were unable to attain functional literacy skills, he questions the utility of mother tongue literacy in contexts where teacher training, appropriate material and teaching techniques as well as motivation and support for literacy are lacking.

On the other hand, Alisjahbana (1984) sustains that it is a difficult task for mother languages in developing countries to catch up with modern languages. Given this situation, the author explains that minority languages will lose their importance through compulsory education, use of modern national languages and universal communication. He concludes that in order to avoid the dry rationality of modern languages, language planners of modern official national languages need to transmit as much as possible of local culture and poetry from the mother languages into the modern ones.

To deal with this controversy, Srivastava (1984), who believes in the *Transfer Model*, which consists in initiating literacy in the mother tongue and subsequently introducing the official language, states that literacy as a skill is better achieved when the language of literacy is the mother tongue. Literacy as a function, however, is better attained when the language of instruction is the language of wider communication. On the other hand, Shaw (1983) suggests that language choice for adult literacy programs in multilingual settings should be based on the language which better answers the language needs of the learners.

**The official language experience**

Other campaigns and programs were launched in the official language of their countries. Such a policy, however, has been identified as a negative experience in certain situations. In this respect, the *Experimental World Literacy Program* was criticized for propagating a dominant language that was unknown to the linguistic minorities. This resulted in a situation where the learners failed to learn the language and the information displayed in that language. In this respect, UNESCO (1976:170) concludes that "the closer the language used to present the content and materials of the course to the workers' everyday language, the more effective the literacy program."

Evaluation reports reveal that the non-command of the language of instruction by the learners is one of the most important obstacles to the success of a campaign. The evaluation of the EWLP in Ethiopia, for instance, reveals that the high dropout rates and slow progress of the learners were mainly due to the fact that over 60 percent of people from the rural industrial area did not know Amharic, the language of literacy. Likewise, a Tanzanian literacy evaluation's report shows that about 65 percent of the male Tanzanian population and 95 percent of the female one do not speak Swahili, which results in serious language problems in teaching literacy (Shaw, 1983).

Other studies, however, report the success of using a second language in Ethiopian adult literacy programs (Ferguson, 1971). Ferguson's findings reveal that Ethiopian learners are able to achieve literacy in languages that are unfamiliar to them, namely classical and religious languages such as Geez or Arabic and even in the national language, Amharic. He adds that in some cases, the non-speakers of Amharic do better than the native-speaker group. In the light of his findings, Ferguson suggests that, rather than claiming mother tongue literacy, decision-makers have to consider the status of the languages of literacy and the motivational and religious values associated with their role in teaching literacy. Six years later, Sjostrom and Sjostrom (1977) came out with similar results showing that the non-native speakers of Amharic acquire literacy as well and even better than the Amharic speakers' group. In both studies, however, no reference is made to the degree of mastery of Amharic by their non-native informants.

This review of language and literacy reveals that several approaches to the language of literacy exist, each with advantages and disadvantages. Therefore, no definite answer as to which approach would work best in adult literacy is available. While an approach may work in some situations, it would not in others. Even Shaw's study which attempts to offer decision-makers guidelines as to which language to be used in adult literacy programs, comes to the conclusion that there is no perfect choice that would work for all situations and suggests that the best language for adult literacy is a functional language which answers the literacy needs of the learner, whatever that may be. By analysing the literacy needs and attainments of Moroccan adult literacy graduates, the present research will provide data on the extent to which teaching literacy in the official language, which is Standard Arabic, answers the learners' literacy needs and learning needs and prepares them to handle everyday literacy.

## ADULT LITERACY AS A BASIC SKILL: WHERE DOES THE PRESENT STUDY STAND?

In the present book, basic literacy is defined as school-based literacy. More specifically, it refers to the reading skills that the learners have acquired through their literacy training. These include pre-reading skills and reading comprehension skills. Evaluation of the learners' basic literacy is done through an achievement test, the contents of which are drawn from the textbooks used in Moroccan adult literacy programs. For more details, see chapter 4. This evaluation seeks to answer the research question which deals with the extent to which the informants of the present research master what they have learned from the literacy course that has been designed for them. As already explained the relevance of this work lies in its assessment of the efficiency of the designed literacy course on the basis of skill ability rather than self-report. In addition, by comparing the learners' achievements according to their mother tongue, in this case Arabophones and Amazighophones, this study will fill the gap in the research on the impact of language policy in Moroccan adult literacy. As noted above, there is some evidence as to the impact of language policy on the basic literacy attainments of non-literate adults. No such information, however, is available in the Moroccan context. In fact, no official document has ever explicitly stated the language policy that is adopted in Moroccan adult programs. Even the *Commission Spéciale d'Education et de Formation* (1999) "Special Commission for Education and Training" made no reference to the language(s) to be used in adult literacy programs despite the document's focus on the necessity to give priority to adult literacy and its "modest" call for the teaching of Amazigh for rural children. It is to be noted though that considerable research in teaching in the mother tongue and the choice of the language(s) of literacy for the teaching of Moroccan children in an L2 context, namely in the Netherlands, is available (Ruiter, 1990; Ruiter, 1994; Ruiter, 1995).

Adult illiteracy in Morocco persists despite the governments' attempts to eradicate it. Part of the problem is probably that no attention has been paid to how non-literate adult learners need literacy and equally important how they acquire it. While Boukous and Agnaou's study (2001) deals with the problem, it does not address the language issue as a learning process nor does it deal with it as a predictor variable. This limitation pertains to the assessment procedure it uses in determining the literacy levels of informants. Based on the United Nations assessment technique (1989), this procedure consists of assessing the learners' literacy levels and, accordingly, assigning them to appropriate literacy categories. One limitation of these categorical breakdowns is that they are based on product tests rather than process tests—that is to say, they investigate literacy in terms of the results of learning rather than in terms of the skills needed to learn. Second, such categorization does not permit the researcher to deal with literacy as an individual phenomenon. Hence, important diagnostic information as to the learners' reading and writing difficulties, comprehension strategies, language problems, and attitudes is not taken into account.

Aware of these limitations, the present study adopts another technique, which is a combination of an assessment of the learners' literacy levels, their reading strategies and their scores. In so doing, it investigates literacy as both a learning process and an end product process. Chapter 4 provides ampler description of the investigation of this issue.

## FUNCTIONAL LITERACY

Toward a clear definition, the present section attempts to review studies related to the concept of functional literacy, present the historical events that contributed to its emergence and application in adult literacy programs, clarify which aspect of the definition is adopted by the present study and show how it is measured.

### Definition

Functional literacy refers to the ability to use reading and writing skills sufficiently well for the purposes and activities which normally require literacy in adult life or in a person's social position. An inability to do this is known as functional illiteracy. People who are functionally illiterate are illiterate with regard to all functional purposes. For instance, they may be able to write their names and read simple signs, but they can do little else. According to Gray (1956:24) "a person is functionally literate when he has acquired the knowledge and skills in reading and writing which enable him to engage in all those activities in which literacy is normally assumed in his culture or group." Hence, functional literacy is closely connected to a person's culture and community.

### The multi-facets of functional literacy

Illiteracy and literacy are relative and so is functional literacy as regards the general area of skills covered by its definition. For instance, Gray's linking literacy to culture or group gives a *relativistic* understanding of functional literacy. In fact, there is a wide variety of literacy tasks that an individual may be required to perform and these change as a function of the various and different societal and occupational roles that s/he may occupy within his or her culture or group. Gray's definition also implies that there are no limits to functional literacy. It involves reading and writing competencies related to the performance of essential tasks in daily life, and often regarded as essential by the learners, such as gleaning information from television and newspapers, reading a train schedule, making out a bank deposit, understanding advertisements and election posters, interpreting maps, following instructions, comprehending medicine labels, and the like. Functional literacy may also include other literacies: graphic literacy, technological literacy, scientific literacy, cultural literacy, religious literacy, computer literacy and so on. The ability to accomplish adequately these specific tasks is what Kirsch and Guthrie (1977) refer to as "functional competence". Therefore, the levels of qualifications for socio-economic integration are difficult to discern as they change according to individuals, groups, and societies.

Functional literacy is also coupled with the ability to enter and survive in the work force. It is, then, defined as the ability to use the acquired skills to function productively and effectively in the workplace or in society at large. In this respect, the *World Conference of Ministers of Education on the Eradication of illiteracy*, held in Teheran in 1965, defines functional literacy as "linked to a vocational training program and encouraging the rapid growth of the individual's productivity" (Hamadache and Martin, 1986:30).

## The historical background of functional literacy

Historically, the concern for "functional literacy" emerged as a consequence of industrialization and the need for the working mass to survive in the job market. According to Stercq (1993), functional illiteracy originated as a problem in 1876 with the discovery of electricity and the invention of the light bulb, the phonograph, the electric locomotive, the telephone, and so on. The functionally illiterate then became the product of a new era of industrialization and socio-economic changes that generated new requirements in terms of work skills and organization.

Functional illiteracy has been rediscovered in the early 1970's with the first oil crisis and the spectacular rise in unemployment, especially among young people. It was then correlated with poverty and marginalisation. In the late 1980's, functional illiteracy was viewed as an educational problem closely linked to the mechanisms of social discrimination and it became the center of an alarmist economic issue. The costs it entailed were measured in terms of billion dollars in developed countries, namely the United States, Canada, and France (The UNESCO Courier, 1990). Thus, the concept of literacy gained a new dimension as it became associated with economic development and social transformation.

**Functional literacy and adult education programs**

To answer the economic and development needs of the functionally illiterate, many vocational and adult literacy programs have been developed in the economic sector, the most widely known being the EWLP. In this program, learning takes place in actual work situations, where the workers are required to apply the acquired literacy skills to their occupational tasks to increase productivity and economic development.

In 1961, the United Nations Assembly asked UNESCO for a report on World illiteracy and recommendations for action. UNESCO responded with a plan for a World massive action that would involve 330 million illiterates. Despite the 1963 General Assembly's support, the project was abandoned at the 1964 session of UNESCO's General conference. This was due to the huge cost it would entail and because of the economists' belief that better returns are to be expected from selected programs rather than from mass designs and large-scale campaigns. In 1965, the *World Congress of Ministers of Education on the Eradication of Illiteracy* took place in Tehran and gave the political and technical support for the EWLP, which was initiated one year later.

Between 1966 and 1974, UNESCO implemented the EWLP, which aimed at selectivity and functionality. The main concern of this program was to provide quantitative assessments of the correlation between work-oriented literacy and worker productivity (Coombs 1985, Jones 1988). To this effect, the program set three objectives: the development of a new functional approach to literacy, associating it to job requirements in eleven national programs, namely Algeria, Ecuador, Ethiopia, Guinea, India, Iran, Madagascar, Mali, Sudan, Syria, and Tanzania; the design of teaching programs for carefully selected learners and the assessment of the impact of training on worker productivity and generation of universal comparisons. In agreement with the guidelines of the Tehran's *World Congress of Ministers of Education on the Eradication of Illiteracy*, Morocco also developed selective and work-oriented adult literacy programs. Information on such programs is given in chapter 3.

The EWLP generated a big deal of controversy. For instance, Paulo Freire (1973) criticised the program for its monolithic definition of literacy, which is restricted to functionality and socio-economic returns at the expense of the learner's critical awareness of his or her condition within the society. In the same vein, UNESCO (1976) reports on some problems inherent to the program. These relate to the existence of different definitions of functional literacy, insufficient preparation to deal with administrative structure, diversity of educational methods and learners' attitudes as specific to each country, lack of interdepartmental coordination, unstable socio-economic and political situations of some of the target countries, unreliable evaluation procedures, to name but a few. Jones (1990) states that while the first two objectives of the EWLP were successful, as illustrated by the number of countries that continue to adopt the program even after the financial support had been consummated, the last aim was hampered by a set of methodological difficulties, namely, the absence of reliable quantitative data and inexperience in processing cross-national data for generalization.

In the nineties, many developing countries developed functionally-based programs especially for women. Examples of these approaches to women's literacy and development are described in Ouane (1992). They include: Literacy for Income Generation Programs, Employment-Oriented Learning Programs, Skill Training Programs, and Small Farmers Development Projects. In addition to teaching literacy, these programs, which exist mainly in rural areas, encourage the learners to expand their own business thanks to special learning funds or loans. The main objectives of these programs are to combat illiteracy through income generating activities, and to pursue personal development, which in turn has an important impact on the family and the social environment of the learner.

## Assessing functional literacy

Functional literacy is gaining an increasingly outstanding place in the domain of reading instruction. According to the United States National Reading Center "A person is functionally literate when he has command of the reading skills that permit him to go about his daily activities successfully on the job, or to move about society normally with comprehension of the usual printed expressions and messages he encounters." (Ouane, 1992:72). Thus, teaching and eventually assessing functional literacy and numeracy skills necessitates a better understanding of the printed materials that one is likely to encounter in his or her daily life and analysing the problem-solving skills they require

While some researchers investigate adult functional literacy skills in terms of their application in the workplace (Mikulecky, 1982; Stitch, 1975), others assess the use of these in everyday activities as "document literacy" (Kirsch and Jungeblut, 1986). For both purposes, a wide range of tests has been developed (Bowren and Zintz, 1977). Gaining insight from Bowren and Zintz, the present research seeks to analyze functional literacy as the ability to recognize and comprehend written texts that are directly associated with everyday literacy experiences such as filling out self-related information forms, understanding ads and messages, reading drug prescriptions, bills, and the like. The learners' priority functional needs are also surveyed and assessed.

## LITERACY AS AN EMPOWERING SKILL

Literacy as an empowering skill extends the cognitive and functional knowledge of reading, writing and mathematics. It is a process of reflecting critically upon one's situation within society and acting collectively with the objective of changing what is repressive about it. As explained in chapter 1, this *emancipatory* view of literacy emerged in the seventies with the works of Freire who considers literacy as a process of empowerment for oppressed people all over the world, and believes that it can bring about change and combat inequities and injustices in society. In becoming literate, what is important is not the possession of a set of literacy skills and the ability to perform functional tasks in specific socio-cultural settings but rather the process of gaining a new position in society. In this way, literacy is no longer an individual attribute but rather a collective *emancipatory* political act providing the mass with adequate intellectual forces to reflect on illiteracy as a manifestation of underdevelopment and oppression. Within this school of thought, illiteracy is regarded as a violation of human rights and an injustice (Ramdas, 1989; Walsh, 1991; Auerbach, 1992), a sign of cultural deprivation (Harrison, 1981), a means of perpetuating the gender gap, and a power to subdue women (Stromquist, 1990; Carmack, 1992) and other oppressed groups (Freire, 1970a; Harrison, 1981).

Injustice, oppression, deprivation and subordination are features of the marginalized groups including the poor, the disabled, the illiterate, the indigenous and, cutting across these categories, women. Examples of women's subordination include insignificant representation in the governing system, restricted participation in the economic sector, reduced wages, exclusive responsibility for domestic work, family and children, wife beating, and huge gender gaps in literacy, to name but a few. Aware of this alarming situation, the concept of literacy as an empowering means has been developed within gender scholarship.

### Definition of empowerment

According to Stromquist (1993), empowerment involves women's awareness of their conditions, their capability and belief that they can successfully act at personal and societal levels to improve their conditions, and finally their ability to analyze and criticize their environment in both social and political terms. Indeed, the author claims that a full definition of empowerment must include cognitive, psychological, political and economic components. She explains that the cognitive component is related to addressing women's condition of subordination. The psychological component would involve the development of feelings that women can act to improve their conditions. The political component encompasses the ability to organize and mobilize society for social changes. Finally, the economic component of empowerment embodies the aptitude to obtain some degree of financial autonomy. Stromquist concludes that while women can be empowered individually, their collective awareness and action is fundamental to attaining social transformation.

The cognitive and psychological components of empowerment as suggested by Stromquist (1993) involve women's mobilization for reflecting on their status and redressing the imbalance in that status. The political and economic dimensions of empowerment would require collaboration from other parties, namely the government. This implies that the potential agents of empowerment are women themselves together with other agencies whose contribution would consist of changing the pre-established partition of power and supplying means and resources to ensure women's full integration and empowerment. Such enterprise would consist of providing the measures needed to give women more control over their lives through participation in decision-making and increasing self-reliance and self-confidence. For example, these measures may consist in providing knowledge, training, skills and credit needed for productive work and having access to decision-making processes inside the family and the community.

The definition of empowerment as a means to achieve a democratic distribution of power and knowledge within society has many implications for gender. Gender is understood as a socio-cultural construct rather than a biological one where women and men are ascribed specific social roles within society (Haider, 1996). This culturally-based definition of gender explains that the division of social roles between men and women is the product of culture rather the human physiology or anatomy. As Simone de Beauvoir (1949) explains:

> One is not born, but rather becomes a woman. No biological, physiological, or economic fate determines the figure that the human female presents in society; it is civilisation as a whole that produces this creature.

Being dependent on culture, gender relations in society can be transformed and changed through the transmission of empowering values and education. It follows from this that the concept of empowerment as applied to gender implies a change toward a democratic distribution of power within society. The important agents of this change are women themselves and an encouraging policy climate that would be favourable to involving women in the economic, political and social decision-making processes through raising gender issues within the national policy and securing girls' and women's access to education and information.

## APPROACHES TO WOMEN'S LITERACY

As explained in chapter 1, addressing women's condition and position through literacy has been carried out by the WID movement and the GEA, respectively. The WID approach examines the current condition of women and advocates their integration in any development endeavor. Hence, it connects literacy work to issues related to development such as health, fertility, nutrition, and employment. The GEA claims that actions should be directed to the basic determinants of the position, status and role of men and women. It focuses on the gender relationships that govern and sustain the existing inequities. Its perspective is based on analysing the gender relations in terms of difference and dominance and works toward reshaping these relations as they constrain efforts to redress women's condition. In so doing, it deals with measures required to give women more control over their lives such as their participation in decision-making, increase of their self-reliance and self-confidence so as to become active agents in the society. By implication, it aims at eliminating any reproduction of the stereotyped roles in teaching adults. Accordingly, it takes into consideration women's literacy needs that are linked to the processes of social questioning and transformation. For instance, Stromquist (1992:63–64) states, "Literacy for women has to provide access not only to the written world but also to the information they need to transform the world." This means that literacy content and procedure should be both *practical* and *emancipatory.* But to achieve this, Stromquist contends that women should play an active role in the implementation of literacy programs. She notes, though, that women's involvement in designing literacy programs has been opposed by many government bureaucrats.

### Gender approaches to literacy as applied in the present research

The present research assumes that both WID and GEA are needed to combat female illiteracy and to redress women's condition and position. In fact, Molyneux's (1987) theory of *practical gender interests* and *strategic gender interests*, which the present research advocates, embraces both approaches. The *practical* side of literacy would include the learners' capacity to use and understand daily encountered document literacy. The strategic side of literacy, on the other hand, would refer to the learners' right to be made literate through an empowering content that is free from any forms of reproduction and re-domestication.

## Measuring empowerment

Immediate effects of empowering literacy are very difficult to measure in empirical terms. In many respects, empowering literacy is conceived of as a philosophical orientation toward social change. Usually, the effects of social change are attested only over long stretches of time, hence their investigation could be achieved only within a longitudinal design. The results of such an investigation, however, would undoubtedly be contaminated by interfering historical and social factors. Perhaps due to these constraints, very few scholars have undertaken to study the role of literacy from this perspective. To my knowledge, only Bhola (1984) and Arnove and Graff (1987) investigated the issue and its impacts on a national level. Their historical investigations of literacy campaigns following the communist revolutions have shown that literacy for empowerment, beside other historical and social factors, has indeed played an important role in transforming the system of values of illiterate adults and in restructuring oppressive relations in society at large (Arnove and Graff, 1987; Bhola, 1984).

In the field of female literacy, empowerment entails not only a change of women from the category of the non-literate to the literate, but involves processes that trigger their awareness of their condition and contributes to its change in a positive way. Accordingly, empowering literacy takes on a fundamentally transformative power in the psychological as well as the material lives of non-literate women all over the world. Accessible studies show that positive transformations associated with female literacy within this perspective have so far been assessed only through the use of questionnaires and testimonies (Lind and Johnston, 1990). The learners are asked how much literacy has affected their attitudes, behaviors and status at home, in the workplace and in society as a whole. Central in this type of research, then, is the learner's own opinions and experiences, which, while being very important, may be highly subjective. Hence, one possible way to extend this research is to investigate these effects in terms of longitudinal and anthropological studies. The present study does not claim to undertake these studies because this would have necessitated a different research design, which would require much time and specialized expertise, which is beyond the scope of the present research. Hence, rather than dealing with the empowering effects as perceived by the learners, the present study deals with the orientation adopted toward the attainment of these effects through an assessment of the contents of the designed textbooks.

The messages conveyed by the text or images of the teaching materials determine the direction followed in teaching and eventually transforming the minds of the learners, men or women. Indeed, teaching materials can blur women's aspirations for change or potential by assigning them in conventional roles and representing them in stereotyped traits. At the same time, they can be used to convey ideas that promote task-sharing between men and women both inside and outside the home and project images that highlight the status of women, assert their rights and stress the importance of their participation in society. This provides an opportunity to investigate such materials and identify the orientation which they adopt in inculcating the literacy skills in the target learners. Criteria used for the evaluation of these materials are explained in chapter 4 and their analysis is provided in chapter 8.

## CONCLUSION

The present review has set out to address the concept of literacy in terms of three skills. These skills constitute a conceptual framework for understanding the phenomenon of adult illiteracy among men and women, as both are victims of socio-economic and human underdevelopment, notably in developing societies. In such societies, however, women are further marginalized through traditional and cultural practices to the extent that we now speak of the *feminization of poverty* and *the feminization of illiteracy*. Hence, it is necessary to deal with women's literacy within a broader perspective, which regards literacy as basic, functional and empowering. In sum, and in view of what has been said in the present chapter, literacy is understood as the ability to acquire a set of instrumental reading skills which are necessary for women to function effectively in life contexts and to reflect on their condition of subordination with the aim that they can change it in collaboration with well-advised male partners. Chapter 4 provides technical information on how each element of this literacy construct is assessed in the present research. But first, it is necessary to examine Morocco's efforts to combat adult illiteracy. This is what is dealt with in the next chapter.

3

# The Planning and Organization of Moroccan Adult Literacy Campaigns and Programs

The present chapter provides a historical description of the planning and organization of adult literacy campaigns and programs that were carried out in Morocco from Independence in 1956 to the year 2000. The chapter is divided into three parts. The first part relates the government's efforts to combat illiteracy since Independence to the celebration of the international year in 1990. The second part deals with the new directions that have taken place in Moroccan adult literacy programs and campaigns since the celebration of the international literacy year to the publication of The National Charter of Education and Training in 1999. The last part investigates the place of adult literacy in the Charter and in the education decade (200–2010) that was launched by King Mohammed VI in September 2000. Related information is taken from documents supplied by the Ministry of National Education, the Ministry of Youth and Sports, the Literacy Directorate, and the Charter.

The aim of this chapter is threefold as it seeks to bring to light the triggering events of the literacy action in Morocco and explain its goals, mobilization, and implementation, to unveil the inherent obstacles to its realization, and to explain the period and the type of the literacy programs investigated by the present study. Before proceeding to these descriptions, brief definitions of the concepts *adult education, campaign* and *program* are given hereafter.

## DEFINING ADULT EDUCATION, CAMPAIGN AND PROGRAM

Adult education, adult literacy and adult basic education are used in the present study interchangeably to refer to literacy activities that are designed for people who never attended school at their child age or who dropped out of school before attaining literacy threshold levels. These include the educationally disadvantaged people who, because they do not possess basic literacy skills, resort to basic education training to acquire those skills through adult literacy campaigns or programs.

In keeping with (Bhola, 1987:211) *literacy campaign* is defined as "a mass approach that seeks to make all adult men and women in a nation literate within a particular time frame" On the other hand, *literacy programs*, while being established all over a country or region, are selective in nature as they focus on particular communities, professional groups and sectors. Bhola distinguishes between the *program approach* to literacy and the *mass approach* to literacy. The author claims that while both involve planned and systematic objectives, the *campaign approach* denotes "war" as it is viewed in terms of *urgency* and *combativeness* within a limited time. A *program approach*, however, does not involve such urgency and enthusiasm. Bhola adds that literacy programs' objectives are mainly economic, technological, and developmental rather than political and ideological.

According to the Moroccan Adult Literacy Directorate, a literacy campaign, called *'al-ḫamla 'al-3a:mma*, the general campaign, is meant to refer to the adult literacy courses that are organized by the Directorate in collaboration with the Ministry of Education. On the other hand, a literacy program, called *bara:mij maḫw 'al-'ummija*, anti-illiteracy programs, refers to the literacy courses that are supplied by every Ministry or by voluntary and non-governmental associations. In the present study, *campaign* and *program* are used interchangeably to refer to both the general campaign and anti-illiteracy programs.

## LITERACY CAMPAIGNS AND PROGRAMS: FROM 1956 TO 1990

Since Independence in 1956, Moroccan governments have made great efforts to eradicate illiteracy through various means: expansion of primary education, development of secondary and tertiary education, and adult basic or vocational training. This section deals with the Moroccan governments' endeavor to combat illiteracy through adult education. The periods dealt with start from independence in 1956 to the celebration of the international literacy year in 1990.

### The political side of literacy

According to Arnove and Graff (1987), literacy by itself has not always been an absolute goal worldwide. Based on a historical and comparative approach, the authors claim that literacy campaigns have aimed at the transformation of societal structures and belief systems through massive mobilization which usually involves compulsion and social pressure to disseminate a specific doctrine or to attain particular goals such as maintaining social and political order. By way of illustration, they explained that in the sixteenth century, the German, Swedish, and Scottish literacy campaigns sought to achieve religious reformation and propagation. Likewise, the twentieth century campaigns, namely in USSR, China, Cuba, Nicaragua headed a new political culture and economic development through revolution and war. Other countries struggled for independence from colonial domination, as is the case in Vietnam and Tanzania.

In view of these situations, where literacy is linked to religious transformation (Protestants versus Catholics), political education in specific doctrines such as Marxism-Leninism, or nationalist movements like Sandinismo, the authors contend that literacy provision is not designed to gratify the specific needs of the learner but rather the learner is confined to a particular text or doctrine for fear of perceiving the world differently and questioning the established socio-political order.

In Morocco, the government's first efforts to combat illiteracy were predominantly linked to the country's liberation from the colonizer and aimed to contribute to a new political order and language policy. Later on, particularly in the sixties, there has been a change in perspective and literacy provision became mainly based on functionality and economic development. Therefore, the literacy efforts in Morocco have been national, selective and sectorial.

At the national level, the Moroccan government launched two literacy campaigns immediately after independence in 1956 and 1957. These campaigns were organized by the Moroccan League for Basic Education and Adult Literacy under the patronage of the late king Mohammed V. While the campaigns were designed to answer the learner's basic needs in literacy, they were linked to the Nation's will to celebrate independence and engage in a new era. This governmental will and involvement was supported by massive mobilization from both literate and non-literate people. Indeed, the two campaigns involved more than three million beneficiaries and led to the publication of *Manar Al-Maghreb*, a specialized newspaper for the neo-literates. This post-literacy material, however, stopped from being issued a few years after the campaign.

## The functional side of literacy

From 1961 to 1963, adult literacy became selective and took the form of programs rather than campaigns despite the huge number of the non-literate people who represented 87 percent of the adult population, according to the first population census which took place in 1960. This selection concerned rural women and agricultural workers in specific regions.

The rural women's literacy program was organized by the Ministry of Youth and Sports. 335 regional offices supervised its action. It was mainly addressed to non-literate girls whose age ranged from 10 to 15. The course was meant to teach basic literacy. Its contents include topics on child development, food, nutrition, family health and family planning. This program, however, did not succeed to attract sufficient participants from the target population.

The rural developmental literacy program, designed to educate agricultural workers, was organized by the Ministry of the Interior. Its objective was to heighten the beneficiaries' awareness of the importance of the use of new agricultural methods and techniques for better production. Fifty rural centers were open to receive the target beneficiaries. Their effective participation, however, was very limited. The province that benefited most from the rural development program was that of Beni Mellal. This project was sponsored by UNESCO. Its originality lies in the fact that it used the local radio broadcast along with schools to combat the illiteracy of 53,000 citizens within a period of thirteen weeks only. Unfortunately, this experience was not generalized to other regions due to limited funds.

## The Experimental World Literacy Program (EWLP)

As stated in chapter 2, EWLP was also launched in Morocco. This program was mainly functional and was meant to increase the quality of the workers' production and ensure their efficient use of the production machines within the industrial sectors. Four industrial sectors benefited from this program. These are: The Sherifian Phosphate Office, The National Electricity Office, The National Railways Office, and Foreign Marketing Office. The course lasted six months and took place inside the work place. About 13,000 workers followed this program within the Phosphate sector.

Notwithstanding the efforts of these programs to *alphabetize* important proportions of the non-literate population, their strategy was marked by limited pedagogical configurations and patterns of mobilization and was rather situational and unstructured.

## Looking for a responsible body

From 1965 to 1982, the main role of adult literacy rested with the education authorities. The Population censuses which took place in that period revealed a 12 percent decrease in 1970 with 75 percent illiterates but only 10 percent decrease twelve years later in 1982 with 65 percent illiterates. The absolute number of illiterates, however, increased from 6,560.00 in 1960 to 10, 61, 3,100 in 1982. In addition to that, the absolute number of unschooled children whose age ranges from seven to eleven rose from 1,097, 807 in 1960 to 2,601, 274 in 1982, which resulted in a child illiteracy increase rate that attained more than 236 percent (Ibaaquil, 1994, cited in Essaknaoui, 1998).

In the late 1970s, the problem of adult illiteracy was no longer regarded as a disease to be eradicated within a specified time, but was rather considered as a social phenomenon with multi facets. Hence, a proclamation was published in 1978 to transfer the responsibility of adult literacy to the social affairs' authority. In April 20, 1982, a decree was promulgated to create an adult literacy administration service within the Ministry of Traditional Industry and Social Affairs. At that time, the national adult illiteracy rate was 65 percent.

In the 1981–1985 *quinquennial* plan, the government allocated symbolic funds for the establishment of yearly adult literacy programs. The target population was non-literate adults whose age was between 10 and 45 with a focus on the centers and cooperatives that belonged to the supervising ministry. 81,000 non-literate Moroccans took advantage of these programs. In 1986, another literacy program was launched. The interesting thing about this program is that it was spread over a two-year period. The course was provided through evening classes for four hours a week and six months a year. The first year course was intended to teach basic literacy and numeracy. The second year course was meant to teach the first year graduates basic socio-cultural skills. Special textbooks were published in Standard Arabic for each grade level. The total population that benefited from this literacy program involved about 50,000 people. Due to limited funds, this program approach was restricted to five provinces that were marked by heavy demographic concentrations. These were Casablanca, Fès, Marrakech, Agadir and Oujda.

In view of what has been said in this section, one can realize that Morocco's efforts to combat illiteracy are indeed colossal, but they have not kept pace with the demands of the explosive rates of population growth. And yet in some ways, one can say that things have not changed considerably. Illiteracy still prevails as it affects more than half of the adult population whose age is 10 and above. According to the World Literacy Report (1993), Morocco's national illiteracy rate was 50.5 percent in 1990. Illiteracy was then linked with poverty, isolation and women. This situation was prevailing in many other developing countries and UNESCO declared that there were an estimated 963 million illiterate adults whose age was fifteen years and more and over 125 million children between the ages of six and eleven, who were not enrolled in school and were hence at risk of becoming the adult illiterates of the twenty-first century. Likewise, women's education trends were serious: one woman out of three is illiterate as compared to one man out of five. Industrialized societies made no exception, one fifth or more of the adult population was unable to cope adequately with the literacy demands of the technological revolution associated with the use of the computer in telecommunications and the job market. Against this backup, UNESCO proclaimed the year 1990 as the International Literacy Year.

## LITERACY CAMPAIGNS AND PROGRAMS: FROM 1990 TO 2000

The present section deals with the new directions and innovations that have been taking place in the Moroccan adult education since the International Literacy Year in 1990 when the problem of illiteracy became essentially linked with the gender gap, rural and urban differences, and lack of professional expertise as regards policy making, organization, budgets, teachers and methods of evaluation.

### The Jomtien call and Morocco's response

As stated in chapter 1, in 1990, the *World Conference on Education for All* took place in Jomtien, Thailand and considered adult literacy and particularly female literacy, as one of its important worldwide goals. The conference's recommendations stressed the importance of reducing the number of illiterates to half of the current rate by the year 2000 and the adoption of a new approach to literacy which focuses on learning as a measurable achievement rather than just mere participation. The Jomtien call triggered international interest in literacy and adult education. Morocco was no exception as adult literacy gained special attention on January 8, 1990, with the call of the late king, Hassan the second, to combating illiteracy. Since then, adult literacy became an integral part of national development plans. A national committee for combating illiteracy was created to coordinate efforts toward adult literacy, to advise on the program and to publicize the campaign. It was composed of the representatives of the governmental and non-governmental agencies as well as political, social and industrial figures and authorities.

The committee launched a general literacy campaign, which was addressed to all illiterates in all provinces of the kingdom; 254,987 people were made literate. Several ministries, local communities, state and private agencies, and non-governmental associations participated in this action under the responsibility of the social authorities which have launched annual campaigns ever since. The establishments involved were: primary schools, the centers of Education and Work, Youth and Sports centers, cooperatives and workshop centers and non-governmental centers. These synergies and collaborations between all the governmental and the non-governmental sectors constituted a turning-point in dealing with the issue of adult illiteracy in Morocco as they planned to eradicate it on a country-wide scale by invoking the following objectives: launching annual campaigns for the benefit of 200,000 non-literates, reducing the gender gap in literacy, increasing public awareness and motivating the target population to participate in the literacy action, developing post-literacy material for the new literates, increasing the training duration from six months to nine months a year, and establishing legislations and laws. On January 13, 1991, the supervising .ministry created the adult literacy department within the Social Affairs Directorate. This department included three administrations that were responsible for:

1. Curriculum Development and Teaching materials.
2. Planning, Programming, Evaluation and Monitoring.
3. Staff Training.

The Adult Literacy Department's efforts to reduce the illiteracy of 200,000 illiterates, which represented only 2 percent of the total illiterate population, were in vain. The 1992–93 campaign covered 166,025 people only. This rate decreased dramatically to 91,575 in the 1993–94 campaign. According to the supervising ministry, this campaign covered only 45.6 percent of the target population. In addition, 76 percent of the involved centers functioned with only one class, which means that only 24 percent of the graduate level classes were available. The reported reasons are the following:

1. Budget constraints and limited infrastructure.
2. Unqualified human resources.
3. Lack of a well defined strategy and policy.
4. Absence of legislations and laws.
5. Non-existence of field-based research, monitoring and follow-up activities.
6. Non-use of publicity to encourage effective participation.
7. Non-sufficient remuneration for the teachers involved.
8. Limited participation of the female population as teachers and learners.
9. The problem of climate and harvests in rural areas.

In 1994, the idea of creating the National Adult Literacy Agency to handle the above-mentioned problems was presented before the Parliament. The Ministry of Employment and Social Affairs, which was the supervising institution at that time, decided to create instead the Adult Literacy Directorate.

### The Moroccan Adult Literacy Directorate

In 1997, the Adult Literacy Directorate came into existence and became the body responsible for the execution of the government's adult literacy policy through partnership with all the actors involved. Upon its creation, the Adult literacy Directorate operated under the aegis of the Ministry of Labour and

Social Affairs. This Directorate is now the authority responsible for the design of the adult literacy programs, textbooks and teacher training, as well as co-ordination and partnership with other government departments which are mobilized for collaboration. These operators include the Social Affaires authority in collaboration with the Ministry of National Education, Youth and Sports, National Cooperation, the Marines, the Royal Armed Forces, Justice, Agriculture, Industry, Tourism and Non-governmental associations.

Among the duties of the directorate are the design, the implementation and evaluation of adult literacy education at the national level; the planning and programming activities take place at the ministry. Implementation occurs at the local provincial level. The regional office acts as a coordinating link between the center and the province through the Provincial Office of Social Affairs and National Cooperation which is composed of inspectors and coordinators who are assigned control evaluation and monitoring. Upon its creation, the Adult Literacy Directorate came out with a policy outline. The next section describes the conditions of its creation and its contents.

## The planning process: a policy outline

Forty-years after independence, the national illiteracy rate was 55 percent and the development of a national strategy and policy to combat adult illiteracy was still a project. On January 8, 1996, the Ministry of Employment and Social Affairs celebrated the Arab day for adult literacy with the presentation of a policy outline concerning the general organizational framework, the services to set up, and the financing procedures. The policy outline included the following recommendations that the Directorate of Adult Literacy set as objectives:

1. To examine and assess the extent of the problem in the light of the number and the geographical distribution of adult illiterates and other local circumstances through the creation of the illiteracy map.
2. To define the timing for the eradication of illiteracy by planning to reduce its rate to 10 percent in 2010 through the organization of yearly literacy campaigns for 680,000 adults.
3. To establish formal legislation.
4. To provide continuing adult education by integrating the adult literacy graduates in formal schooling or vocational training.
5. To develop partnership with all active governmental authorities and non-governmental associations.
6. To involve the local communities in the action.
7. To create a national treasury to finance the literacy action.
8. To undertake evaluation and monitoring as an essential part of the action.

9. To use audio-visual media to publicise the literacy action.
10. To encourage academic research.
11. To provide in-service training for the mobilized teachers.

**Organization and coverage**

At the organizational structure level, the directorate is trusted to execute the following procedures:

1. Publication and distribution of teaching textbooks and reading materials for the new literate.
2. Recruitment and training of teachers.
3. Selection of classrooms.
4. Registration of learners and opening classes.
5. Evaluation.
6. Presentations of certificates to the new literate and rewards to the teachers.

At the coverage level, the directorate adopted three methods of intervention:

1. The general campaign organized by the Social Affairs Authority in collaboration with the Ministry of Education. The former pays the teachers and delivers the teaching materials while the latter provides the teachers and classrooms. This campaign is addressed to all non-literate people whose age is between 10 and 45 throughout Morocco. The course takes place twice a week in the evenings.

2. Selected programs addressed to the centers that operate under the Ministry of Youth and Sport, the National Cooperation and Non-Governmental associations. These programs are designed for women. The course takes place trice a week in the afternoons in Youth and Sport centers and in the morning in the National Cooperation centers. As for Non-Governmental associations, the courses take place in their own centers or in public primary schools. Some provide literacy courses twice a week, others offer daily classes.

3. Sectorial campaigns *al-ḫamala al-iqṯa:3iyya* designed for the workers in the industrial and agricultural sectors where illiteracy rate was about 52 percent (Résultats de l'Enquête Nationale sur le Budget Juin 1997–Juin 1989). These campaigns came into effect only recently in 2000 and special textbooks were published for each sector. The course takes place at the workplace.

The general literacy campaign and the selected programs described above are directed to the illiterate masses, particularly adult women, who are not wage earners or who have very limited participation in non-formal economic sectors. It is noteworthy that these women constitute the majority of the informants of the present research.

## Textbooks and method

The literacy course lasts nine months for a two-year period upon which the literacy graduate is awarded a literacy certificate and given a post-literacy textbook to use at home. Very few classes were designed as a post-literacy grade and all of them were established by non-governmental associations. The lessons are given in Standard Arabic, the national language of the country. The textbook that was used is called *al- qira:'a li al-jami:3* , henceforth Literacy for All. It is composed of two volumes: the basic stage and the follow-up stage. These textbooks were used in all the adult literacy centers that worked under the general campaign and the selected programs irrespective of the learners' age, origin, sex and mother tongue. Their aim, as scantily stated in the textbooks, is to make the learners contribute to the development of their country. Thus, one of the main priorities of the course is to combat religious illiteracy, civic illiteracy, health and family planning illiteracy, ecological and agricultural illiteracy. Information concerning the acquisition of literacy as a skill, however, is inexistent. These textbooks were distributed free of charge for the targeted groups.

The method used in the textbooks is eclectic as it is a combination of the synthetic method and the global method. The synthetic method is based on three techniques: recognition of letters, recognition of sounds, and recognition of syllables. The global method involves recognition of the letters at the level of the word, the phrase and the sentence level. The eclectic method as used in the textbooks starts with the global method and ends with the synthetic method. In other words, it starts with the sentence as a text and moves to the individual words that compose the sentence, and then to the target letter, which is usually written in red in all the presented material. Last, new words and sentences are made up with the new letter.

## Limited returns

Despite the Directorate's efforts to deal with the problem of illiteracy, the 1996–1997 campaign's efficiency was less than 28 percent of what was expected as the dropping-out rate reached 72.24 percent. To handle this situation and in accordance with the guidelines of national cooperation, the National Literacy Committee launched *barna:maj al-mi'at yad* "The One Hundred Hands Program" whose aim was to involve civic society as an efficient and professional agent in the literacy action to ensure a yearly literacy campaign for the benefit of 500,000 and to reduce the national illiteracy rate to 37 percent in the year 2004.

In 1998–1999, the Ministry in charge changed the name under the new government and became The Ministry of Social development, Solidarity, Labor and Vocational Training. Due to the contribution of the One Hundred Hands Program, the number of enrolees (181,000) exceeded the expected one (130,000) and the dropping-out rate decreased to 25 percent as 135,614 beneficiaries participated in the final exams.

It is important to note, though, that at that same period, 60 percent of the female population was still illiterate (Direction de la Statistique, 1998). At the same time, the generalization of child schooling, which is linked to adult literacy, was still a challenge for Morocco. For instance, in 1998 the primary schooling rate in Morocco decreased by 20 percent. (UNESCO's World Report on Education, 1998). More than two million children were deprived of schooling. In fact, only 70.7 percent of children whose age was between seven and twelve were schooled at that time and the schooling rate was less than 50 percent for rural girls. School coverage in the rural areas was less than 42 percent, the number of villages deprived of schools was 1900 and 7830 children had to walk more than two kilometres to reach the school. Moreover, out of 100 children of schooling age, 85 enrol at school, but only 45 complete primary education, meaning that 15 percent remain illiterate and 47 percent would relapse into illiteracy. All these estimates are found in an unpublished official document produced by the Ministry of National Education in July, 1998.

Eight years after the Jomtien call, Moroccan illiteracy campaigning efforts to meet the basic learning needs for all children, youth and adults remain limited due to educational, social and economic factors. This wastage, together with the World's concern about global competitiveness and workforce skills, stimulated the Moroccan nation's interest in reforming its educational system.

## The National Charter of Education and Training

One of the most salient factors affecting adult literacy rates is child schooling. The previous section shows that this is still far from being attained in Morocco. Indeed, illiteracy is expected to prevail until the next century's quarter unless fundamental changes and measures are made in the formal educational system and non-formal education is given high priority. Aware of this alarming situation and realizing the inadequacy of the educational system for the job market and the globalization's constraints, the late king, Hassan the second, launched an appeal for the creation of a special commission charged to reform the Moroccan educational system on March the third, 1999. In October

1999, the commission published the National Charter of Education and Training where literacy and non-formal education aimed the following:

1. Reduction of the national illiteracy rate to 20 percent in 2010 and its total elimination around the year 2015 by giving top priority to the workers in the production sectors, the jobless illiterate adults especially rural and semi-urban women, and the non-literate or drop-outs whose age is less than twenty.
2. Mobilization of schools, educational and training institutions, non-governmental associations, and local communities.
3. Provision of suitable teaching materials for the aimed categories.
4. Reduction of illiteracy in the industrial sector from 50 percent to 10 percent in the year 2010.
5. Generalization of primary education by the year 2004.
6. Public information by spreading literacy through the use of television.
7. Organization of yearly competitions for both the beneficiaries and the supervisors of the literacy action by awarding prizes for individual and collective realizations.

In keeping with the guidelines of the National Charter of Education and Training, the Adult Literacy Directorate started to implement the national policy plan called *'al istra:tijiyya al-waṯaniyya li al-qira:'iyya wa at-takwi:n al-'asa:si:* "the national literacy and basic training strategy". The aim of this policy is threefold: to reduce the illiteracy gender and regional gap among adults, to involve the workers in the industrial sector in functional literacy programs, and to produce new suitable teaching literacy materials.

**The Education Decade: 2000–2010**

The Education Decade (2000–2010) was declared by King Mohammed VI in September 2000 as an important era for the achievement of the goals that have been set up by the Charter as regards to the generalization of child schooling and literacy provision for the adults. Indeed, education has become the second national priority after the national integrity. This political will resulted in a 10 percent enrolment increase in primary education for the school term 2000–2001 in comparison to the preceding year *(L'Economiste,* September 15, 2000:20).

Non-formal education for the eight to sixteen years old, however, is lagging behind. The enrolment rate is less than 1.5 percent of the non-schooled children whose total number is two million and a half. Only 35,855 children have benefited from the 1999–2000 literacy program but 1,214 have succeeded to integrate formal teaching (*L'Economiste,* September 15, 2000: 22).

Concerning adult literacy, one major innovation in the academic year 2000–2001 is the expansion of the use of mosques as non-formal schools in addition to their being places of prayer. Accompanying this is the use of the radio and television for heightening the masses' awareness in Colloquial Arabic, of the problems of illiteracy and gender gaps in education. This information, however, is denied to a significant proportion of the Moroccan population, which consists of monolingual rural Amazigh speakers who undoubtedly suffer from high illiteracy rates. Further innovations consist in the publication of new teaching materials, the reduction of the literacy course period, and the teaching of literacy in the workplace.

## The organizational framework

The administrative framework of the organization of adult literacy is composed of:

1. The Adult Literacy Directorate, which is composed of four departments that handle the following tasks: syllabus management, teaching materials design, adult literacy, and common affairs.
2. The regional delegations, which organize implementation and evaluation.
3. The Consultative staff.
4. The regional literacy committee.
5. The national literacy committee.

After the setting up of the program, the Ministry in charge, whose name changed with the government's shuffle in 2000 and became The Ministry of Labor, Vocational Training, Social Development and Solidarity, the literacy Directorate has adopted four methods of achieving national coverage. These are shortly described hereafter.

## The General-campaign-based literacy program

This is the most orthodox method in implementing the program in the country at large and attracting as many participants as possible. This campaign is organized by the Ministry in charge, which designs and finances the literacy courses in collaboration with the Ministry of Education which provides the classrooms and the teachers, enrols the participants, executes the program, evaluates the teaching activities, and makes reports for the Ministry in charge. As already explained, this campaign is addressed to non-literate people from all social categories in both urban and rural areas with a special focus on the latter and on the 15–45 age groups.

### The Government-sector-based literacy program

This program consists of a partnership between the Ministry in charge and other government departments which provide the literacy centers and institution's as well as the managerial staff. This program is financed from the National Budget. The Ministry in charge covers expenses related to the publication of the textbooks, the teachers' allowances, and teacher training costs. At the implementation level, the concerned government department has to accomplish the following steps: sensitisation, provision of sites for literacy centers and institutions, textbook design, staff recruitment, participants' enrolments, collection and distribution of the materials to the beneficiaries, and the launching of the program in coordination with the regional delegation.

### The Civic-society-based literacy program

This program is executed by the non-governmental associations which adhere to the agreement of the partnership contract with the Ministry in charge upon completion and acceptance of their membership application by the Regional Delegation or the Literacy Directorate. The partnership contract is renewed upon condition that the association executes its guidelines. This program is also financed by the National Budget to cover the costs of teacher training, teaching materials and equipment, and the instructors' salaries. The implementation procedure is similar to the one followed by the Governmental literacy Program. The textbooks, however, are designed by the Directorate.

### The Industrial-sector-based Literacy Program

The aim of this program is to improve the workers' basic skills to prepare the Moroccan industry for the global competition. The concerned firm pays only 20 percent of the costs if the literacy training is done by one of the following institutions: a representative association, the Literacy Directorate (LD), the Vocational Training Office (VTO). The remaining 80 percent of the expenses of this program are financed by the Ministry in charge. The maximum annual cost of a learner is 2000DH. If the program is totally self-funded, the concerned industrial sector has to provide its own instructors. In both cases, the launching of this program takes place only when the concerned firm is a member of the social security and has a special contract with the VTO. The target sector is free to determine the program contents, the timing and the setting for the literacy action. The VTO provides the LD with the names of the sectors and the lists of the beneficiaries. If the program is self-funded, it is the regional delegate, which provides the LD with those names and lists. It is to be noted that no reference is made to the language of literacy in these sectors.

Whatever the type of the program, the literacy course is spread over a nine months instead of a two year period and requires 200 hours for its completion. Apart from the general-campaign-based program which grants the courses in the evening on one hour and a half basis trice a week, the other programs have the right to choose the time that suits them most while taking into consideration the specificities of each region and target group.

**New teaching materials**

New teaching materials for both the learner and the teacher have been published. The learner's textbook *al- qira:'iyya wa at-takwi:n al-'asa:si: li al –kiba:r*, henceforth Literacy and Basic Training for Adults. The new textbook is composed of three volumes. The First volume aims at teaching basic skills in reading, writing, and numeracy for a period of 60 hours, trice a week. The second volume teaches matters related to civic society, social services, population concerns and ecology. It is programmed for an 80 hours course. These two volumes are used as a common course for all the existing adult literacy programs and campaigns.

The third volume is program-specific and is designed for another 60 hours. Its contents are related to the learners' specific functional needs. The so far published volumes that are program-specific are designed for women, agriculture, milk cooperatives, and prison administrations. Still, no reading post-literacy material for the new literates is available. In addition, the final report of the evaluation of the One Hundred Hand Program (July 2000), reports that many associations claim that the new timing load is too short for an efficient training.

It is to be noted that since the constituting of the new Moroccan government in September 2002, a secretary of state for adult literacy has been nominated for the first time in Morocco and it is a woman. The Secretariat depends on the Ministry of Education and Youth. No information on the Secretariat's strategy, organisation and action plans concerning adult literacy is available for the present.

## CONCLUSION

The present chapter provides information concerning the planning and the organization of Moroccan adult literacy campaigns and programs from Independence in 1956 to the year 2000. Reference is also made to the triggering events of each reform. No claim is made that this description is exhaustive or definite. Its aim is mainly of practical nature and targets the reader who may need some guidance in the Moroccan Adult literacy experience. It is important to note, though, that the reviewed campaigns' or programs' efficiency is measured only quantitatively. In most cases, impressive figures involving thousands or millions of beneficiaries have been reported. These figures, however, tell nothing about the real literacy attainments of the beneficiaries. Yet, it is known that judging the success of a campaign or a program should also involve an evaluation of the skill levels and tasks achieved through learning and training. Thus, empirical studies dealing with the outcomes of the literacy campaign at the level of the individual learner are needed. The present study is hoped to fill this gap. Thus, by examining the literacy needs and attainments of the participants in the 1998–1999 literacy campaign, which has been so far the most efficient in terms of massive participation, this work will be able to assess other important aspects of this campaign, namely its effectiveness in satisfying the beneficiaries' learning needs and preparing them to deal with the demands of the literate ecology they live in. Information regarding the instruments used and the research design adopted for this assessment is presented in the next chapter.

# 4 Research Design, Data, and Sample

Investigating women's issues in developing countries necessitates the adoption of an approach that ensures women's development as well as their empowerment, because the gender question is not only a matter of socio-economic development, but also a part of the bigger issue of human rights. So, first, it is necessary to satisfy women's practical interests through developmental processes such as education, employment and integration to eradicate their poverty, illiteracy and malnutrition. Second, there is the need to answer women's strategic interests through an equitable division of gender roles within the family, society and decision-making positions to attenuate the weight of tradition and discrimination which continue to affect women all over the world and constitute an obstacle to their emancipation. Starting from this assumption, the present research postulates that women's literacy teaching in Morocco is designed to:

(a) answer women's practical needs through:

1. combating their illiteracy and sustaining their effective participation,
2. answering their literacy needs and learning needs,
3. preparing them to use the acquired basic skills to deal with everyday life skills,

(b) satisfy women's strategic interests through:

4. emancipatory and empowering teaching material that is free of any forms of sexism and discrimination.

Based on the foregoing points, the present research is made up of four main research questions which seek to check the propositions stated in 1 to 4 respectively. As explained in chapter 1, these issues, which constitute the empirical part of the present research, involve the learners' characteristics and literacy obstacles, the learners' literacy needs and learning needs, the learners' literacy attainment, and the learners' empowerment. It is to be noted that the first three issues are field work based and the fourth one is a textbook-based analysis. Combined together, the analysis of these issues is expected to provide insights into the factors that contribute to the feminization of illiteracy in Morocco, the problem of dropping out, the profiles of the participating women, their literacy needs as compared to the ascribed ones, their proficiency, the circumstances under which they learn and the content through which they are made literate.

The present chapter is divided into five parts. The first provides information on the population, the date, the setting, and implementation of the field work studies. The remaining parts describe the methodological procedures that are used in the empirical studies respectively.

## RESEARCH DESIGN

Data for the field work studies, which took place in 1998–1999, are collected from current learners (N=204), graduate learners (N=140), post-literacy learners (N=40) and drop-outs (N=75). It is to be noted that only the learners who were selected for graduation and for a literacy certificate composed the graduate and the post graduate group. The informants of the present research are mainly taken from Rabat, the administrative capital of Morocco. Other participants are selected from Salé, Temara, Casablanca and the province of Tiznit. Geographically, Salé and Temara are close to Rabat. Salé is a small town in the north of Rabat and Temara is a semi-urban area in its south. Casablanca is the economic capital of Morocco. It is located about sixty miles south of Rabat. The province of Tiznit is a rural area in the anti-atlas, south of Morocco.

The selection of Rabat is motivated by two factors. First, it is the administrative capital of the kingdom and, consequently, it offers its inhabitants auspicious literacy ecology and a challenging environment for the non-literate who represent an important proportion of its population. According to the last population census provided by la Direction des Statistiques, Rabat has a total of 614,820 Moroccan inhabitants and a rate of 26.45 percent of illiterates comprising 16.56 percent men and 35,89 percent women. It is composed of five municipalities: *Agdal Riyad* with 70,492 inhabitants and 28.28 percent illiterate women, *El Youssoufia* with a 193,038 of inhabitants including 40.40 percent illiterate women, *Hassan* with a number of 144,217 Moroccan comprising

30.90 percent non-literate females, *Touarga* counting 8056 people and 32.96 percent illiterate females and finally *Yacoub El Mansour* counting 199,017 citizens 38.12 percent of whom are illiterate women.

Second, Rabat was chosen for its significant contribution to the Moroccan literacy campaign in terms of the number of enrolees and successful graduates. Information related to this contribution was collected on December 15, 1997, that is, one month before the undertaking of the fieldwork studies. This information, which is given in a document available at the Literacy Directorate, states that Rabat is the urban province that has the largest number of enrolment rates with a total of 4,565 beneficiaries including 4,520 women. In addition, Rabat is classified as the first urban province with the highest number of successful graduates; 834 participants have succeeded in the final graduation exam (*Séminaire de formation au profit des coordinateurs d'alphabétisation; Direction de la lutte contre l'analphabétisme, le 15/12/1997*).

Salé, which according to the same document is the urban area that has the second largest number of enrolment rates (3.680), was also chosen because in addition to the important literacy ecology which it offers, it enriched the sample of this research with participants from a non-governmental association which was praised for its literacy action.

Informants from Temara and the province of Tiznit are investigated as rural informants and because they belong to different linguistic communities, the former being Arabophones and the latter monolingual Amazighophones. Informants from Casablanca are selected from the enrolments of *Illigh*, a non-governmental association which offers up to five years post-literacy training. As explained in chapter 1, subjects from this association together with two others from Rabat, namely *Ribat al Fath* and *L'Action Féminine*, are investigated in order to see whether literacy acquisition improves with further training.

To conclude, in addition to the above mentioned reasons, the five settings were selected as they represent contrasting development contexts and living conditions ranging from urban to semi-urban to remote rural areas. It is important to note, though, that this purposeful selection does not claim to be representative nationwide.

## The visited adult literacy centers: organism, location and schedule

The present section provides information as to the names, location and schedule of the schools and literacy centers that were visited for the collection of datas. These centers fall in three categories:

a. The centers that operate under the general campaign organized by the authority in charge in collaboration with the Ministry of National Education.
b. The institutions that work under the Ministry of Youth and Sports, namely Youth Clubs and Women's Clubs, and Education and Employment centers.
c. Non-Governmental Associations.

It is to be noted here that the institutions in (a) and (c) refer to the selected adult literacy programs that are mainly designed for women (see chapter 3). These institutions were selected for the implementation of the present research's instruments mainly because they are the ones that participated most in the Moroccan literacy campaign addressed to women. For instance, their contribution to the literacy campaign which took place in Rabat in 1997 exceeded 90 percent. The enrolment figures provided by the Literacy Directorate reveal that the total number of the participant women in the graduate grade in Rabat was 1470. The above mentioned governmental institutions contributed to this total with 640 participants and the non-governmental ones did with 800 beneficiaries.

With respect to the informants of the present research, 51 percent are randomly selected from non-governmental associations, 49 percent from governmental institutions, 29 percent from the general campaign, 18 percent from the Ministry of Sports and Youth and 3 percent from the Education and Employment centers guided by the Ministry of Labour, Vocational Training and Social Affairs.

The list of the names and addresses of the visited adult literacy centers and their beneficiaries was collected from the Ministry of Labor and Social Affairs in 1997. The general campaign's sample was drawn from seven schools in Rabat: *Allal Ben Abdellah, Al Fath, Attawhid, Hassan AL Mourrakouchi, Mohammed Ben Youssef, Sahat Chouhada,* and *Soukayna Bent AL Houssine.* These schools grant instruction for non-literates in the evening from 6.30 P.M. to 8 P.M.

The data from the Ministry of Youth were collected from five Youth Clubs: *Al Amal, Al Laymoune, Takadoum, Ennour,* and *Temara,* where the courses take place every Tuesday and Friday from 4 P.M to 6 P.M. Additional data were collected from two women's foyers in the province of Tiznit: one is in Tafraoute and the other is in Amanaouz.

The beneficiaries from the Education and Employment centers were interviewed and tested in two centers from Temara, namely *Mers El Kheir* and *Massira* where the courses take place from 9 A.M. to 11.30 A.M. daily.

The non-governmental sample was collected from the most operative associations in Rabat, namely *l'Action Féminine, Zhour Azzarqa* and *Ribat al Fath.*

Additional data were collected from the associations *Abi Raqraq* in Salé and *Illigh* in Casablanca.

The association *L'Action Féminine* grants literacy training on Mondays and Thursdays from 3 P.M. to 5 P.M. at the association's locale. The *Zhour Azzarqa* association provided literacy courses daily from 8 A.M. to 12 A.M. and from 2 P.M. to 6 P.M. The beneficiaries are free to choose the course schedule which suits them most. Each course takes two hours time and is given at the association's center.

The *Ribat al Fath* is the association that has the largest number of enrolees in Rabat. At the time the present field work took place, it had about 1134 participants and 23 classes. Actually, it established a partnership with the Ministry of social affairs regarding anti-illiteracy action in January 1996 and won the UNESCO prize for combating illiteracy. The classes it uses for literacy training belong to the Ministry of National Education. The schools that were visited are *Anachia Al Mohammadia* and *Moulay Rachid.* The former is in the municipality of *Yacoub Al Mansour*, a popular underprivileged district counting 38.12 percent non-literate females. According to the association, this school is the most efficient in terms of quantity of the participants and the quality of their attainments. It is to be noted that this school uses one of its graduates as a teacher for the basic grade level. The *Moulay Rachid* School is located at the Hassan municipality, a more or less prosperous community counting 30.90 percent illiterate women. The total number of the participants in this school is 178 distributed over four classes: two basic ones comprising respectively sixty-two and forty-four learners, a complementary one involving thirty seven learners and a post-literacy one including thirty five participants.

At the *Abi Raq Raq* Association, literacy training is dispensed in five schools: *Ezzahraoui, L'éveil, Said Hajji, Ibn Tofail* and *Ibn Battouta.* The respondents belonging to this association were drawn from the centers *Ezzahraoui* and *Said Hajji.* This was done for two reasons. First, these are the only schools which had a graduate level. Second, these schools are located in totally different districts: a popular one called *Hay Errahma* and a middle class one named *Hay Essalam.* The former is composed of young working class participants and the latter comprises middle class non-working women. This association won the Islamic Educational, Scientific and Cultural Organization's prize for its anti-illiteracy action.

All the above mentioned literacy centers use the same textbooks. As explained in chapter 1, these textbooks are analyzed to see the extent to which they promote women's empowerment. Criteria for the investigation of these materials are described later in the present chapter.

## THE CAUSES OF WOMEN'S' LITERACY: SAMPLE AND DATA

As explained in chapter 1, the analysis of the learners' characteristics and literacy obstacles seeks to provide data on the learners' profiles and the obstacles to their literacy as children and as adults. In so doing, it addresses three sub-questions:

a. *What are the characteristics of female participants in Moroccan adult literacy programs?*
b. *What caused their illiteracy?*
c. *What are the causes of their dropping-out of the literacy course?*

To answer the first two questions addressed above, a sample of 204 current learners in the graduate level was randomly selected from a total of 1224 beneficiaries. To obtain data for the question 1.1., whose aim is to see whether the investigated learners constitute a homogenous group, the informants were interviewed in their respective classes about their personal characteristics (age, and birthplace) family status, origin (rural versus urban), mother tongue (Arabic versus Amazigh), occupation (wage earner or not), and their literacy experience (schooled versus non-schooled). Additional data concerning their husbands' profession and literacy levels are also collected through the same interview. These data are presented and analyzed in chapter 5.

Data concerning the second question, 1.2., are collected from the same interview and the same sample. Informants were interviewed on the causes of their non-schooling or dropping out as a child. They were also asked to give reasons for their absenteeism from the courses, if applicable.

As for the last question, 1.3., a sample of seventy five drop-outs was interviewed through another different oral interview on the reasons of their dropping out of the literacy course. These drop-outs were interviewed in their homes. As explained in chapter 1, the aim of these two last questions is to investigate the variables that contribute to the *feminization* of illiteracy. Analyses of these data are given in chapter 5.

## WOMEN'S LITERACY NEEDS AND LEARNING NEEDS: SAMPLE AND DATA

Investigation of the learner's literacy needs and learning needs is meant to see whether the designed program is consonant with women's needs in terms of objectives (target needs) and implementation (learning needs). The questions addressed in this regard are:

2.1. *What are the literacy needs and learning needs of female participants in Moroccan adult literacy programs?*

2.2. *To what extent are their needs satisfied by the designed course?*

To obtain data for these questions, the same sample and instrument employed to answer the questions 1.1 and 1.2, investigating the learner's profiles, are used. In other words, 204 current graduate learners are involved in the learners' needs' analysis as well. To answer question 2.1., addressed above, informants are asked to describe the motivations that triggered their participation in the literacy course and to identify their *real needs* in terms of incapacity to deal with situations that require their use of literacy. Analyses of these data and a definition of the concepts, *perceived needs, learning needs,* and *real needs* are presented in chapter 6.

To answer question 2.2., the informants are asked to express their satisfaction with the ascribed program in terms of course contents, language policy, timing, and course length. Additional data are collected through an interview with the informants' teachers (N=37). Official documents are also used along with an interview with the head of the teacher-training department at the Literacy Directorate, which, as explained in chapter 3, is the body in charge of adult literacy campaigns and programs in Morocco. Data from these two sources are processed to understand the aims and objectives of the organising institution and investigate their consonance with the literacy needs of the learners.

The interview, used with the 204 current learners, is composed of written questions that were addressed orally to the respondents. Most of these questions are in the form of alternative choices. Notwithstanding the fact that the respondents' subjectivity and bias can be contaminating through the provision of such choices, the data can be easily quantified and processed by the computer. The completion of the interview required about fifty-five minutes. The choice of the interview as the best instrument to collect data on the learners' needs is based on a twofold motivation. First, data regarding the informants' needs is not directly observable. Second, most of the respondents were unable to read and understand the written questions.

## WOMEN'S LITERACY ATTAINMENTS: SAMPLE AND INSTRUMENTS

The learners' attainments analysis investigates the graduate learners' ability to use school-based literacy and to deal with everyday literacy tasks. To this effect, it addresses three sub-research questions related to the learners' mastery of school-based literacy, use of everyday literacy and predictors of reading performance. As already stated in the introduction of this book, these questions read as follows:

3.1. *To what extent do the learners master what they have learned?*

3.2. *Are they able to apply what they have learned to deal with everyday literacy tasks they seek to learn through their participation in the literacy course?*
3.3. *What are the variables that affect their reading performance?*

School-based literacy and household literacy are measured according to two separate tests. The following sub-sections provide information on the informants, who took both tests, describe the contents of each test respectively and the criteria that are used for the scoring of administered tests.

## Sample

A sample of 180 learners was randomly selected to sit for the basic and functional literacy test. It includes 140 graduate learners and forty post-graduate ones. As already explained, the post-literacy group is tested to see whether literacy acquisition increases over a longer period of instruction. Consideration of this issue is expected to provide insight into the efficiency of the assigned teaching length, which is normally two years. Both groups were tested individually in their own classes a few days before graduation. Only the learners who were selected for graduation and for a literacy certificate composed these groups. In other words, only the participants who were judged by their instructors to have finished their training successfully were assigned the tests. Each test took about 90 minutes.

The fact that fewer graduate learners (N=140) were tested than interviewed on their literacy and learning needs (N=204) is no surprise. The interview was administered in March–April, that is, few months before the test, which was administered in June, the last month of the course. Obviously, because only successful graduates were selected for the tests, and due to absenteeism and dropping-out, many informants who had been interviewed did not take the test. As the post-graduate learners did not take part in the interview, they were asked to provide data on some predictor variables that might affect their score achievements in the test. These included: (1) their personal characteristics, such as age, residence, marital status, occupation, mother tongue, and motivation and (2) their previous and current educational experience as well as their attendance frequency. The same variables were taken into consideration when dealing with the graduate group.

## The basic reading test

The basic reading test is an achievement test. It is based on exercises derived from basic to graduate curricula that have been designed for the teaching of non-literate adults. The textbooks used for that purpose were the first and second volume of "Literacy for all". The test is intended to measure how much of basic literacy skill the respondents have acquired with reference to their course of study or program of instruction. One pilot study with twenty respondents was conducted to control for any procedural difficulties and to identify any administration constraints. The test's content validity was assessed by the instructors, who agreed that the test covered most of the language components dealt with in the classroom. This validity is also statistically tested and yields a highly significant correlation coefficient ($r=.89$; $p<.0001$) between the basic test and the respondent's in-class levels which were supplied by their teachers.

The basic test comprises two sections. The first section tests the respondents' basic reading and the second section assesses their basic comprehension. The basic reading section includes questions on basic reading mechanics such as recognition skills, completion skills, reordering skills and production skills. These skills cover a set of diverse exercises such as word/picture-matching, letter recognition, word completion, word construction, sentence completion, word order and sentence maze.

The basic comprehension section is comprised of a reading text followed by multiple choice questions on vocabulary, true/false questions, yes/ no questions, and Wh-questions.

### The Functional Test

While the basic test was designed to measure how much the respondents have learned from their literacy course, the functional test was designed to measure the learners' proficiency in understanding a series of reading tasks that the learners encounter in their everyday life. The test deals with questions related to consumer economics, health, community resources and problem solving. More specifically, the consumer economics seeks to measure the respondents' ability to scan information from an advertisement, a money order and an electricity bill, and to understand a piece of consumer counselling. Questions related to health are meant to test the respondents' proficiency in reading directions on a medicine prospectus like indication, dose and duration, and filling out the health book. The community resources questions were designed to test the respondents' ability to understand a short message and identify a train's schedule. The problem-solving questions test the respondent's ability to compute an item's sale price and calculate its sales deductions and to find out the consumption date of a medicine based on its indication and dosage.

Before the administration of the test, each respondent was asked to answer questions related to her pre-literacy level, birthplace, mother tongue, age, motivation, attendance, grade level, and class period. Only the respondents who regularly attended the course were selected for evaluation. During the test, verbal behavior and explanations were noted and dealt with qualitatively. These verbal reaction notes helped in the checking of the reliability of the answer and in the explanation and interpretation of the respondents' errors. After the test, the teacher was asked to supply his or her own evaluation of the respondent's current in-class literacy level, that is, the so-called teacher reported literacy ability.

### Scoring criteria

Based on Bowren and Zintz's (1977) method of evaluating adult reading performance under three reading levels, namely the "independent level", the "instructional level", and the "frustrational level", which refer to the learner's high, moderate and low performance, respectively, and based on the classical evaluation criteria that are currently used in many adult and child educational systems, that is, low, weak, moderate and high, the present research investigates the informants' proficiency in the basic test and in the functional test in terms of four levels. These levels are "deficient" (low), "frustrational" (weak), "instructional" (moderate) and "independent" (high). The method consists of calculating the learners' total score in each test separately. Each score is calculated on the basis of the total number of correct answers, which is forty for the basic test and twenty for the functional test. The learners' reading level is, then, calculated in terms of the percentage of correct answers in each test and its sub-components. The obtained percentage is evaluated according to the four reading levels described above. For example, if the respondent's total percent of correct answers in an exercise or the whole test is between zero and twenty-five, her reading ability is classified as "deficient". If the total percent of her correct answers is above twenty-five and equals or is below fifty, her reading ability is judged "frustrational" (weak). When her percent of correct answers is above fifty and equals or is below seventy-five, she is classified under the "instructional level". When the percent of her correct answers is above seventy-five she is scored under the "independent level".

Motivation for choosing to assess the respondents' literacy skills within these four learning levels resides in the applicability of this assessment model for any type of exercise and skill at any stage of learning. Furthermore, it can be used as a means of evaluating or monitoring educational programs. In other words, it can be used as a learner assessment and/or as a course evaluation. Finally, it regards literacy acquisition as an ongoing process, which may change and evolve with further instruction or post-learning. Based on these criteria of evaluation, an ideal literacy program would be one where the majority of the beneficiaries have attained the independent learning level in all the investigated literacy skills. In addition to investigating the learners' reading proficiency under the reading levels explained above, the respondents' calculated total score in each test is used as a dependent variable in statistical techniques such as ANOVA, the analysis of variance or correlations to assess the impact of such independent variables as the learners' age, motivation, pre-literacy levels, area, and mother tongue. This technique served to answer the sub-research question 3.3., which deals with predictor variables of literacy attainment.

Last but not least, the learners' reading strategies are noted down and analyzed qualitatively. This is backed by the fact that the informants are tested individually. This method is adopted as it helps to account for the individual reading or writing difficulties of the respondents.

## ASSESSING WOMEN'S EMPOWERMENT: DATA AND TECHNIQUES

Women's empowerment is assessed through an examination of the content of the textbooks that are designed for their literacy training. As already stated, the aim is to see whether adult literacy teaching in Morocco is consonant with a perspective that seeks women's empowerment and emancipation. The question that has been addressed in this respect reads as follow:

> *To what extent is the designed content consonant with a perspective that seeks women's empowerment?*

In view of the definition of empowerment as a process which entails an equitable and democratic distribution of power between men and women within the family and throughout society (Chlebowska,1992; Stromquist, 1992) and in view of the fact that sexism is 'an attitude which demeans, excludes, underrepresents and stereotypes people on the basis of gender' (Abu Nasr, Lorfing, and Mikrati, 1983:15), the research question addressed above is analyzed in terms of the following three sub-questions:

4.1. *How much space is given to women in the textbooks under study?*
4.2. *What functions do they occupy in such a space?*
4.3. *What characteristics and traits are they assigned?*

These issues are investigated according to ready-made criteria that are used in the determination of sexism and stereotype in school-based materials (Michel, 1986). The checklist that has been adopted is that of Michel (idem.) because it is the most adapted for the analysis of the research questions addressed above. The checklist is designed for three types of analyses:

1. A comparative analysis of the number of male and female references such as proper names, common names (man versus woman, girl versus boy) and pronouns like she, he for humans in both singular and plural forms.
2. A comparative analysis of *conventional* versus *non-conventional* activities (CA versus NCA) attributed to women and girls in the family, work, politics, society and leisure.

3. A comparative analysis of *conventional* versus *non-conventional* character traits attributed to women and girls (C T versus NCT).

These analyses are mainly quantitative but are qualitatively explained and discussed in terms of their relevance to the research questions addressed above respectively. Hence, by examining the number of female and male occurrences in the textbooks, the present research will be able to determine the place women occupy in the textbooks. The aim is to see whether women are underrepresented in comparison to men. A consideration of the number of the traditional roles and the non-traditional roles they occupy in the textbooks will make it possible to determine the functions they occupy in the textbooks and assess the extent of their exclusion or integration in public roles which have so far been identified as men's domains. Assessing the conventional versus the non-conventional characteristics they are assigned will make it possible to evaluate the extent to which these textbooks reproduce the sex-related stereotypes that stress the importance of men but deny the worth of women. Investigation of all the three issues will provide insight into the use of the literacy materials as a means of female emancipation and liberation from the constraints of illiteracy and tradition or re-domestication.

While the adopted checklist allows assessment of the extent to which women are underrepresented, excluded and stereotyped, it is difficult to identify the *conventional* roles or traits and the non-*conventional* ones. To deal with this limitation, the present research investigates these categorical comparisons in terms of the society's gender ideology which reduces women's responsibilities to domestic duties and child rearing and limits their potential outside the house to the same traditional roles of handling food and children. In so doing, this analysis claims to be anti-traditional but not anti-natural, that is, not against maternity and child rearing.

The present study may also be criticised for adopting a checklist that has been conceived in an *alien* environment with different socio-cultural values. Still, this checklist works for the Muslim context, where women experience discrimination because of sexist tradition and culture.

The content parts, which are considered for these analyses are the illustrations, titles and texts. These analyses have the advantage of breaking down sexist manifestations in several ways: according to a numerical representation of male and female characters and according to the distribution of their social roles and character traits. This makes it possible to locate and identify the content area and the category that is mostly marked by sexism.

After the application of the checklist, the identification of sexism is carried according to the following criteria. A textbook is considered as non-sexist if it contains an equitable distribution of words, activities and traits. While the ideal distribution is normally 50 percent for each sex and because it is difficult to design textbooks with such a perfect equitable distribution, the attribution of conventional versus non-conventional traits and activities for each sex should not deviate by more than 10 to 20 percent; otherwise the textbook is judged sexist. Qualitatively, a textbook is considered sexist when it relegates women to specific conventional roles and negative or stereotyped behavior patterns.

The textbooks that are assessed are the two volumes, basic and graduate, of Literacy for All. These textbooks are used in the schools and centers that were visited during the fieldwork. As explained in chapter 3, these textbooks have been replaced by Literacy and basic training for adults since the year 1999. Therefore, their analysis is also taken into consideration.

## CONCLUSION

It may be useful to conclude this chapter with a brief summary of the informants and instruments that have been used in the investigation of the issues addressed in the present book. 204 current learners are interviewed on their personal, educational and language characteristics. The same sample is also interviewed on their literacy needs and learning needs. 180 are assessed on their literacy attainments and their background information. These include 140 current graduate learners and forty current post-graduate learners. Seventy five women are interviewed on the causes of their dropping out of the literacy course and thirty seven teachers are asked to provide information on the objectives, aims and evaluation of the course they are assigned to teach. A brief description of the profiles of these teachers reveals that 60 percent are females and 40 percent are males. Their average age is forty. Forty-three percent work as part-time volunteers in addition to being full-time primary school teachers. They receive an annual honorarium of about 1500DH from the Moroccan Adult Literacy Directorate. Twenty-two percent work as full time civil servants and receive a monthly allowance of about 2000DH from the Ministry of National Education. Nineteen percent work as full time youth leaders who are paid monthly by the Ministry of Youth and Sports. Sixteen percent work as volunteers, usually university students, who are hired by the non-governmental associations as volunteers. The questionnaires and the tests have been piloted to control for any administration and time constraints. The data obtained are coded and analyzed through the use of Statview, a computer-based statistical program. The statistical techniques that are used are descriptive statistics, correlations, and analyses of variance as presented in the remaining chapters.

# 5
# Women's Literacy Obstacles

The present chapter provides information regarding the profiles of the female participants in Moroccan adult literacy programs and elucidates the causes of their childhood illiteracy and obstacles to their effective participation in the literacy courses. As explained in chapter 4, this is done through the analysis of two interviews addressed to 204 current participants and seventy-five drop-outs respectively. The analysis of data collected from both interviews is done in three main sections. The first section is devoted to a description of the personal, educational, linguistic and socio-economic characteristics of the current learners. The second section is concerned with the causes of women's childhood illiteracy. More specifically, it provides data on the non-schooling of the respondents and their dropping-out of the primary school. This section also identifies the reasons for their absenteeism, and dropping-out of the literacy courses. In the last section, the data are summarized and discussed.

## THE TARGET BENEFICIARIES: A HOMOGENEOUS GROUP OR A DISPARATE POPULATION?

The aim underlying the investigation of the profiles of the participants in literacy courses is twofold. First, it is an important step to take into consideration in a needs analysis study. Second, it provides data on the extent to which target beneficiaries of adult literacy programs form a homogeneous or a heterogeneous group, which has important implications for the design of appropriate literacy programs. The learners' characteristics such as their age, family status, mother tongue, occupation, literacy experience as children, and their husbands' occupation and literacy levels are presented subsequently in terms of percentages.

### The respondents' age

The learners are classified under five age groups. The distribution of the informants by age group is almost the same. Most of the groups contain a minimum of 20 percent of the learners and a maximum of 24 percent. The oldest group, whose age is between fifty-one and sixty years, contains only 10 percent of the learners. The minimum age of the learners is twelve, their maximum age is sixty and their average age is thirty-two. It is to be noted that 70 percent of the investigated current participants are less than forty years old.

These results bear significance to three issues. First, the majority of the sample is relatively young which provides a good justification for combating their illiteracy. In fact, the sample answers the objectives of the Literacy Directorate, which, as explained in chapter 3, aims to attract women whose age ranges from fifteen to forty-five years. Second, old women's participation is quite low despite their being the most affected by illiteracy. In fact, their illiteracy is high in almost all developing countries, because of the long-term effect of having no or very limited educational opportunities. According to the latest population census, the illiteracy rate for Moroccan females constituting this age group is higher than 90 percent. Possible reasons for the weak participation of this group in the literacy programs may be of biological, psychological, and socio-cultural nature. So, it is likely that a significant majority of women aged fifty and older in Morocco remain illiterate for the rest of their lives. Third, there is a disparity within the age groups of the learners. In fact, it is not unusual to find participants from various ages within the same class. Accordingly, this may constitute some pedagogical difficulty for the teaching/learning activity.

### The respondents' family status

Regarding the learners' family status, it was revealed that the majority of the participants are either married (44%) or single (46%) representing an important sample of current and potential mothers who need to benefit from the program contents, especially as regards development issues such as nutrition, family planning and strategic issues such as empowerment and emancipation. It is important to consider the low participation of the divorced sample. Their enrolment in the literacy program is as low as 6 percent. This could be due to economic and/or socio-cultural reasons. The socio-economic obstacles could be explained by women's involvement in the workforce to sustain their children who are often abandoned by their fathers and do not benefit from any custody as attested by some participants. The socio-cultural reasons could be related to the undesirable and suspicious status of the divorced whose life is most often controlled by male tutor(s), a fact which makes them confined to the home or to subsistence activities especially in needy cases. It is possible to claim that the same thing could apply for the widows as well. Their participation is only 4 percent. Concerning this group, two informants reported that it was only after their husbands' death that they were able to join in the literacy course. They explained that during their husbands' lifetime, it was impossible to get involved in such emancipating activities.

## The respondents' mother tongue

The analysis of the question related to the learners' mother tongue reveals that 69 percent of the learners have Moroccan Arabic as their mother tongue. The same analysis reveals that the remaining 31 percent speak Amazigh. It is to be noted that while standard Arabic is the language of literacy, most of the teaching activities are carried out in Moroccan Arabic, namely, the explanation of vocabulary and the use of instructions. Amazigh, which is quite different from the language of literacy, is not used despite the fact that many Amazigh participants are monolingual. Pedagogically as attested by some monolingual Amazigh informants, this puts the Amazighophones, whose language in this case does not compete with Standard Arabic but with Moroccan Arabic, at a disadvantage.

## The respondents' occupation

The statistical analysis of the informants' occupation shows that the majority of the learners (63%) are unemployed housewives receiving no wages. It is interesting to note, tough, that a fair proportion of the women (37%) are wage earners. Their jobs, however, consist of small wage professions such as dressmakers (14%), factory workers (8%), and cleaners (7%) in private institutions such as banks, supermarkets, and hotels, maids (6%) and shop assistants (2%). Notice the low participation of maids who are the most affected by illiteracy due to socio-economic problems. In fact many rural families send their daughters, whose age in some cases is less than eight years, to work as maids in middle-class or rich families. These young girls are thus deprived of schooling and undergo various forms of exploitation.

The above-mentioned occupations bear significance to the informant's poverty as the result of their illiteracy. While some are involved in the job market, the natures of the jobs they occupy afford them only small wages. In addition to that, note that the majority is economically dependent either on their husbands or tutors. It would be interesting then to describe their husbands' or tutors' profession as well to have an idea about the nature of such socio-economic dependence.

## The respondents' husbands' or tutors' profession

Investigation of the informants' husbands' or tutors' profession shows that 33 percent are blue-collar workers. 23 percent are involved in small trade, 22 percent work as civil servants. 6 percent of the respondents give no information about their husbands or tutors jobs. These are in fact the divorced sample that was reluctant to answer that question. The remaining 16 percent of the respondents answered that their husbands work as seasonal farmers (2%), are retired (8%) or do not work at all (6%).

These results reveal that the majority of the learners depend on their husbands' low paid work, which consists of subsistence work activities. While 22 percent are civil servants, most of them work as janitors and caretakers. It is to be noted that only 5 percent of the civil servants work as lawyers, doctors or university teachers. These findings along with those concerning the respondents reflect the poor socio-economic status of the learners. This status is further confirmed by their husbands' or tutors' literacy levels as explained in the next section.

## The respondents' husbands' or tutors' literacy levels

Analyses of the respondents' husbands' or tutors' literacy levels reveal that 31 percent have never been to school, 25 percent have reached only the primary school level, 23 percent have attained the secondary school level, 13 percent received Koranic teaching. Only 5 percent have attained the university level. It is to be noted that this *highly* literate sample is composed of the employers of the maid informants.

These results are suggestive as they reveal that a quite important proportion of the learners' male partners are illiterate (31%). They also show that the majority has attained only the primary learning level (69%). At the same time, the figure indicates that the *highly* literate tutors are concerned by their maids' literacy, which reveals a remarkable participation of the civil society in combating their maids' illiteracy.

## The respondents' literacy experience in chilhood

Investigation of the question related to the literacy experience the respondents had in their childhood reveals that illiteracy is both a matter of non-schooling and of school leaving. By way of illustration, it is revealed that 53 percent of the informants were left out of formal primary school and 47 percent dropped out of it when they were children.

The number of school years the schooled respondents has is at most three years. This early school leaving is, of course, not enough to ensure sufficient threshold levels for literacy retention, which explains their enrolment in literacy courses in their adult age.

Considering these results, one can say that non-schooling, early school leaving and adult illiteracy are highly related. In fact, illiteracy among adults is closely linked to the problem of primary school coverage and high drop-out rates worldwide.

## The causes of illiteracy

Investigation of data related to the causes of the respondents' illiteracy shows that it is a matter of parents' opposition (40%), lack of schools or distant ones (20%), school failure (17%), personal refusal (13%), economic reasons (8%) and administrative such as lack of a birth certificate (2%).

When arranged by groups of schooled versus non-schooled, descriptive statistics show that the pre-schooled informants dropped because of school failure (17%), parents' opposition (15%), personal refusal (10%) and economic reasons (4%). Among the personal reasons for leaving school, some reported antipathy towards school due to beating by the teacher, others cited anxiety over exams, and very few referred to the death of a parent. As for the economic reasons, most respondents cited the necessity to be involved in a job as a maid or worker in the carpet industry or agricultural cooperative to help their poor family.

As for the non-schooled group, the same analysis reveals that 25 percent of the respondents claim that their illiteracy is caused by their parents' resistance to their schooling, 20 percent associate their illiteracy to the lack or distance of schools, 3 percent attribute it to economic reasons and 2 percent allude to lack of a birth certificate.

Considering these estimates, it is to be noted that the most significant causes of illiteracy in a descending order are socio-cultural, logistic, inherent to the system, motivational and economic. These findings give credence to some studies, which deal with obstacles to literacy in other developing countries. Jones (1990), though not dealing with the relative importance of the causes of illiteracy, refers to the inaccessibility of primary school education to girls, rural and minority groups in the world population and to the phenomenon of dropping-out as a result of repetition, failure, distance, or poor socio-economic conditions. The author explains that these problems contribute to the failure of the primary school to prepare its graduates for their roles in life because of inappropriate literacy provision and relapse into inadequate literacy. Likewise, Belarbi (1991) deplores the lack of schools, distance, poverty, and resistant parents. Manzoor (1992) and Hill and King (1993) allude to social discrimination, poverty and limited budgets.

## The causes of non-regular attendance

Adult literacy has been designed primarily to make up for the waste that has been generated by lack of access to primary education or early removal from it. In many developing countries, including Morocco, these programs are addressed particularly to women who are the most affected by basic education inequity mostly due to socio-cultural pressures as explained above. However, even when women and girls are given chance to acquire elementary skills and to some extent compensate for their illiteracy, there are some obstacles that go against their effective participation. In the present study, for instance, only 11 percent of the learners attend regularly their literacy courses.

Investigation of the reasons for irregular attendance in the courses relate to work either inside (26%) or outside (32%) the house. In other words, the problem of earning a living or running a house is so crucial that it prevents women from attending regularly their courses. The second reported reason is rather complex and is related to some social events such as weddings, funerals, or guest entertaining. Such events are socially regarded as being more important than class attendance, especially that the presence of women in such events is primary. In other cases, frequent absence has been reported as the result of the fact that many rural-born families still keep contact with their place of origin and, thus, travel there for various reasons which are economic, social or judicial and, thereby, miss classes. Sickness constitutes a natural and biological impediment to regular attendance and accounts for 14 percent of the factors against regular attendance. In fact, due to their manifold social roles as wives, child bearers, mothers, family rearing, and in some cases 'bread seekers', women are more stressed and tend to become sick quite often. Unfortunately, though such reasons are either socially or biologically founded, they sometimes lead to failure to attend the program altogether.

## The causes of dropping out of the literacy course

While there are many motivating reasons for non-literate adults to participate in literacy courses, their diverse activities as heads of families and/or money earners do not leave them much time for continuous participation and efficient learning. The problem of earning a living is of a great value to both men and working women; therefore, these do not have enough time to participate in the literacy course. For instance, during the present field work, the headmaster of a primary school in Rabat said that two literacy classes for men, who were involved in occupations such as barbers, carpenters, locksmiths and ironsmiths, were closed two months after they have been launched due to work constraints and time unsuitability. The reason for dropping-out of the course is linked to the timing of the course, which did not suit the participants. Their claim is that six in the evening, when the literacy course normally begins, is their most busy time of the day as they receive their *best* clients who due to their work as civil servants are available only at that time.

Likewise, women and girls, who are the focus of the present research, tend to be overburdened with domestic tasks such as cooking, cleaning, and child rearing. Frequent child bearing leaves little time and energy for mothers to learn how to read and write. While these factors are being considered as the most determinant causes of dropping-out of the literacy classes worldwide, other reasons are reported by the informants of the present study.

The most recurrent obstacles to continuing literacy training are the domestic duties and family constraints (36%). According to the respondents, these responsibilities do not leave them much time for regular attendance and efficient learning. Subsistence work to feed their kids is another cause of giving up training. During a fieldwork in the province of Tiznit, south of Morocco, some women reported that they dropped out of the literacy classes because of poverty. They revealed that because their husbands found no job in the towns, and because their job in the village is only seasonal, they had to work either as maids in houses and/or integrate the co-operatives as seasonal workers. In addition to their roles as housewives and mothers of more than five children, their job consists of fetching wood and water, farming, cropping, animal feeding, and so on. Another cause of dropping out in this region is migration. Some families spend six months in towns and six months in villages. Some women also dropped the literacy course because they have to assume the responsibilities left out by their men folk who have immigrated to the towns in search of work. On the whole, they report that they are involved in priorities of life, which do not include literacy and many have the feeling that it is too late to learn and to read.

Program interruption constitutes another significant obstacle to effective participation and accounts for 21 percent of the dropping out. In fact, out of the visited centers, three rural and two urban ones interrupted the program. Reasons for such interruption include political reasons such as designing literacy courses just before the elections, the changing of the headmaster of the school, the instructor's non-remuneration for the literacy work, non-availability of volunteer teachers, and insufficient number of participants.

The next reported obstacle is distance. 16 percent of the respondents from both rural and urban areas interrupted the course because they had to walk long distances. The urban ones explained that they are often victims of sexual harassment after the course, which ends late in the evening. The rural ones reported the badness of the weather and the unsuitability of the road conditions.

The problem of sight constitutes another important obstacle against women's effective participation in literacy programs. This problem was reported by aged urban women who could not afford to buy glasses. It is worth noting that some non-governmental associations distribute glasses for the needy participants. In most cases, however, the glasses are not adapted to their sight requirements, though the frames may be.

Husbands' opposition is another reason for women's dropping-out of the literacy course. Twelve percent of the interviewed women, all rural, revealed that their husbands, who lived in the towns, ordered them to stop attending the center. The respondents' explanation for their husband's objection is jealousy on the part of their mothers or sisters in law who convinced either their sons or brothers to urge their wives to quit the center. Yet, as they attest, learning how to read and write would help them correspond in an intimate way with their folks. If they were literate they would read their husbands' letters and write back without having to call on other people.

## SUMMARY OF THE RESULTS AND DISCUSSION

The data analyzed in the present study, while not claiming to be representative, reveal that the current participant learners constitute a heterogeneous group. Their difference is related to their age, mother tongue and literacy levels but not their socio-economic status as most come from poor families. This heterogeneity bears significant implications as to the design of literacy programs that would answer the learners' needs according to their age, linguistic and educational backgrounds.

The causes of illiteracy are mostly external to women's control as it is not based on personal attitude. Parents' opposition, lack or no access to schools, school failure, and poverty are the most important obstacles to their illiteracy in their child age. Likewise, the causes of their irregular attendance find their sources in their multiple social roles as workers, mothers and heavy demands of family life. The causes of dropping out among former participants are also independent of their will. Gender roles, the weight of tradition, physical disability, poverty, and lack of commitment from some providers of the literacy course are beyond the learner's control. Overall, the causes of the illiteracy of the subjects under study and their non-effective participation relate to tradition, the quality of primary education and poverty. These are discussed hereafter.

### The impact of tradition

The parents' objection to their daughters' education accounts for 40 percent in the present study. In fact, until recently, many Muslim traditional families would mind educating their daughters. Yet, in Islam men and women enjoy equal rights regarding literacy. Islam's support for the education of women is evident in the saying of the prophet "*the search for knowledge is the duty of every Muslim, man or woman*". In practice, however, this equality is not implemented. Within the Muslim culture, it is tradition and culture, rather than Islam itself, which stands as a barrier against girls' education.

Actually, objections to female literacy and education are predominantly based on traditional stereotypes of women's roles in society as perpetuated by customary patriarchal systems. Unfortunately, these socio-cultural factors and attitudes continue to reinforce resistance against the advancement of women especially in rural areas and in very conservative families. Accordingly, these girls and women are deprived from any advantages accruing from available opportunities. Yet, one knows how important is the education of mothers for the welfare of the family and the society where they usually constitute half of the population. In fact, it has been found that many indicators of underdevelopment, such as malnutrition, child decrease, lack of hygiene, ignorance of family planning, are partly a result of women illiteracy as is reported in Isenman (1978) and Hicks (1979).

Parents' opposition to their daughters' education has in turn a bad effect on the girls' own motivation for education and literacy. Accordingly, girls refuse to enrol in schools and even when they do so, they drop out very early. In fact, in many traditional families, literacy practices are believed to be rather masculine. As a child, a girl is socialized into accepting that marriage and raising a family should be her ultimate goal. The result of this value system is sexual segregation, early marriage, and rigid sex roles and practices leading to education deprivation as explained by the high illiteracy rates among women in such societies and as attested by the majority of the informants in the present study. Early marriage and the restriction of labor in the home explains the fact that many women from underdeveloped societies depend financially on their male guardians, namely their fathers, brothers, husbands or older sons, a fact which does not create the need for them to join the labor force to earn a living and to be educated. As a result, they are often allowed a lower social and economic status where there is no room and eventually no valorization for literacy.

Examples of reported impediments to female literacy include the fear of too much freedom engendered from schooling and its negative effects on the girls' sexual conduct, the need for girls' housework or agricultural labor, a preference for investing limited resources in their sons' education with a view to parental support in old age as daughters move out of their parents' household to become part of their husbands' family where they are financially dependent (El- Sanbary, 1993).

## The quality of education

World illiteracy is not only inherent to socio-cultural factors as explained above but is also a matter of other issues, namely the quality of education and non-sufficient budgets. In the present study, for instance, 20 percent of the non-schooled group is illiterate due to lack of schools or to their distant locations. In addition, 17 percent of the schooled sample relates their dropping out to failure.

In Moroccan rural areas, especially in mountainous regions, schools are not available and if so, they are not accessible as the children have to walk long distances before reaching the school, a fact which does not encourage parents to send their daughters as it involves many moral and physical risks (Belarbi, 1992).

Lack of schools or their insufficient number is often linked to the non-sufficient budgets allotted to primary education. Heyneman (1997) cited in (Maamouri, 1998) notes that some countries, namely the Arab ones, allot more budget for higher education than the primary one. The budget allotted to higher education is four times more in Gulf States and 15 more in Morocco. In this respect, Ibaaquil (1996) notes that the budget allotted to the pedagogical material in the Moroccan primary school is in most cases less than 6 percent of the whole budget. He adds that due to lack of material, teaching methods are rather traditional and based on memorization and authority.

In fact, non-sufficient budgets, and the quality of education are highly correlated. In many developing countries, reduction in educational spending often leads to larger classes, fewer materials and lower teacher motivation. Moreover, compensatory programs, remedial tuition and additional tutoring for the weak are considered costly and are, thus, inexistent. Given this situation, children whose parents cannot compensate for what is lacking in school inevitably fall behind and, consequently never possess self-sustaining skills.

In addition to the impact of insufficient financial resources on the quality of education, Bokamba (1992) reports the non-accordance between educational development objectives and educational systems, inappropriate language policies, and insufficient teaching. The author claims that the battle against illiteracy in Africa will not progress unless fundamental changes are made in the formal educational system and unless non-formal education is given high priority.

Inappropriate language policies is in fact peculiar to many developing countries including Morocco where instruction is provided in the dominant languages of the society, while important portions of the population may speak quite different language(s) which have no place in education. This equal treatment where all children are taught in the same language whatever their linguistic backgrounds often produces very unequal outcomes especially at the early stages of basic education. While students who speak a variety of the dominant language are linguistically prepared to master a particular learning task, others who come from a different linguistic community may need remedial work before doing so. Still, in many countries the only available remedial form is grade repetition. In Morocco, for instance, it has been reported by the Ministry of National Education that monolingual Amazigh speaking children are at a disadvantage in comparison with the Arab speaking children with a difference of 20 pointsin their school achievement. Likewise, Wagner (1993) found that Berber monolingual children catch up with the Arab-speaking peers only at the last year of the primary education, which implies that before the attainment of that grade, many Amazigh children dropped due to school failure.

Aware of this problem, along with the inadequacy of the educational system for the job market and development demands, the special Commission charged to reform the Moroccan educational system (see chapter 3) came out with recommendations in this respect. Among its objectives is the adaptation of education to the demands of the job market, the implementation of public kindergarten education, the re-examination of the status of foreign languages, namely French and English, and the teaching of local dialects, namely Amazigh, which can be used for initial literacy instruction as a bridge to literacy in the official language. Many of these objectives, however, are still waiting to be implemented hopefully not later than September, 2004.

**Illiteracy and poverty**

The obstacles to literacy are not always a factor of school coverage and failure, but are socio-economically determined as well. Indeed many studies link illiteracy to poverty. Lourié (1990), for instance, states that the map of world illiteracy coincides with that of world poverty. The statistics he presents support his statement as they reveal an important concentration of the totally illiterate in the poorest and most populated areas of the globe, namely Asia and Africa. The author adds that even in richer countries, namely Canada, France and the United States of America, the functionally illiterates are almost found among the poor and the unemployed. He explains that it is not unusual for the poor to be unable to communicate as they speak languages or dialects, which have no written forms by which exchanging information would be possible. The author contends that their poverty and, consequently, their isolation prevent them from integrating the "mechanics" of social life.

Likewise, Hill and King (1993) report that the gender gap in educational attainment, measured by years of schooling, is greater in low-income countries than in middle-income ones. They explain that in those countries, many families cannot afford sending their sons, let alone their daughters, to free public schools given the high cost of books, clothes and transportation. In fact, children from households with a low income or small land holdings are much more likely to drop out or never attend school. Likewise, El-Saadawi (1985) and Mernissi (1987) argue that in addition to the impact of tradition, the reasons that make the parents keep their daughters out-of-school are economically based. Wagner (1993) states that it is the poorest sectors of the Moroccan society that are most affected by illiteracy. He says that children from very poor Moroccan urban and rural areas are at risk of "continued educational poverty". The author explains that estimates from the Moroccan government show that 90 percent of the heads of the poorest households have never been to school. He adds that even when children in such families are schooled, their educational resources remain limited and under-utilised.

Manzoor (1993) relates the problem of illiteracy to social injustice affecting the poor from ethnic and cultural minorities in both industrialized and developing societies. He adds that it touches women more than men as a result of social discrimination. In so doing, the author contends that literacy is not associated with a nation's economic status, and the 30 million functionally illiterate in developed countries such as North America is a good illustration of this. He maintains that the ironical side of illiteracy is that it is those who most need literacy to ameliorate their socio-economic conditions that are deprived of it. He concludes that dependence of illiteracy on social phenomena makes it impossible to predict its eradication at a determined and fixed date. He recommends the involvement of all the sectors of society in fighting illiteracy and makes an appeal for additional resources to promote literacy as an integral part of the effort to meet basic education needs.

In the same vein, El Bindari in collaboration with Mulholland (1992) state that the elimination of illiteracy should not be carried out in isolation. It should rather take into consideration other sectors of society, namely, health and economics as they are largely linked to each other. They sustain that women's education, for instance, may reduce child mortality but will not guarantee access to food for the surviving children. They assert that this can be achieved only through programs enhancing functional literacy and economic activities. Aware of this, many developing countries including Morocco developed measures to retain girls and women in schools and in literacy programs. In so doing, they turn to the private sectors and voluntary associations for help. In such cases, small-scale projects in the form of income generating resources for women, and collecting educational stationery for girls take the place of long-term public commitment. Yet, we all know that non-governmental efforts can only complement but not replace public provision.

In the present study only 8 percent of the respondents declared that they are illiterate because of poverty. A consideration of their profession, however, as explained above, reveals that the majority are unemployed or involved in low paid jobs. One may be tempted to draw the conclusion from these findings that part of their parents' refusal to enrol or stay at school might be due to lack of means.

What has been said so far shows that a factor of some significance concerning female illiteracy as a social issue is its link with poverty. This, however, does not mean that better socially integrated informants are not affected by illiteracy. From the fieldwork investigation and class observations, a good proportion of the participants come from middle classes and rich families. In fact, some go to the literacy center by their own car, which is an indication of good economic conditions. When asked about their illiteracy causes, these women explain that their illiteracy does not draw its source from poverty but from resistant parents who are influenced by societal mandates that are supported by stereotypes about the role and status of women in society.

## CONCLUSION

In view of the results presented and discussed above, the causes of female illiteracy are linked to cultural, economic, and school-based reasons. Unfortunately the same obstacles continue to affect women's effective participation in programs that are designed to compensate for their non-schooling and combat their illiteracy. This means that the effort to deal with the problem of illiteracy at its source and compensate for the work that has been left out by the primary school still represents an enormous challenge for the country. In fact, these women are trapped between past discriminations and present constraints. As they explained themselves, due to this situation they feel that they are socially marginalized, and economically lagging. It is worth mentioning, however, that these respondents are culturally strong, cognitively sane and possess a wealthy experience and a large repertory of skills. Yet, they all report that educationally speaking, they feel poor as they lack the literacy means necessary for challenging the demands of the written communication and coping with the technological development of the literate world. Still, the ingenuousness of their eyesight is very impressive as it reveals remarkable talent and intelligence that would have shown their effects had they been given the chance of being educated.

In fact, illiteracy doesn't preclude knowledge or wisdom. History and research have shown that there is genius in the oral traditions of people from all nations. In Morocco, for instance, nobody can deny the wealthy and aesthetic aspects of oral tradition (Boukous, 1977), the amazing rationalization and intellect of riddles (Bentolila, 1986), the flawless memorization of the illiterate (Wagner, 1987), the fabulous imagination of folk tales (Mouhsine, 1992), the genius and abstraction of proverbs (El Attar, 1992), the unconscious calculated improvisation and creativeness of unwritten poetry and songs (Jouad, 1995), and the measured and premeditated rhythms of indigenous dances (Boukhris, 1996). Yet, today's rapid progress in technology requires that the acquisition and measurement of human competencies be based on the knowledge of printed languages, which have become a primary mode of transmitting and acquiring information.

Aware of the importance of the script as a means of power and as an empowering mean many non-literate women become involved in literacy training. It would be interesting, then, to assess their literacy needs and analyze the conditions under which they learn literacy. These issues are dealt with in the next chapter.

6

# Identifying Women's Literacy Needs and Learning Needs

The present chapter provides a survey of the literacy needs and the learning needs as collected from a sample of current female beneficiaries of Moroccan adult literacy programs. The starting point of the chapter is a brief review of the literature on the definitions and theories of *need* in education. The aim is to clarify to the reader what is meant by *need* and what theory is adopted by the present study when investigating the informants' literacy needs and learning needs. The second section outlines the learners' literacy needs as determined by the program designers and as expressed by the teachers. The third section gives a survey of the literacy needs of the respondents. A sample of related testimonies is also presented. Note that they have been translated for the readers' convenience. This section also analyses the respondents' learning needs through their own evaluation of the designed program in terms of the ascribed contents, the adopted language, the resources used, the programmed timetable and training length. The respondents' perceived satisfaction with the designed program as a whole is also taken into consideration. The last section summarizes and discusses the results of the needs analysis survey in the light of the hypothesis stated below.

Investigation of literacy needs as perceived by women and ascribed by literacy designers is done with the intention that awareness of a need is a matter of perception and perception may vary according to one's standpoint. More explicitly, it is possible that the women's views concerning their necessities in the target situation will conflict with the perceptions of other interested parties such as course designers and teachers. Thus, it is hypothesized that target literacy needs as ascribed by the course designers and as perceived by the learners may not be in agreement.

## THE CONCEPT OF NEED

One important feature of adult literacy and education is its dependence on need analysis, a necessary step for the development of syllabus contents and design. In fact, it is the awareness of a target situation, in this case, a definable need to be literate, which distinguishes adult literacy from child literacy. In this respect, Jones (1990) draws the educators' attention to the importance of the value judgement associated with the concept of need in education for it is the educators themselves who decide on the type of training to be sponsored. The author's argument is that individuals may have their own value judgements about their needs and the ways they can be met, thus probing efforts to find out what real needs are. But what is meant by need? And what kind of information should a need analysts provide?

The concept of need as viewed by Kowalski (1988:122) means the "gap between what is and what is required". The author distinguishes between common needs among humans such as eating, drinking, and sleeping and educational needs which are more disparate. He defines the latter as "the gap between present competencies and desired competencies". He explains that these *competencies* may include cognitive growth, skill improvement, and changing attitudes. In this way, educational needs involve a change in the behavior of individuals and, hence, can be thought of as a gap between a present and a changed set of circumstances. This gap can be perceived by individuals and/or by or their communities. It can be considered as something that is inexistent, deficient or incompatible with certain social values, linguistic norms or literacy standards. This discrepancy nature of need as a missing condition is the most adopted one in education and social policy studies (Packwood and Whitaker, 1988).

### Wants, needs and interests: What's the difference?

The concept *need* reveals ambiguity and confusion. For instance, *wants* and *needs* are frequently confused (Brackhaus, 1984). Kowalski (1988) identifies *wants* with motivation as they both express the internal energy and drives that determine a person's desire to do something as aroused or stimulated by experience. The author explains that *wants* or motivations alone do not fully reflect *needs.* He argues that *educational needs* represent gaps between present competencies and desired competencies. *Educational wants,* on the other hand, describe an individual's predisposition to remove selected needs.

Likewise, Knowles (1982) distinguishes between *wants* and *interests* as the latter refer to demonstrated preferences between alternative modes of overt behavior. In fact, the distinguishing characteristic of an interest is that it involves a choice between activities. Therefore, interests imply acceptance or rejection. The author explains that it is this element of choice between alternatives that differentiates between *interests, needs,* and *motivations.*

To sum up, the various meanings attributed to the concept of *need* such as *interests, wants* and *motivation* make it slippery in nature. Besides, *needs* are not fully developed facts that can be easily grasped and described. In addition, the adjectives attached to the concept add to its confusion. Thus, *real needs, perceived needs, ascribed needs, target needs* and *learning* needs are frequently used in adult education, each having a specific meaning. These are defined hereafter within the most well known theories of need, namely the *target situation approach* and the *learning centred approach.*

## THE TARGET SITUATION APPROACH VERSUS THE LEARNING-CENTRED APPROACH

In the late seventies, Munby (1978) developed the target situation approach. In this approach, which Chambers (1980) names as the *target situation analysis* (TSA) two years later, the need analyst is concerned with the identification of the situation where the learner needs to use what s/he has acquired. Thus, the concept of need is analysed in terms of the communicative competence that is needed in the target situation through a needs processing instrument called *Communication Needs Processor* (CNP). In this respect, it can be considered as a pre-course need analysis. The CNP seeks to identify two sets of parameters. The first involves the non-linguistic constraints on the learner such as the occupational, physical and psycho-social settings where s/he will use his or her competencies. The second set of parameters, on the other hand, includes all the linguistic means required by the learner to accomplish a communicative event in the target situation.

Almost a decade later, Hutchinson and Waters (1987) came out with a different model of needs analysis. The *learning-centred approach* considers the learner and learning as the most important elements to be considered before and during any teaching activity. Hence, the learners' needs, desires, attitudes and motivations are taken into account at all the stages of the learning process and course design. In so doing, Hutchinson and Waters distinguish between *target* needs and *learning* needs. The former refers to what the learner needs to do in the target situation and the latter is concerned with what the learner needs to do in order to learn. One advantage of the *learning-centred approach* lies in its analysis of the learners' needs in terms of the discrepancy between a desired state and an actual one, as well as the problems inherent to the ascribed remedy to fulfil the desired goals.

## Target needs

Hutchinson and Waters (1987) explain that *target needs* include three types of needs: *wants, lacks and necessities. Wants* are defined as the learner's own perception of his or her needs. *Lacks* are referred to as the gap between a required proficiency in the target situation and the existing proficiency of the learner. Finally, *necessities* are described as what the learner has to know to function effectively in the target situation. It is to be noted that Knowles (1982) uses other concepts to refer to *wants, lacks* and *necessities*; these are *felt needs, real needs* and *ascribed needs* respectively.

*Felt* needs as defined by Knowles are self-identified as they represent a conscious awareness by the learners of the needs they desire to gratify. In this respect, it is possible to say that *felt* needs may be viewed as *wants* or *motivation. Real* needs, on the other hand, stand for the gap existing between a present competence and a desired one. In this way they can be referred to as *lacks* which are described as the gap between a desirable standard and a standard that actually exists. *Ascribed needs* reflect the observer's determination of a learner's need in a given situation. In other words, ascribed needs refer to what the educator thinks necessary for the learner to know in order to function effectively in the target situation. In this way ascribed needs may be comparable to necessities which reflect the type of need determined by the demands of the target situation.

To sum up, it is possible to say that with respect to adult education, felt needs are psychologically based, real needs are skill based and the ascribed needs are the remedy used to fill the lacks and possibly satisfy the wants. The present chapter investigates the learners' literacy needs in terms of these three categories of needs. Hence, felt needs or wants refer to the motivations that drove the learners to enrol in the literacy course; real needs reflect respondents' own evaluation of their skill ability or deficiency with respect to the target situation; ascribed needs correspond to the course designers' objectives and aims.

## Learning needs

Hutchinson and Waters (1987) compare the fulfilment of a need as a journey where the starting point are lacks, the destination are necessities and what the destination should be are wants. The authors argue that learning needs could be defined as the route that the learners have to take to get from the starting point to the destination. This route, as the authors clarify, may include conditions of the learning situation, the learners' knowledge, skills, strategies and motivations to arrive at the destination. Viewed in this light, learning needs analysis seeks data related to both the learning and the teaching conditions, namely, the availability of human and technical resources, the objectives of the course, curricula, syllabus and teaching methods as proposed by the course .designer and evaluated by the learner. In this way, learning needs analysis is much concerned with collecting information on how the learner undergoes the learning process, particularly the conditions under which learning takes place and the constraints that affect such learning. As explained above, the present chapter investigates the learners' learning needs in terms of the respondents' evaluation of the ascribed contents, the language of instruction, the employed logistic, namely the teachers, proximity of schools, and practicality of the time table.

Given the importance of *target needs* in the development of adult literacy materials and contents and given the significant effect of the *learning needs* on the learning process and motivations of the learner, the consideration of both needs in the present study is imperative. What follows is a survey of *target needs* as determined by the literacy providers, and expressed by the teachers and also importantly by the female learners, who constitute the majority of the participants in literacy programs. Investigation of their learning needs is given subsequently.

## TARGET NEEDS AS DETERMINED BY THE PROGRAM DESIGNERS

Target needs as ascribed by the course designer can be analysed in terms of objectives and aims. Widdowson (1983: 6–7) defines objectives as "the pedagogic intentions of a particular course of study to be achieved within the period of that course and in principle measurable by some assessment device at the end of the course". On the other hand, the author defines aims as "the purposes to which learning will be put after the end of the course". For example a course may have as one of its objectives the acquisition of some specific mathematical operations. The aim of this exercise would be a more general capacity for problem solving and rational enquiry which learners could apply to later experience even if they have no further contact with mathematics for the rest of their lives. In a language teaching course, for instance, the objective of the course would be the development of a set of lexical items, syntactic structures, or notions or functions. The aim of the course, on the other hand, would be the development of an ability to exploit knowledge of these elements in effective communication. In brief, objectives are related to pedagogy and teaching methods. Aims, on the other hand, are related to the concept and nature of education. Hence, aims refer to what the learner has to do with what s/he has learned after training. Objectives refer to what the learner needs to know in order to learn.

The present sub-section gives an overview of the objectives and aims of the Moroccan adult literacy programs in which the informants of the present research have participated. As explained in chapter 3, these programs include the general campaign, which is organized by the Social Authority in collaboration with the Ministry of Education, and the courses which are supplied by the Ministry of Youth and Sport, the National Cooperation, and non-governmental associations.

On the basis of an interview with the head of the department of Teacher Training at the Literacy Directorate, the objectives of teaching non-literate adults may be said to be implemented in accordance with UNESCO's definition of literacy in 1958, which defines a literate person as the one "who can, with understanding, both read and write a short simple statement on his everyday life". The respondent explains that the levels of literacy that should be attained by the graduates of adult literacy courses should be equivalent to the completion of four years of primary schooling.

Investigation of the annual proceedings published by the Literacy Directorate reveals that the objectives of the Directorate are explained only in terms of program coverage at the national and regional levels, and the distribution of beneficiaries according to grade level, sex, residence and host institutions. Reference to the pedagogical objectives of adult literacy education is explicitly stated in the introduction of the textbooks used for that purpose. For research purposes, these objectives are explained with regard to the textbooks that were used during the fieldwork of the present research, in this case the two volumes of Literacy for all. As stated in the textbooks, the objective of the course is to teach reading, writing and arithmetic skills for functional purposes to ensure positive participation of the new literate in the society. The textbooks are divided into two main parts: reading and arithmetic. The aim of the reading part is to combat religious illiteracy, civic illiteracy, health and family planning illiteracy, ecological and agricultural illiteracy. The arithmetic part aims at teaching basic arithmetic, measurements, and geometrical shapes and financial transactions such as income, expenses, loans and percentages. The syllabus is grammatically based. It mainly consists of stimulus-response procedures, pattern practice, mechanical drills and rote learning of grammatical rules and vocabulary items.

To sum up, the adult literacy program designers aim at the teaching of basic literacy through a content that seeks to develop a set of language skills and knowledge that are related to religion, civic society, health and development matters.

## Target needs as expressed by the teachers

The teachers play a key role in the implementation of the course objectives and in the development of appropriate learning conditions which would facilitate the achievement of the objectives and goals of any educational program. Therefore, their objectives and goals in combating female illiteracy are taken into consideration.

The response to the question "what are the objectives of the literacy course that you are supplying at the center?" was unanimous and reads as follows "to combat ignorance, underdevelopment and illiteracy". A consideration of this answer reveals that the objectives and the aims of the course are confused. When further explanation was supplied, all the interviewed teachers agree that the objective of the literacy course in the basic grade is to teach mechanical reading and writing, oral skills, basic chapters of the Koran, and arithmetic such as: measuring and weighing units, the four basic mathematical operations, time, bills and price tags, and monetary conversion of the *riyal* into the *dirham*, which makes twenty riyals, and which is the currency in use in the monetary systems and domains such as banks, bills, shops and services, and supermarkets. It is to be noted that *riyal* is the smallest unit of Moroccan currency. It is in use especially among non-literate people instead of *centime*, which is normally used in the formal economic sector along with the dirham.

The objectives of teaching literacy at the follow-up level or the graduate level, as expressed by the teachers under study, consist in the teaching of language structure, reading strategies, written expression, dictation, arithmetic, and religious instruction. With respect to the aims of the course, the interviewed teachers came up with the following points:

1. Make the learners attain a level of literacy that can help them to read any sources of knowledge and written culture.
2. Prepare the learners to express themselves in the Arabic language.
3. Love the Arabic language, the language of the Koran.
4. Broaden the learners' religious knowledge and Islam based issues.
5. Prepare the learners to develop self-sustaining literacy skills.
6. Participate in the creation of a safe and healthy society.
7. Respect productive work.
8. Respect the nation and the established constitution.
9. Develop a sense of patriotism.
10. Acquire agricultural and sanitary matters.

A consideration of these objectives and aims reveals that they do not differ much from those stated by the course designers whose objective, as already explained, is to teach basic literacy for religious, civic, agricultural and sanitary purposes.

Note though that some of the foregoing objectives are language related and aim at high levels of literacy.

### Target needs as expressed by the learners

Nowadays, societies witness a daily evolving mutation in communication and information practices as they rely more and more on the script as a means of diffusing information and knowledge, posing new and heavy challenges to those who, while possessing other skills and competencies, were not previously given chance to use literacy or failed to acquire it. Letters and figures are everywhere in houses, streets, cinemas, cafés, hospitals, stores, administrations, and so on. They are shown on documents, television, bills, papers, and posters. As a result, the ability to use the script to handle everyday matters has become a fundamental need and a required qualification for social and vocational integration. Accordingly, many non-literate people seek such ability through massive enrolment in literacy courses and the informants of the present study are a case in point. But what are their literacy needs? Are they of a utilitarian use? Integrative use? Or empowering use?

The following sub-section seeks to answer these questions through an analysis of the learners felt needs and real needs. Data related to the learner's felt needs is gathered through the question: "What drove you to participate in the program?" Information concerning the informant's real needs is collected through an investigation of the question "In what situation(s) do you feel the need to read but couldn't do so? The same question was asked for writing and computing needs.

### THE RESPONDENTS' FELT NEEDS

The answer to the question "what drove you to participate in the literacy course?" was almost unanimous for the whole sample. The majority responded as follows: "I came to the center to know how to *read* anything I come across". In sum, the learners' primary objective in acquiring literacy is simply to become literate. In fact, the verb "qra" in Moroccan Arabic has three meanings. The first is associated with mechanical reading, the second refers to comprehension and the last one means "become educated or literate". It is this last meaning that the respondents have in mind as it encompasses not only mechanical reading but also comprehension and other literacy skills such as writing and arithmetic. The rest of the respondents, namely the pre-schooled ones invoked reasons such as restoring their reading skills, improving their handwriting and mathematical skills, and learning the French language.

To gain insight into their motivations in becoming literate, the respondents were asked another question which reads as follows: "why do you want to become literate?" The respondents came out with many answers. These are examined and analyzed in the form of individual variables for each respondent. The variables are, then, grouped under related literacy domains. The goals cited as desirable outcomes of female participation in adult literacy classes include the following felt needs in an ascending order: culture-based (10%), education-based (20%) job-related (28%), child education (42%), linguistic (47%), health-related (56%), religious (65%), consumer-based (80%), empowering (86%) and community-based (91%). Presentation and explanation of each need is given hereafter.

**Community-based felt needs**

The most commonly felt need as presented above is community-based. Examples of such a need are mainly of a utilitarian nature. They express the learners' desire to be able to write their names, sign, fill out forms, use the telephone, keep an agenda, read street signs, understand directions and schedules, correspond with relatives and friends, recognize mails and parcels, read and understand community based service documents such as advertisements, news, newspapers, summons, and law documents on divorce, custody, legacy property or heritage as stated by these testimonies:

**Fatna, 33 years old**

*Since my husband's death I had a lot of problems with my heirs-at-law and had a lot of papers I couldn't read. My brother in law wants me to sign anywhere, though I didn't know how to do so. On the other hand, my own brother wants me to confer powers of attorney on him. I came here to know how to handle all those judicial papers.*

**Khaddouj, 50 years old**

*One day, I inadvertently tore a very important document which was littering the floor of my son's room. He never forgave me for that. I felt remorseful and decided to become literate.*

**Khlija, 18 years old**

*My father and my brothers keep a shop in Casablanca. As you know, every month they send us a parcel which contains basic food, medicine, money and a tape where they let us hear from them and give us advice on how to handle some life matters. One day, our neighbour, who used to bring our parcels from the coach station, deliberately exchanged our parcel for another. Maybe he wanted to hear the news our father sent us as we had a problem concerning a shared well with our uncle at that time. Since then, my father urged me to enroll in the center to learn to read and write. Now thanks to our dishonest neighbor, I'm here. God bless him, ha, ha, ha.*

**Empowerment-based needs**

The informants' community-based needs consist in applying a set of language skills to a set of knowledge areas. On the other hand, empowerment-based needs consist in gaining a positive social value which is missing due to the inability to apply literacy as a functional skill. In other words, community-based needs, like any other functional needs, are skill based while empowerment needs are personality related. To use Molyneux's terminology, it is possible to say that community-based needs, like any other functional skills, reflect the learners' *practical* interests and the empowerment-based needs stand for their *strategic* needs. In this case, empowerment needs or strategic interests are self-related and can be considered as an aspiration to a better socio-psychological position within the family, the community and society at large. Within this category of needs, which is highly desired, the respondents claim that they seek literacy to combat their ignorance, dependence and exclusion, to develop their personality, to ensure self-reliance, self-esteem, self-confidence and self-respect, as expressed in the following translated testimonies:

**Rabha, 45 years old**

*One day I went to the hospital to pay a visit to a sick relative. Being illiterate, I was unable to find his room number. Suddenly I found myself in the surgery room. The doctor screamed: "put that donkey out." Since then I decided to enroll in adult literacy courses.*

**Hlima, 32 years old**

*I came to the center to combat my exclusion and to develop self-esteem especially vis-à-vis my literate brothers and their wives who avoid me because of my illiteracy. One is a doctor and his wife too, another is a lawyer and his wife a teacher, the remaining one is a chemist and his fiancée studies in France. My parents didn't send me to school because it was far from home. Of course my brothers went to school and completed their college and university studies at my uncle's in Rabat, as for me I remained in the village and stayed there till I was left out by school. Now I'm just an animal who is good for nothing.*

**Zaina, 20 years old**

*Every month my boyfriend used to send me a letter from Paris. A friend of mine used to read and answer them for me. When he came for the summer holiday, he married her. I never knew what happened. Since then I came to the center to become independent and gain self-esteem.*

**Hajja Keltoum, 60 years old**

*I want to become literate to write my biography. Yah, the story of my life, as an oppressed woman. Of course I can tell it orally, but I want it to enter history.*

**Yamna, 30 years old**

*Because of my illiteracy, I always feel deficient. My language is imperfect, my knowledge is limited, my personality is weak, and my life is useless. I earn no money but I'm good at spoiling bread. I pray God that the literacy course I'm taking will open new horizons for me and make me efficient, capable, and productive. But the problem is that an old monkey never learns!*

**Consumer-based needs**

Just like community based skills, consumer-based needs are sought after for utilitarian reasons. They are needed to apply a set of skills to a set of socio-economic situations. Among these are the following: to know items' prices and compute their sums, to understand sums on bills, cheques, money orders, rent papers and tax forms, to handle the problem of monetary conversion of the *dirham* into the *riyal* and vice versa, count expenses and income, understand use-by dates of goods or medicine, avoid being cheated by checking labels, measurements, weights and prices of items as expressed below:

**Aicha, 34 years old**

*Whenever I come back from the grocer's I check my money and I always realize that I have been cheated. Sometimes the grocer pays me back, but sometimes he doesn't. Had I known how to count on paper and check with him the prices once in his shop, I would never have been involved in such trouble. Now I guess you know why I'm here.*

**Mina, 45 years old**

*When I go to supermarkets, I feel very frustrated as I cannot read the prices on the items. Of course I feel very embarrassed when I ask someone for help and my frustration becomes bigger when s/he gives me the price in dirham. Now, I'm here to handle those prices and money conversions.*

**Religious needs**

Religious needs are another sort of functional skills. In this case, they are sought after to answer the learner's inability to read and understand the Koran, though the majority explain that they know how to recite the verses that are necessary for the prayer. Their claim in this respect is to understand what they recite, learn more *suras* and gain a better understanding of a good Muslim's duties and rights as dictated by God's words. The majority also regret their inability to read the holly book especially in sacred periods such as Ramadan, and during the pilgrimage, or at the mosque as their *literate sisters* would do.

**Hajja Hachuma, 55 years old**

*When I went to the pilgrimage, I was hung up to see that women of my age and even younger could read the Koran at the mosque. When I came back I decided to learn to read.*

**Oummi Fatna, 55 years old**

*People say that women are religiously and cognitively disabled. They are right; we don't know how to read the Koran. I'm here to compensate for this handicap.*

### Health-related needs

Health-related needs is another type of functional skills that more than fifty percent of the respondents highly seek to acquire. Data related to this skill include the learners' desire to understand directions on medicine bottles and pills, know their use-by dates, make a better use of contraceptive methods, namely the pills, follow a doctor's directions, note down special treatments and diets, and recognize vaccination dates as marked on the health book.

**Ruqayya, 25 years old**

*When my son Karim caught influenza, the doctor prescribed a nasal drop and an eye drop. Because of my illiteracy my dear Karim almost lost his sight as I put the nasal drop in his eyes. Now I'm here to understand all those health matters. Health is the most important thing in life, isn't it?*

### Language needs

As already stated, 47 percent of the respondents claim that they enrolled in adult literacy courses to comprehend the linguistic features of the target literacy situations where Standard Arabic and French are used. A comparison of the respondents by their mother tongue and birthplace through ANOVA reveals that these variables have a significant impact on seeking the satisfaction of the respondents' language needs ($F=120$; df= 1and 200; $p<.0001$) for the respondents' mother tongue and ($F=36.86$, df= 1 and 200; $p<.0001$) for the birthplace. The most significantly motivated group to acquire the languages of literacy is the rural Amazigh group. Although Standard Arabic and French are not the languages of their immediate environment, the rural Amazighophones claim is that they enrol in the literacy classes to learn these languages for their highly prestige and to handle the literacy functions they fulfil. They explain that as Standard Arabic, which is so far the only language used in adult literacy courses, is a new language for them, they first need to learn it as an oral language and use it as a language of literacy later on. The next motivated group is the urban Amazighophone group followed by the rural Arabophone group. Curiously, none of the urban Arabophone group expressed this need. This felt desire for learning and understanding Standard Arabic and French is also associated with their important use in television. This is attested by the following testimony whose author's motivation in this respect is to understand the languages of the media.

**Houria, 21 years old, rural Amazigh**

*Since we had electricity in the village, our father sent us a television set from Tangier where he works as a grocer. Unfortunately, we don't understand a word of the programs it broadcasts. We just look at the screen like donkeys. Now I wish I could learn Arabic and also French to come out of this darkness.*

The learning of the French language is also cited as a literacy goal especially among working non-literate women (Agnaou, 1998). Their motivation emanates from the prestigious and the functional status of the language. French is sought after to impress the other literate mates or simply feel educated like their husbands and children, to read dressing and knitting patterns, hairstyle magazines, cookery books, phone bills, contraceptive methods, and instructional manuals. It is also needed to understand French movies and broadcasts, to help children with homework, to work in French speaking environments for better salaries or to avoid paying extra expenses as illustrated in the following story which is told by Saadia, a middle-aged maid:

*I blame my parents; they didn't send me to school. Now I'm paying for that and the price is too high. I found a nice job as a chambermaid in a big hotel in Agadir but they didn't recruit me because I don't speak French. In addition, I had to pay half of my salary (300Dh) to a literate man for having filled the visa form for me as I'm planning to immigrate to France. I enrolled to study French but they said this year there are no French courses. Now, I think I will have to pay again, ha, ha, ha.*

### Child education related needs

42 percent of the learners enrolled in the literacy classes to satisfy the need to keep up with their children. This percentage refers to the majority of the married sample which represents 44 percent of the respondents. In fact, most of these mothers declare that they enrol in the same school as their children to reinforce links between home and school and have control over their children. Their concern is to approach teachers and headmasters and follow their children's progress at school.

### Job related perceived needs

28 percent of the respondents claim that they integrated the literacy center for job related reasons. When compared by their occupation, it is revealed that the working sample significantly express job related needs. Their means in this

respect (2.58) are significantly higher than those of the non-working sample (1.61), ($F=20.62$; $DF=1-202$; $p<.0001$).

Job related needs is either skill related or socio-economically based. Skill oriented needs are mainly sought after to improve job performance and/or understand matters that are job linked. This type of skill goals are needed by the working sample. Qualitative investigation of their responses came up with various motivations. The dressmakers' group explains that acquiring literacy would help them read dressing and knitting patterns, make use of more sophisticated measures, keep records, use better communication skills with their clients and handle money and cheques. The maid sample refers to the importance of literacy as a memory supported skill for keeping records, writing culinary recipes, noting down telephone messages, and acquiring basic measurement skills for cuisine and pastry purposes. Concerning the workers' sample, they responded that they needed literacy to know how to fill out forms, understand pay slips, and identify their names on duty timetables. The shop-assistant sample's goals are mainly money-based. Tagging items, paying back the clients, using desk calculators, checking till receipts or providing written ones are their main wants. Surprisingly, none of the respondents from the cleaners' group demanded job-related skills. It is important to note, though, that one of these cleaners, who works in an orphanage in the province of Tiznit, explains that a driving motivation that urged her to attend literacy courses was her desire to read and understand the scratch paper she has been collecting in the playground for about ten years. She adds that since she has started the courses, she takes part of this paper home and uses it as a reading material.

The second related job need is socio-economically based. This means that it is not linked to the learners' deficiency in applying literacy to the job requirements but is rather expressed in terms of aspiring to have a better job for the working sample or earn a living for the non-working group. This need is highly expressed by the post-graduate group from *annachi'a al-Mohammadia* school in Rabat where one of its graduate learners teaches literacy in the basic level. It is worth mentioning here that due to this recruitment, this school registers high enrolments and motivations especially from primary school drop-outs or leavers. Unfortunately, though, most of these pre-schooled women register as totally non-literate, a fact which in the long run affects the non-schooled sample's motivation as it is difficult for them to catch up with the pre-schooled participants.

**Continuing-education based needs**

Continuing-education based needs refer to the respondents' need for literacy to pursue their education after graduation from the literacy program to integrate other training institutions which require basic literacy as the minimum level of the enrolees. The cited training fields include: hairdressing, typing and dress design. This desire is significantly expressed by the pre-schooled group whose .means are slightly but significantly higher (0.72) than those of the non-schooled group (0), (F=72.23;. DF=1–202; p<.0001).

**Culture-based needs**

The last cited motivation for acquiring literacy is culture related. Culture-related needs as defined by the participants consist of the understanding of the national as well as the international socio-economic and political issues that are conveyed by media. Despite its lower demand as it is required by only 10 percent of the respondents, it is worth analyzing this need in terms of some predictor variables. Correlation analyses reveal that the most significant variable that has an effect on the respondents' motivation to understand culturbased issues are their husbands' or tutors' literacy levels (r=.47) and (p<.0001). This means that the higher the respondents' husbands' or tutors' literacy level, the higher the learners' motivation for acquiring literacy for cultural purposes. In fact, the learners' means for culture-based needs significantly increase as their tutors' or husbands' literacy level increases. These are 0.10, 0.50, 1.09 for the participants whose husbands' level of education is primary school, secondary school, and university respectively. Qualitative analyses of the data show that these respondents require literacy to be integrated in their milieu. The majority of the seekers of this goal express their desire to follow their literate mates' conversations from which they are excluded due to their deficient knowledge of the concepts employed and the matters dealt with.

When compared in terms the respondents' own pre-literacy experience, the analysis of variance reveals no significant differences between the pre-schooled and the non schooled group with respect to acquiring literacy for culture purposes (F=.80; df=1–202; p>0.5). It is important to note, though, that the pre-schooled group (0.23) feels this need more than the non-schooled group (0.16).

**THE LEARNERS' REAL NEEDS**

To assess their real needs, the respondents are asked to specify three situations where they are unable to use reading, writing and arithmetic. Four situations are reported as marked by the learners' inability to use literacy as a task. These are in a priority order linked to the community (40%), consumer matters (30%), job (20%) and health (10%). Second, these same needs are also expressed by the

**Table 6.1. A Matrix of the Functional Skills Requested by the Respondents**

| | Community-based | Consumer-based | Health-related | Job-related |
|---|---|---|---|---|
| **Reading** | Directions<br>Mail documents<br>Newspapers<br>Services | Bills<br>Money order<br>Advertisement | Labels<br>Directions | Knitting patterns<br>Magazines |
| **Writing** | Correspondence<br>Sign/Fill out documents | Keep records<br>Sign/ Fill out cheques | Special diets & menus | Telephone messages<br>Recipes<br>Menus |
| **Arithmetic** | Date/time<br>Schedules | Item prices<br>Check money<br>Income/expenses | Visit dates<br>Vaccination dates<br>Use by dates | Pay slips<br>Measurements<br>Receipts |

respondents as felt needs with more or less the same order of importance. Qualitative analyses of the respondents' answers in this respect came out with a set of functional skills that are grouped by skill and domain in the matrix below:

This matrix summarizes the language functions needed by skill and by situation. It reflects the knowledge and abilities the learners feel as necessary to function effectively in the target situation For instance, with respect to community based situations, the respondents report that they enrolled in the literacy class because they could not read schedules, street directions, newspapers, correspondence and because they were unable to write letters, sign or fill out forms.

## THE LEARNERS' LEARNING NEEDS

So far, the preceding sections have dealt with target needs as perceived by the learners and ascribed by the literacy designer and teachers. Still, it would be interesting to find out how the learners respond to the learning situation they are undertaking to satisfy their needs. The elements of this learning situation as addressed in the present section include the learner's reaction to the ascribed contents, teaching techniques, the adopted language, the employed logistics namely the teachers, proximity of schools, and the practicality of the time table.

**Reaction to the ascribed contents**

As already stated in the present chapter, the designed literacy courses include topics that are related to religion, civic society, and development matters such as health, migration, agriculture and ecology. The respondents are asked to express their satisfaction with these subjects in terms of a four scaled response. The frequency distribution analysis of these responses reveals that 14 percent report that they are not at all satisfied with the ascribed contents, 17 percent claim they are quite satisfied, 25 percent say that are very satisfied and 44 percent express little satisfaction. This means that more than fifty percent of the respondents are at most little satisfied with the designed content.

The non-satisfied respondents' claim is that the topics they are taught are too elementary and do not bring information of practical value. Some of the respondents, namely the urban ones, suggest that topics dealing with migration, agriculture and popular education should be designed for rural women only. Others suggest that most of the topics dealt with are addressed to men. This last statement is confirmed by the analysis of the textbooks in chapter 8.

To gain insight into the content that would satisfy the respondents, these are asked to suggest a list of topics and subjects they consider as more interesting to learn. 88 percent of the respondents respond by providing four main suggestions. The desired topics include matters that would deal with law (18%), women issues (30%), and vocational instruction (40%). While analyzing the answers to this question, the voices of middle-aged women from the old Medina of Rabat resound in my ears saying:

*God forgive my parents who didn't send me to school and bless the authorities who gave us a chance to learn. They teach us literacy and they do it with a lot of patience. But, please tell them that we want to know, yes we want to know our rights and duties as women. You know, what I mean, heritage, divorce, custody and all those law matters.*

Another voice said:

*Birth control is good for girls not for women of my age. We already have four to six children and can't have any more now. So, it's too late to do family planning. What we need is to know how to deal with such big families, how to handle the problems of puberty and adolescence, not how to feed babies and those pregnancy matters.*

Another informant added:

*First, I would like to thank our teacher. May God protect her! When I came to the center, I couldn't even hold a pen. Now I can write my name and sign. With her help and God's willing I will certainly know the rest. Concerning the topics, I have an objection especially to those dealing with religion, good citizenship, and popular education. The messages they convey are child education based. But we are educated and come from noble families; you know my father is a well known religious scholar. We all know what a good Muslim and a good citizen are like; we know what is good and what is bad. You know, we are not ignorant, what we don't know is simply how to read and write.*

Other respondents require topics that deal with health issues such as breast cancer, and body matters like how to remain young and good-looking. Still, others claim vocational courses such as pastry-making, cooking, knitting, hair dressing, dress making and embroidery to earn a living. Unfortunately, none of the designed textbooks aim at teaching these required topics and only very few programs grant vocational training.

Both the ascribed needs and felt needs include religious literacy, health literacy, and socio-economic literacy. It is important to note, though, that the language contents used for the teaching of such skills does not correspond to the learners' expectations. As already explained, felt/real health-based needs include the learners' desire to understand directions on medicine items, know their use-by dates, make a better use of contraceptive methods, namely the pills, follow a doctor's directions, note down special treatments and diets, and recognize vaccination dates as marked on the health book. A consideration of the ascribed contents, however, reveals that none of these skills exist in the designed textbooks, namely the two volumes of Literacy for All. The subjects dealt with are rather general and most of them can be learnt through other channels such as television or the radio. For instance, the vaccination lesson on pages 27–28 of *the* basic level textbook, reads as follows: "This is a nurse. This is a hospital. Those are children. The nurse vaccinates the children of the village." "Vaccination is necessary. It is done at the hospital" "The nurse vaccinates the children in the village". No indication is given concerning the vaccination types by age nor by dates and no vaccination book is used either at the presentation level of the lesson or at its exploitation stage. Likewise, the lesson on pregnancy on page 34 of the graduate level textbook conveys well known messages such as the importance of having a rich and a varied diet for the good development of the baby. But no information is given as to what a "rich and varied diet" would be.

The sanitary lesson on pages 35–36 of the basic level textbook, deals with well known daily and stereotyped female roles such as cleaning the house, sweeping the floor, washing the clothes, and emptying trash. No explanation, however, is made on how to organise such domestic duties and save time for other activities that would contribute to women's emancipation such as their participation in literacy courses, and associative or cooperative work. Moreover, no information is given on how to avoid certain diseases such as diarrhea by knowing how to store food, sterilize milk, make good use of water and waste vegetables, and how to deal with certain vitamin deficiencies by suggesting healthy and cheap menus.

As already mentioned, religious literacy is mainly sought for understanding the basic chapters of the Koran, acquire other *suras* and understand the principles of Islam. A consideration of the ascribed religious lessons, however, reveals that they are rather general as the texts deal with the qualities of a good Muslim and the advantages of Islam as being the religion of mercy and forgiveness as shown on pages 7–10 of the graduate level textbook.

Consumer-based needs, as already explained, involve the learners' desire to compute large sums, read and understand use-by dates, recognize sums on bills, cheques, money orders, rent papers and tax forms. While the designed contents aim at teaching such skills, none of these materials or documents is used for the completion of that goal. It is worth adding here that the same works for community-based needs as no authentic material is used in this respect.

## Reaction to the adopted language

As stated in chapter 1, adult literacy work in Morocco is mainly carried out in Standard Arabic (SA), the official language of the country. The literacy centers that have been visited are no exception; they all teach literacy in SA. What follows is an analysis of the learners' reaction to the language of instruction in terms of its utility and ease of learning.

All the respondents agree on the important utility of the Arabic language and state that its knowledge is a necessary step to satisfy most of their target needs. However, the majority claim that it is a difficult language to learn. When asked to rate the difficulty of learning Standard Arabic, 48 percent of the respondents consider it as very difficult and 13 percent judge its learning as quite difficult. 36 percent, on the other hand, say that its learning is easy but only 3 percent report that they have little difficulty in acquiring it.

A consideration of these percentages reveals that a quite proportion of the whole sample has difficulty in acquiring the language of literacy. In fact, the ascribed language is not the natural vehicle of thought or expression of the learners who either speak a different variety of that language as is the case for Moroccan Arabic speakers or a completely different language as is the case for the monolingual Amazigh speakers. Given this, it is possible to hypothesize that the group that would experience more difficulty would be the Amazigh group. This is confirmed by the fact that 70 percent of the Amazighophones claim that they have a lot of difficulty in acquiring the Arabic language in comparison to 38 percent of the Arabophones. Only 13 percent of Amazigh respondents claim having no difficulty at all in comparison to 46 percent Arab learners. It is noteworthy that Amazigh is used instead of Berber. In fact, the word "Berber" has been rejected by Amazigh activists for its pejorative and colonial connotation.

They prefer to use instead the original and appropriate word "Amazigh", which means "a free person".

An important proportion of the Arabophone respondents (38%) claim that learning the Arabic language is very difficult, while another 46 percent of the same sample claim that learning in the Arabic language is easy. One possible reason for this discrepancy may be linked to the learners' pre-literacy levels. In fact, it is revealed that 65 percent of the non-schooled respondents have difficulty in acquiring the language of literacy in comparison to 28 percent of the schooled sample. It was also found that 56 percent of the schooled learners claim that learning in Standard Arabic is easy in comparison to 18 percent of the non-schooled group.

## Reaction to the employed logistic

What is meant by the employed logistics are the teachers, the proximity of schools, the nature of the classes, the timetable, the duration of the course and satisfaction with the designed program as a whole.

While addressing female literacy in Muslim countries, the issue of the teacher's sex is often regarded as a key element. Given the weight of tradition, some families would object to send their daughters to school or to the literacy class when the teacher is a male. In addition, some learners themselves would refuse to participate in courses that are given by a male teacher. Their claim is that they would feel embarrassed by the presence of a male teacher especially when dealing with taboo matters. Aware of this problem, the informants of the present research are asked to express their choice regarding a male or a female teacher. The analysis of their responses brings the following findings: 55 percent of the respondents prefer a female teacher. They argue that they feel better at ease with a female teacher especially when dealing with family matters and women issues. Thirty-five percent of the learners have no preference and only 10 percent prefer a male teacher.

An examination of the interview that is administered to the respondents' teachers reveals that 60 percent are female and 40 percent are male. This means that the teachers' sex distribution satisfies the learners' need. It is important to note, though, that irrespective of their sex, the majority of these teachers (78%) never had a pre-service training nor an in-service training in andragogy, which means that they are not adequately prepared for the task they are performing mostly as volunteers (75%) in addition to their job as local primary school teachers (54%), or as students (21%). The primary school teachers receive a yearly remuneration of about $140 from the Literacy Directorate in Rabat. Sixty percent of the interviewed teachers are not satisfied with that sum particularly those who live away from Rabat. They claim that they spend an important part of that sum on travelling expenses and accommodation. As for students, some declare that they have a monthly salary of about $100 from the employing associations while others regret working for free.

The proximity of schools is another question that is addressed to the learners given its effect on continued participation. The participants' answer in this regard reveals that the majority (86%) live near the center and have no distance constraint. Fourteen percent of the respondents claim that they have to walk long distances or even take transportation means to the center. This situation is peculiar to residential quarters, especially in Rabat and Casablanca where there are no literacy centers. The distance constraint also prevails in rural areas where some girls have to walk long distances to reach the literacy center which is located in another village. As explained in chapter 5, due to this constraint, many of these girls end up leaving the center altogether.

The nature of the classes depends on the proximity of the center. Generally speaking, urban classes are crowded with participants from different ages, linguistic communities and socio-economic backgrounds and are instructed by a single teacher. In most cases, the number exceeded the recommended number which is twenty five participants per class. In addition, some women bring their children. While the respondents have no objection to the crowded nature of the classes, their teachers have and explain that an assistant is needed to help with the learners who, unlike children, require more individual support. They add that a second assistant is required to watch over the children while their mothers are taking the course. In addition to being crowded, most of the classes where adult literacy teaching takes place are children's classes. This class furnishing, however, is not suitable for adult use. Moreover, some of the ones that have been visited are not well lit. According to the participants, the comfort issue is not that important as long as they can learn how to read and write. With respect to rural classes, the visited ones are almost empty although special classes have been constructed for the teaching of adults. This results from the fact that many rural women do not consider literacy as their immediate need as expressed by Fadma, a middle-aged woman from Dousderm, in the province of Tiznit, South of Morocco.

*What shall I do? Feed my children or study? Who will cut and collect my wood? Who will fetch my water? Who will light my fire and cook my meals? Who will grind the almonds and argan fruit of my employers? Who will sift their wheat and barley? Who will cook their bread? Who will water their fields and collect their vegetables? Who will bring money and food home? My hands are bleeding and my back is aching, I'm worn out and if I had time, I would only take a rest.*

With respect to the practicality of the time table, 71 percent of the respondents are satisfied with the ascribed course schedule. This is partly due to the diversity of the training schedules on offer. For instance, the Ministry of Youth provides the courses in the afternoon, the Ministry of National cooperation in the morning and the Ministry of Social Affairs in the evening. Non-governmental associations grant the courses in the afternoons, some do it all day. So, the learner is free to enrol in the program that is most convenient. This also encouraged some learners to participate in different centers at the same time. Note, however, that 29 percent of the respondents are not satisfied with their course time. These belong to the programs that operate under the aegis of the Literacy Directorate which provides the literacy courses after six in the evenings. The respondents consider this time not suitable for two reasons. First, they consider that it is not a safe time to go out for a woman especially in winter as it gets very dark at that time. Second, they argue that it is the busiest time of the day due to the children's and husbands' return back home from school and work.

As for the programed length of the courses, 87 percent of the respondents explain that it is too short to answer their target literacy needs. Therefore, they suggest having longer training periods. In addition, 7 percent of the respondents claim that they have more than one literacy certificate and still feel unable to handle everyday literacy. To maintain and improve their skills, many adult literacy graduates keep registering in the same center or enrol in new ones. They argue that they need more literacy training and suggest that the Literacy Directorate designs post-literacy courses.

Last but not least, the respondents are asked to rate the extent to which their training is consonant with their target needs. These ratings are given in the form of five appreciations: high, quite, half, and little and not satisfied. It is found that only 8 percent of the respondents perceive their needs to be highly met by the prescribed program and just 12 percent are quite satisfied with it. 18 percent consider that the designed program moderately meets their needs; almost half of the respondents (49.5%) express little satisfaction and 11 percent report no satisfaction at all.

To determine the extent to which the respondents' satisfaction with the designed program changes according to their host institution, that is, governmental versus non-governmental, the analysis of variance is calculated and reveals that the respondents' satisfaction with the designed program is more or less the same irrespective of their host institution ($F=.28$; $df=1$ and 202; $p>.05$). In fact, this is expected as both institutions teach the same program. A consideration of the respondents' score means reveals that the non-governmental group is slightly but not significantly more satisfied (1.6) than the governmental sample (1.5). Many explanations are possible. One would be the frequency of the courses. While governmental institutions grant literacy at most trice a week, the non-governmental associations do it daily. This of course allows the non-governmental group to have more contact with literacy and accordingly be in a better position to have their needs fulfilled. Second, non-governmental associations, in opposition to the governmental ones, organize extra-literacy activities which consist of lectures by researchers or specialists in the domain of health, religion and sociology. In addition, the size of the classes and their furniture are more convenient and some associations, namely *Zhour azzarqa* association offers childcare which encourages women to participate in the courses in an effective way. Last but not least, other associations, particularly the *Action Féminine* Association grant counselling in the Personal Code and women's issues and the "Illigh" association in Casablanca provides post-literacy training.

With respect to the interviewed teachers, only 35 percent consider that the ascribed program highly meets the learners' needs. Eleven percent think that it is not at all consonant with the learners' needs and 54 percent are just little satisfied with the extent to which the designed courses meet the needs of the learners.

The teachers argue that there is an enormous gap between the basic grade level and the continuing grade level. They explain that the textbook that is used in the graduate level is very difficult for the learners and is of no practical value. Second, they claim that while the learners are highly motivated to learn, they are handicapped by their limited knowledge of the target language which makes the teachers use a lot of translation or shift to the mother tongue while explaining or giving instructions. They add that that the timing and duration of the courses are not sufficient especially in rural areas due to absenteeism which is linked to religious, socio-economic and cultural events such as Ramadan (the fasting month), harvest, ploughing, and reaping. Finally, they claim pre-service and in-service training especially in andragogy, the pedagogy of the adults.

## SUMMARY OF THE RESULTS AND DISCUSSION

The learners' literacy needs are investigated in terms of target needs, which comprise ascribed needs as determined by the program designers as well as the teachers, perceived needs, and real needs as felt by the learners.

Investigation of the ascribed needs reveals that Moroccan adult literacy programs are basically development oriented. Basic literacy, religious literacy, civic literacy, health and family planning literacy, ecological and agricultural literacy make up the contents of the reading part of the teaching materials. This means that the program on offer is a national program based on a universal stereotype that regards the beneficiaries as lacking guidance in religion, family planning, citizenship and popular education. Under such program, non-literate women are regarded as retarding the socio-economic advancement of their countries and are considered as incompatible with the developmental values that are held in society. Such an aspect of literacy includes only economic and social goals for integration and economic development purposes; it does not include personal development nor does it account for socio-economic group differences. Therefore, too much emphasis is put on the learners' practical needs at the expense of their strategic needs. Still the way the learners' practical needs are handled needs to be revised. While the ascribed development-based topics may be of high relevance to the learners, the way they are presented and taught makes them of no practical value. Instead of involving the learners to reflect on their problems and find ways to handle them, the tone of the language is rather lecture-oriented and moralizing as if addressing children. It is grammatically-based and uses education-based discourse which seeks conformity to pre-existing social values and behavior.

Investigation of the learners' perceived needs, which are considered as the most important type of literacy needs with respect to adult learners as they reflect the strongest motivations for enrolment in the programs, reveals a wide range of needs, most of which being development-based. Quantitative analyses of these needs reveal that while some are societal, others are rather individual. Societal needs refer to those literacy needs that are expressed by the majority of the learners. These are hereby presented in a descending order: community-based needs, empowering needs, consumer-based needs, religious needs, and health-related needs. Individual perceived needs are determined by other variables. These include linguistic needs which are mostly required by rural Amazigh respondents. Child-education needs which are mainly sought by married mothers. Job related needs are significantly desired by wage earners. Education-based needs are highly required by pre-schooled informants and culture-based needs are significantly demanded by respondents who live or work in highly literate milieus. In addition, the learners claim post-literacy training and vocational instruction.

In view of these results, literacy acquisition is sought after for socio-economic integration as well as personal development and transformation. The respondents claim that they enrol in the literacy course to acquire *literacy abilities* such as understanding bills, writing letters or reading the newspaper and *literacy functions* like using the language(s) of literacy to deal with religious matters and take part in discussions of cultural issues or deal with literacy situations in the workplace or the community. The respondents also participate in the courses to handle ignorance, to gain self esteem, to combat dependence, exclusion and marginalization, to enlarge their space and manage it, and to reflect on their experience and position. Hence, according to the interviewed learners, female literacy is needed not only for basic and utilitarian purposes but also for personal achievement, the construction of a new identity, the building of a new image of the self and liberation from silence and invisibility. This means that literacy is needed for both practical and strategic interests.

The program designers consider the learners as a homogenous group. However, as stated above, some literacy needs vary according to age, origin, marital status, pre-schooling experience, class and language. This individual dimension of literacy is very important as the learners' literacy needs can only be met by reference to the social group in which the individual operates. Hence, the necessity to deal with illiteracy as a gender phenomenon further characterized by individual, regional, social and linguistic factors.

In view of what has been stated above, there is an obvious mismatch between the curriculum and the immediate needs of the learners. The ascribed program is designed in a top-down way as it focuses on what the policy makers consider necessary to achieve nationally defined needs and interests. Therefore, the adult literacy courses grant education around socio-economic values through a uniform approach which is based on descriptive but not functional language and content.

The respondents are highly aware of the stakes connected with learning the language of literacy. Hence, they feel great interest but experience difficulty. In other words, Standard Arabic answers their target needs but not their learning needs. The linguistic complexity which is inherent to the Arabic language results from the existence of several varieties of language: dialectal Arabic, middle Arabic, modern Arabic, Classical Arabic. While the first two varieties are mainly spoken and are naturally acquired, the last two ones are written and are acquired and used in formal settings and do not have the status of mother tongues, which makes their learning challenging for the adult learner. This difficulty is further emphasized by the teaching approach adopted and the contents offered. From the class observations that have been carried out for the present research, too much time is spent on the teaching about language. In many cases, the teacher spends the whole lesson lecturing on the parts of the sentence such as the difference between sound and defective verbs, conjugation of verbs, the different placement of the glottal stop. Along this heavy concentration on grammar, the social functions of writing are absent. Writing activities are restricted to mechanical exercises and reproduction. Hence, copying and dictation are the sole writing activities. Likewise, reading is dissociated from comprehension and the teaching of vocabulary is done through translation or through synonyms that are not familiar to the learner. The teaching approach that is used is teacher-centred. It is based on memorization through rote repetition and recitation. Oral participation is limited to imitation of the presented model structures. Yet, the approaches that have been proved successful with the adult learners are group discussions, role playing, skill practice exercises, demonstrations, field projects, action projects, case studies and examination of real-life situations (Jurmo, 1987). Furthermore and as already mentioned, the ascribed contents are too general, and the language used is lecture-oriented and not functional. This may be another source of difficulty for acquiring the language of literacy. In fact, the teaching practices that are used during the class observations reduce the object of literacy to a school object divorced from its social functions. Yet, learners require instruction that is practical and applicable to their situations. The present study reveals that the learners' real needs are expressed in terms of situations where the literacy seekers feel ineffective. These situations can be used as support for developing adult literacy teaching and evaluation materials as they comprise the reading and writing skills that the learners need in their daily lives. Hence, rather than focussing on subject matters, teaching adults should use authentic documents and situations that require problem solving and rely on the background knowledge of the learners as well as their needs.

As suggested by the Freirean approach to adult literacy, the learners' background knowledge should be highly stimulated as it eases learning. Named after the Brazilian educator Paulo Freire, this approach bases the contents of the language lessons on learners' cultural and personal experiences. In this way, the approach is also referred to as the problem-posing approach (Auerbach and Wallerstein, 1987) or the learner-centred approach (Anorve, 1989). Freire's approach (1970b) is also called "deeply contextual" (Chacoff, 1989, p.49) because its language teaching flows from the discussion of themes of importance to the adult learner. These are drawn from their real-life experiences. Hence, formal language study plays only a secondary role to learners' conceptual development. In addition, this approach rejects what Freire (1970b) calls "the banking concept of education" which refers to any teaching activity that is based on the lecture format, where the teacher deposits information into the learners as s/he would deposit money into a bank. Instead, Freirean education rather relies on the "culture circle" where teachers and students face one another and discuss issues of concern in their own lives. Hence, the first codifications of the words consist of reactive reading which involves questioning, reflecting, and rethinking the socio-economic, historical, cultural, and political conditions of the learners.

Freire's method of teaching is based on a syllabic phonemic technique. It places the generative and generated meaningful words in the context of associated ideas and familiar objects or concepts. In so doing, it prepares adult learners to read newspapers, write and read simple letters after only six months of training. Unfortunately, none of the interviewed teachers knew about this approach as most of them received no training in andragogy as explained above.

## CONCLUSION

The purpose of this chapter was to assess the learners' literacy needs and learning needs. Its aim was to see whether the designed program is consonant with the learners' needs. Findings related to these issues reveal that adult literacy designers aim at the teaching of basic literacy through a structural syllabus and course contents that are related to religious, civic, health, and ecological matters. The learners, on the other hand, need basic literacy through the learning of a functional syllabus to know how to handle everyday literacy such as reading street directions, newspapers, correspondence, understanding law documents on divorce, custody, legacy or heritage, and write letters, sign and fill out forms. In addition, they require gender specific programming which links school literacy to community-based literacy, job and self-empowerment. Furthermore, they claim post-literacy training to improve and maintain their literacy skills, and their teachers call for pre-service and in-service training in adult literacy teaching. In sum, the program on offer does not answer the learners' literacy needs and their learning needs as hypothesized above. In view of this particular finding, there is a conjecture that, the learners under study are not appropriately prepared to handle the literacy skills they sought to learn through their participation in the literacy courses. One aim of the next chapter is an attempt to check this null hypothesis.

# 7
# Responding to Women's Literacy Needs

In the preceding chapter, it was found that women come to the literacy classes with a specific need in mind, namely to learn how to read in order to functionally deal with everyday life tasks. Starting from this practical need, this chapter seeks to measure the literacy attainments of 180 certified female graduates of Moroccan adult literacy programs in terms of basic literacy achievement and functional literacy proficiency. Three major questions are examined in this respect:

*To what extent do graduates of Moroccan adult literacy campaigns and programs master what they have learned from their literacy training?*

*Are they able to apply what they have learned to deal with the everyday literacy tasks they sought to learn through their participation in the literacy courses?*

*What are the variables that affect their reading performance?*

Briefly, these questions seek answers to how well the learners are keeping with what they have learned from the assigned program, and whether they can functionally use what they have learned to handle everyday literacy. These basic and functional competencies are computed as dependent variables in comparative statistics with independent variables such as the learners' age, motivation, mother tongue, and area (urban versus rural). Consideration of these variables is motivated by their important significance in second language acquisition in general (Skutnabb-Kansas and Toukomaa, 1976) and in Standard Arabic literacy acquisition among Moroccan children in particular (Ezzaki, Spratt and Wagner,

1987; Aarssen, de Ruiter, and Verhoeven, 1992 (cited in Saidi, 2001); Wagner, 1993). Hence three null hypotheses have been stated:

a. *Whatever their age and motivation, the learners will have the same performance in the assigned basic and functional tests.*

b. *The Amazigh sample and the Arab sample will get more or less the same score in both tests.*

c. *The rural group's and the urban group's performance in the tests will not be significantly different.*

While analyzing the learners' literacy attainments, sample differences such as pre-schooling experience and grade level are taken into consideration to reject any causal effects that might have resulted from such differences and, hence, affect the obtained results. This technique helps to analyze and compare the examinees' performance while controlling for the effects of sample differences. In other words, it controls for the initial differences that exist between the groups and provides detailed data on the performance of the target group and compares it with other groups, namely the pre-schooled graduate group, the non-schooled post-graduate group and the pre-schooled post-graduate group as these groups reflect the profiles of the beneficiaries of the investigated adult literacy programs. These sample differences are also important to analyze as they provide data on the effect of pre-literacy and post-literacy on literacy acquisition. It is to be noted that the target group is composed of non-schooled graduate learners.

## THE LEARNERS' BASIC LITERACY ATTAINMENT

As already explained in chapter four, the learners' basic literacy attainment score is calculated on the basis of the total score in both the pre-reading exercises and the basic reading comprehension exercise. It is calculated to answer the question quantifying the extent to which the tested learners master what they have been taught. Investigation of this question reveals that irrespective of grade level, all the investigated learners scored above average. The score means of correct answers is (31.6) out of a total of forty questions. Based on the percentage of correct answers in the overall test, 68 percent of the learners have attained the independent learning level and 32 percent scored under the instructional learning level as shown in table 7.1 below. This means that the majority of the tested learners have achieved good levels of performance in recognizing, producing and comprehending a piece of written Standard Arabic text at the letter level, the word level, the sentence level and the paragraph level. When split by grade level, the same table shows that the majority of the respondents who have attained the instructional level belong to the graduate level. The table also displays that basic literacy is highly attained by 93 percent of the post-graduate respondents in comparison to 61 percent of the graduate respondents. It is to be noted that the score means are (30.61) and (35.27) for the graduate sample and the post-graduate sample respectively.

**Table 7.1. Basic Literacy Attainment by Grade Level**

**Frequency Distribution for Basic Literacy**
**Split By: grade**

| | Total Percent | Graduate Percent | Post-Graduate Percent |
|---|---|---|---|
| Instructional | 32 | 39 | 8 |
| Independent | 68 | 61 | 93 |
| Total | 100 | 100 | 100 |

When further split by prior literacy level, table 7.2., reveals that the group that comprises the lowest number of independent basic readers is the target group (51%), which is composed of non-schooled graduate learners. At the same time, the table shows that the group which comprises the highest number of independent readers is the schooled post-graduate sample (96%). Note that "PriorLitevel" refers to the learners' pre-literacy experience.

On the basis of the figures displayed in table 7.2 below, and considering the score means, which are (29.64), for the non-schooled graduate group, (32.53), for the pre-schooled graduate group, (33.35) for the non-schooled post-graduate group and (36.69) for the schooled post-graduate group, the following hypothesis may be stated:

*The learners' basic literacy attainment increases with grade level and pre-literacy training.*

To test the foregoing hypothesis, a correlation analysis is calculated. Its aim is to analyze the magnitude of the relationship between the learners' basic literacy attainment, grade level and pre-literacy experience. The analysis reveals moderate but highly significant positive correlations. The coefficient correlations are ($r=.40$; $p<.0001$) for grade level and ($r=.39$; $p<.0001$) for pre-literacy experience.

**Table 7.2. Basic Literacy Attainment by Grade Level and Pre-literacy Experience**

**Frequency Distribution for Basic Literacy**
**Split By: grade, PriorLitlevel**

| | Instructional | Independent | Total |
|---|---|---|---|
| Total Percent | 32 | 68 | 100 |
| Graduate, non-schooled Percent | 49 | 51 | 100 |
| Graduate, pre-schooled Percent | 19 | 81 | 100 |
| Post-Graduate, non-schooled Percent | 12 | 88 | 100 |
| Post-Graduate, pre-schooled Percent | 4 | 96 | 100 |

To conclude, the learners' basic literacy attainment turned out to be good for the learners irrespective of grade level and pre-literacy experience. When these variables are controlled for, it is revealed that the learners' achievement increases with grade level and pre-literacy experience meaning that the least performing group is the non-schooled graduate group and the most performing group is the schooled post-graduate group. Now, it would be interesting to examine the subjects' performance in the sub-skills of the basic reading test, namely their score means in the pre-reading exercises and in the basic reading comprehension text.

## The learners' performance in the pre-reading exercises

The learners' basic pre-reading level is obtained from the percentage of the total correct answers of the pre-reading questions which are part of the basic test. Overall, the learners' competence in the pre-reading exercises is good. 78 percent of the respondents have attained an independent pre-reading level and 22 percent of the whole sample scored under the instructional level as displayed in table 7.3 below. Note that none of the respondents scored under the weak or deficient reading levels.

When split by grade level and pre-schooling experience, it is revealed that the most performing group is the pre-schooled post-graduate group. Ninety-six percent of the respondents from this group performed as independent readers and only 4 percent scored under the instructional literacy level. The least performing respondents belong to the non-schooled graduate group with 69 percent independent readers.

**Table 7.3. Pre-reading Achievement by Grade Level and Pre-literacy Experience**

**Frequency Distribution for Basic Reading Level**
**Split By: PriorLitlevel, grade**

| | Instructional | Independent | Total |
|---|---|---|---|
| Total Percent | 22 | 78 | 100 |
| non-schooled, Graduate Percent | 31 | 69 | 100 |
| non-schooled, Post-Graduate Percent | 12 | 88 | 100 |
| pre-schooled, Graduate Percent | 17 | 83 | 100 |
| pre-schooled, Post-Graduate Percent | 4 | 96 | 100 |

As the respondents' competence in the pre-reading test may be misleading, it would be interesting to investigate their performance in the individual exercises which compose the test. Results related to these individual exercises are given hereafter.

### The word picture matching exercise

The word picture matching exercise was designed to measure the examinees' ability to recognize and comprehend a piece of written text at the word level and associate it with the corresponding picture. Six questions were asked in this respect and all the respondents answered them correctly. The learners' perfect achievement in this exercise is possibly due to their exposure to the global method which is mainly used in the early literacy teaching stage.

### The letter recognition exercise

Unlike the word picture matching exercise, which deals with whole-word recognition, the letter recognition exercise is designed to assess the learners' ability to recognize within a set of words the Arabic letter /3ain/ in its three positional configurations: initial bound, middle, and final free. As these positions play an important role in determining word boundaries, they may be regarded as good predictors of text decoding and comprehension. The exercise is also meant to measure the learners' ability to distinguish the letter /3ain/ from the letter /Ra/ which is similar in shape but different by the presence of a dot above it.

On the basis of a quantitative analysis of data, it is found that the learners' overall performance in this exercise is good (3.9). The highest score, which is four, is obtained by the pre-schooled graduate and the pre-schooled post-graduate groups. It is important to note though that some learners from the target group and others from the non-schooled post-graduate group still confuse the two letters even after two years of training or more. This means that when teaching literacy, these confusing letters should be given more attention.

### The letter production exercise

The letter production exercise is meant to evaluate the learners' ability to produce a missing letter in different positions of verbs and nouns. The aim is to see whether the learners can produce appropriate Arabic clusters. At the same time, this exercise tests the learners' spelling competence. Only meaningful words are scored correct. Incorrect positional configuration are scored zero and are analyzed qualitatively. The quantitative analysis of the respondents' performance in this exercise reveals that all the learners scored above average (3.6). The highest score means is (3.9) for the pre-schooled post-graduate group and the lowest is (3.5) for the non-schooled graduate group.

A consideration of the respondents' minimum scores in this exercise shows that whatever their grade level and pre-literacy experience, some learners have scored just average which means that they produced 50 percent incorrect answers. In terms of percentages of the learners who scored just average, 13 percent belong to the non-schooled graduate group, 11 percent are from the pre-schooled graduate group, 6 percent come from the non-schooled post graduate group and 4 percent belong to the pre-schooled post-graduate group. This reveals that pre-schooling does have an impact on literacy acquisition. Still it is important to analyze its relative effect.

Qualitatively, the errors the learners came out with fall into two types: L1-based errors and L2-based errors. L1-based errors are those errors that can be traced back to the learner's mother tongue, in this case Moroccan Arabic or Amazigh. On the other hand, L2-based errors are the product of the learners' limited knowledge of the target language in this case Standard Arabic. The identified L2-based errors consist of:

a) A non-appropriate configuration of the position of the letters /3ain/ and /shin/. For example, the letter /3ain/ is written as if it were in its initial bound position and not in its correct final free position in the production **/azzar3u/** "crops" and the letter /shin/ is given in its final free position in the word **/al-'ashja:ru/** "trees" and not in its bound initial position. In sum, the learners who came out with these mistakes still confuse the final free position of the letters and their initial bound position.

b) Confusion between the final free position of the letter /3ain/ and the final free position of /3ain/ /h̲a/ in the production **/azzar3u/**, which lead to the production of the meaningless word **/azzarh̲u/**.
c) Confusion between letters and numbers as for the letter /h̲a/ and the number **(5)**
d) Use of the long vowel instead of the short vowel with the consonants /qaf/ in **/al-qaryatu/** "village" and /h̲a/ in **/al-h̲urriyatu/** "freedom".

The L1-based errors resulted in assimilated borrowing forms of the verb. In this case, instead of producing the required letter /h̲a/, to complete the verb **/yah̲ruthu/** "to plough", the examinee produced the letter /sin/ **(s)** and came out with **/yasruthu/** which is an assimilated but non acceptable form of the Amazigh verb **/srut/** "to tread out".

### The word construction exercise

The word construction or derivation exercise consists of building words from a familiar set of three letters /3ain/, / lam/, and / mi:m/. The aim is to find out the extent to which the learners can use transformational skills to construct words with the same letters but with different meanings. In other words, this exercise tests the learners' knowledge of the Standard Arabic morpheme structure which is based on the *triliteral root.* So in this case, the triliteral root **(3,l,m)** forms the basis of many words such as **/3alima/** "to know", **/ma3lu:mun/** "known" **/3ilmun/** "science", **/3alla:ma/** "scholar", **/ma3lamatun/** "encyclopaedia" and so on.

Investigation of the learners' score means in this exercise shows that all the learners scored above average (3.6) with the non-schooled graduate group as the least performing group (3.5) and the pres-schooled post-graduate group as the most performing one is (3.9).

Qualitatively the mistakes that have been reported consist of avoiding to give the word altogether due to non sufficient knowledge of Standard Arabic. Given this limited knowledge of the language of literacy, the respondents also resort to a learning strategy where they replace the unknown word by another one which contains at least one of the letters of the *triliteral root.* In this case, they come out with familiar first names such as **/3alla:lun/**, and **/sa3i:dun/** or known words like **/muslimun/** "a Muslim". Still others wrote odd productions like

**/ma3ala/** or **/malula/**. Note, however, that the constructed meaningless words respect the pattern of the Arabic *triliteral root* **/fa3ala/** and **/fa3ula/**.

Another incorrect word construction consists of changing the order of sounds within a word construction as in **/3aimulm/**, which may be due to metathesis. In this case, the respondent may have meant to use the word construction **/mu3allim/**. Finally, other related mistakes consist of weak knowledge of the plural masculine form which is marked by irregularity in Standard Arabic. The reported error in this respect is **/3ulama:tun/** instead of **/3ulama:'un/** "scholars". Another possible explanation for this mistake may be related to deliberate avoidance of an incorrect use of the **hamza** (glottal stop) placement. In fact, the rules governing the placement of the **hamza** have been proved to be difficult to acquire even among schooled children (Saidi, 2001).

Other incorrect word constructions are spell related. The reported ones consist of lengthening short vowels in **/3a:li:mu:n/** instead of the correct word construction **/3a:limun/** "scholar. This may be due to an overgeneralization of vowel lengthening which is not a feature of the respondents' mother tongues.

**The word production exercise**

This exercise consists of producing six Arabic words irrespective of their part of speech. Each of these words must contain one letter which is given by the examiner. The aim is to assess the learners' ability to produce, through writing, appropriate and meaningful vocabulary items from the minimum unit of the language which is the letter.

The analysis of data shows that the respondents' score means is above average (3.9). It also reveals that the learner's achievement increases with grade level and pre-literacy experience. The obtained score means are 3.6 for the non-schooled graduate group, 3.7 for the pre-schooled graduate group, 4.4 for the non-schooled post graduate group and 5.1 for the pre-schooled post graduate sample. A consideration of the respondents' minimum scores, which are 3 for the pre-schooled post-graduate group and 2 for the remaining groups, shows that the pre-schooled post-graduate learners had at least 50 percent correct answers. Learners from the remaining groups came out with a minimum of 33 percent correct answers. It is to be noted that a quite important proportion of the total percent of the learners scored under the weak learning level in this exercise (39%). When split by grade level and pre-literacy experience, 45 percent belong to the pre-schooled graduate group, 44 percent to the non-schooled graduate group, 29 percent to the non-schooled post-graduate group and 17 percent to the pre-schooled post-graduate informants as shown in table 7.4 below. This means that post-literacy has a relatively more important impact than pre-schooling.

**Table 7.4. Learning Levels of Word Production by Grade Level and Pre-literacy Experience**

**Frequency Distribution for Word production L.L**
**Split By: PriorLitlevel, grade**

| | Frustrational | Instructional | Independent | Total |
|---|---|---|---|---|
| Total Percent | 39 | 29 | 31 | 100 |
| non-schooled, Graduate Percent | 44 | 38 | 18 | 100 |
| non-schooled, Post-Graduate Percent | 29 | 0 | 71 | 100 |
| pre-schooled, Graduate Percent | 45 | 38 | 17 | 100 |
| pre-schooled, Post-Graduate Percent | 17 | 0 | 83 | 100 |

Qualitatively, the errors that have been made in this exercise are either L1-based or L2-based. The analyzed L1-based errors are mainly related to spelling. They are associated with the problem of shifting from the speaking form to the written one. One consists of shortening long vowels as is the case for the word **/xa:lid/** "a boy's first name" which is written by the respondents as **/xalid/** following its Moroccan Arabic or Amazigh pronunciation. Another L1-based errors pertains to the Amazigh group, who due to absence of the glottal stop in the Amazigh phonological system, handle the problem by using other letters like /kaf/ or /3ain/ , which are also back consonants. Thus, the word **/mas'alatun/** "problem" is written as it is pronounced by many monolingual Amazigh speakers as **/maskalatun/** and the word **/asma:3/** is used instead of the correct Arabic word **/asma:'/** "the plural form of the word *noun*". This last error can also be labelled as an L2-based error given that the learner may have confused the glottal stop **/'/**, which is written as a small /3ain/ in its initial bound position, with the letter / 3ain/ in its final position.

L2-based errors are also related to spelling problems. Some are due to the non-sufficient mastery of the distinction between some letter pairs which are phonologically distinguished just by a dot as a superscript. These errors consist in the use of the letter /jim/ instead of /xa/ , /ra/ instead of /za/ and /da: l/ instead of /dha:l/. Other mistakes reflect the learners' weak knowledge of the rule concerning the final open /ta:'/ versus its closed form. Still, other errors are due to inappropriate shift from speaking to writing as the learners attach short vowels (*'al ḫaraka:t)* as real letters to the produced word. These short vowels are normally added to indefinite singular or plural nouns as diacritical marks that are put above or below the letters for vocalization and comprehension purposes especially in the early stages of reading.

## The sentence completion exercise

This exercise consists of completing a simple sentence with one of its essential elements in the form of a verb, a subject or an adjective. The learners' overall mean score in this exercise is just above average (1.7). The sample who obtained the lowest scores in this exercise is that of non-schooled graduate learners (1.3) and the one who received the highest scores is the pre-schooled post graduate group (2.6). This means that post-literacy training and pre-schooling might have a significant effect on the learners' literacy attainment. Still this has to be statistically proved.

A consideration of the respondents' minimum scores reveals that some learners from the investigated groups scored under average. To gain insight into the number of the learners who scored below average, scores are calculated in terms of percentages of correct answers and evaluated in terms of four learning levels as displayed in table 7.5 where sentence completion is highly acquired by only 30 percent of the whole sample. The same table shows that only 14 percent of the target sample has a perfect knowledge of sentence completion rules. 51 percent of that same sample scored under the weak learning level "Frustrational" and 12 percent did under the deficient level. Note that none of the pre-schooled groups have a deficient knowledge of that skill and that the majority of the pre-schooled post group have attained the highest learning level (74%). Note also that 6 percent of the post-graduate non-schooled group have a deficient performance in that exercise.

In view of these results, it is important to say that sentence completion is still challenging for graduates of adult literacy programs. Actually, it is reported from their testimonies that sentence completion and construction are the language skills that are the most difficult to acquire.

**Table 7.5. Learning Levels of Sentence Completion by Grade Level and Pre-literacy Experience**

**Frequency Distribution for Sentence completion L.L**
**Split By: grade, PriorLitlevel**

| | Deficient | Frustrational | Instructional | Independent | Total |
|---|---|---|---|---|---|
| Total Percent | 7 | 37 | 26 | 30 | 100 |
| Graduate, non-schooled Percent | 12 | 51 | 24 | 14 | 100 |
| Graduate, pre-schooled Percent | 0 | 32 | 30 | 38 | 100 |
| Post-Graduate, non-schooled Percent | 6 | 12 | 47 | 35 | 100 |
| Post-Graduate, pre-schooled Percent | 0 | 13 | 13 | 74 | 100 |

(Sentence completion L.L refers to the learners' learning levels of sentence completion)

The errors that have been identified with respect to sentence completion fall into three types: case ending, agreement, definiteness. Unrelated errors have been termed as "odd" or "novel".

### Case ending errors

Unlike Moroccan Arabic, the Standard Arabic grammatical system displays case marking which consists of nominative, genitive and accusative suffix forms which appear on nouns, adjectives and participles depending on their syntactic function. The nominative signals the subject function; the genitive signals the possessive or oblique function, while the accusative signals the objective function. Being tangential to meaning, case endings are often dropped in speech. In basic formal literacy learning, full vocalisation is obligatory. The qualitative analysis of the learners use of vocalisation came out with the following errors: **/attalqi:h̲u muhi:mman/** instead of **/attalqi:h̲u muhimmun/** "vaccination is important"; **/at-talqi:h̲u wa:jiban/** instead of **/at-talqi:h̲u wa:jibun/** "vaccination is obligatory".

### Agreement errors

Noun/adjective agreement in Standard Arabic encodes gender, number, person, case, and definiteness. Subject/verb agreement in terms of gender and number is not systematic. For example, some masculine plural nouns take feminine singular verbs such as **/t̲a:rati al-3as̲a:fi:ru/** "The birds flew" and **/bayyad̲ati al-3as̲a:fi:ru/** "the birds laid eggs". These are incorrectly realized by the informants of the present study as **/t̲a:ru: al-3as̲a:fi:ru/** or **/bayyat̲u al-3as̲a:fi:ru/**. This error is probably contrastive-based because in Moroccan Arabic and Amazigh the word "birds" always takes a masculine plural verb. Note that the learner replaced the letter /d̲a/ with the letter /t̲a/ in **/bayyat̲u/**. This may be due to the learner's confusion of the two letters. While having the same shape, the letter/t̲a/ is written with a slash on it and the letter /d̲a/ is written with a dot on it but without the slash. Other L1-based agreement errors include the feminization of masculine nouns as in the example **/attalqi:h̲u muhi:mmatun/** "vaccination is obligatory" instead of / **attalqi:h̲u muhi:mmun/**. This feminization may be due to the impact of transfer from the learners' mother tongue where the word "vaccination" is feminine and realized as **/jjlba/**. In fact, unlike Standard Arabic, the majority of the words which end in **/a/** in Moroccan Arabic take the feminine form. Following this logic, some respondents put the word **/mustashfa:/** "hospital", which is masculine in Standard Arabic, before feminine adjectives as in **/mustashfa maRribiyyatun/** "Moroccan Hospital". Actually, the respondents were expected to come out with **/imara'atun maRribiyyatun/** "A Moroccan woman". This L1-based agreement error is possibly due to the fact that the learners still confuse the Moroccan Arabic feminine gender morpheme **/a/** with the Standard Arabic masculine long vowel **/a:/** as in masculine words like **/maqha:/** "café" and **/mabna:/** "building".

### Definiteness

Definiteness in Standard Arabic is realized by the use of the article **/al/** as in /al-qamaru/ "the moon" and /al-kita:bu/ "the book". In this case, the article is referred to as "lunar". When immediately followed by the consonants *t,d,n,l,r,s,z,sh,* the consonant /l/ of the article is assimilated as in **/ash-shamsu/** "the sun" and in **/atta:ri:xu/** "history". In this case, the article is referred to as "solar".

Vocalisation of definite nouns is marked at the end of the nouns and carried out through the use of short vowels **/a/**, **/u/**, or **/i/** depending on their syntactic function. On the other hand, indefinite nouns never take an article and their vocalisation is done through the indefinite bound morphemes **/an/**, **/un/**, or **/in/** depending on their function in the sentence. The error example that has been identified with respect to this grammatical category is the use of the definite lunar article in cases where the non-definite bound morpheme is required as in **/al-mar'atun maRribiyyatun/** "the a woman Moroccan" instead of **/mar'atun maRribiyyatun/** 'a Moroccan woman". Another error is related to spelling and consists of deleting the bound solar article as in **/dhdhubabu/** "flies" instead of the correct form **/adhdhuba:bu/** "the flies".

### Novel Errors

Weak knowledge of L2 grammatical rules and vocabulary involved the learners in a learning process through which they use some strategies that are either L1-based or L2-based. Quite often, this procedure ends up in the production of novel errors. Some of the reported errors in this regard may be named "substitution errors" where the informant substitutes an L2 word for another target form. This is due to some phonetic or phonological similarities between the missing word and the substituted one as in **/mar'atin al-3aṣa:fi:ru/** "a woman the birds" instead of **/marrati al-3aṣa:fi:ru/** "the birds passed". Other odd errors could be traced to the learners' reliance on the semantic field of the proposed word in the sentence to be completed. For example, the informants were given the word "vaccination" and were asked to complete the sentence with appropriate words of their own choice. In so doing, they come up with the following errors: **/attalqi:ḥu aẓ-ẓiflu/** "the vaccination the child" **/attalqi:ḥu mumarri-ḍatun/** "the vaccination the nurse". These errors are the product of the retrieval process through which the learners go by first identifying the semantic field to which the word **/at-talqi:hu/** "vaccination" belongs and associating it with the word(s) it has been learned with. Hence, they produced the words "child" or "nurse" as these are commonly used in the same context where the word "vaccination" is utilized. Likewise, these errors could be explained by a weak knowledge of the possessive construct as the correct answers would be **/talqi:hu at-tifli/**. Note that the letter /ta/ in **/at-tiflu/** is written as **/za/**. Two possible explanations can be given here. Either the respondent still confuses the letter /za/ and /ta/ as they are written in the same way except for the presence of a dot on the letter /za/.

Other novel errors' types produced by the subjects of the present study include productions such as **/'annay maRribiyyatun/ instead** of **/'ana: maRribiyyatun/** "I'm Moroccan". This error can be traced back to the learner' reliance on Moroccan Arabic, where the first person singular pronoun 'I' can also be realized as **/anaya/**. One last novel error type could be due to metathesis as for the word **/'aln/** in the sentence **/'aln maRribiyyatun/** instead of **/'ana: maRribiyyatun/** "I'm Moroccan". Note that the long vowel **/a:/** in **/'ana:/** changed into /lam/ in **/'aln/** as it was written attached with the letter (**n**).

### The word order exercise

The word order exercise consists in arranging a set of scrambled words to produce readable complete sentences. With regard to this exercise, the respondents were asked to rearrange three strings of words into syntactic structures. These are composed of a verb phrase (VP), a noun phrase (NP) and a prepositional phrase (PP). It is to be noted that the structure of the PP is not the same in the three sentences. In the sentence **/ha:jara al-badawiyyu ila: al-madi:nati/** "the countryman immigrated to town", PP is composed of a preposition and a noun. In the sentence **/yataRadhdha: adh-dhuba:bu bi al-'aRdiyyati al fa:sidati/** "flies nourish themselves with spoiled food", the PP is made up of a preposition, an adjective and a noun. In the sentence **/yajibu 'an nada3a al-'adwiyyata fi: maka:nin ba3:din wa murtafi3in 3ani al-'atfa:li/** "we must put medication in a safe place far from the children", the PP comprises a preposition, a noun and another PP with a preposition and a noun.

Investigation of the learners' score means in this exercise reveals that all the learners scored above average. This may be explained by the fact that the target language and the mother tongues of the learners follow the same sentence pattern which is SVO, subject/ verb/ object and VSO, verb/subject/object. Qualitatively, the mistakes that have been made with respect to the use of the word order rule consist of avoiding to apply the rule altogether or failing to apply the rule correctly. Incorrect use of the rule consists of resorting to a set of simplification strategies that can be classified as follows:

a) Omission of the preposition /**ila:**/ "to" in the sentence /**ha:jara 'al-badawiyyu ila: 'al-madi:nati**/. This is probably due to the assimilation of the preposition with the lunar determiner as is the case in Moroccan Arabic. This, however, resulted in a different meaning of the sentence which reads /**ha:jara 'al-badawiyyu 'al-madi:nata**/ "The countryman left the town".
b) Omission of the bound morpheme, the preposition and the adjective in the sentence /**yajibu 'an nada3a al-'adwiyyata fi: maka:nin ba3i:din wa murtafi3in 3ani al-'atfa:li**/. This resulted in the following non-grammatical and non-acceptable production /**al-'adwiyya nada3a maka:nin 3ani al-'atfa:li**/ "medication we put in a place from children".
c) Reduction of the length of the sentence by omitting the PP /**3ani 'al 'atfa:li**/ "from children" in the sentence /**yajibu 'ann nada3a al-'adwiyyata fi: maka:nin ba3i:din wa murtafi3in**/ "we must put medication in a far and high place".
d) Deletion of the modal /**yajibu**/ (we must) and the subordinate conjunction /**'an**/. This ended up in a simplified form of the sentence /**nada3a al-'adwiyyata fi: maka:nin ba3i:din wa murtafi3in**/ "we put medication in a far and high place".
e) Deletion of the main verb which resulted in the following incorrect realization: /**adh-dhuba:bu al-'aRdiyyati al-fa:sidati**/ "flies food spoiled". Keeping in mind that Standard Arabic and the learners' L1 (Moroccan Arabic or Amazigh) follow the same syntactic pattern, this error type is normally unexpected. One would suggest then that this is probably due to the fact that the noun /**aRdhiyya**/ "food" and the verb /**yataRadhdha:**/ "to nourish" have the same root in Standard Arabic. This semantic similarity might have been a source of confusion.

The omission processes mentioned above could be explained by the learners' use of simplification strategies which consist of omitting grammatical elements in a sentence. These simplification strategies are normally used by any second language learner as a learning and production strategies through which s/he simplifies the burden of learning the target language by unconsciously activating some rules and deleting others (Ellis, 1986). As Ellis explains, these simplification strategies, along with the use of L1, constitute the *natural route* of a learner's interlanguage. It is to be noted that such strategies are also used under conditions of language loss and attrition (Agnaou, 1999).

## The cloze procedure exercise

The cloze procedure exercise consists of a sentence maze type exercise where the informants are asked to complete the sentence with three missing words: a verb, a noun and a prepositional phrase. The aim of this exercise is to measure the informants' reading comprehension at the level of the sentence. Descriptive analyses of the respondents' scores show that they all scored above average. The most performing group is the pre-schooled post-graduate group, and the least performing is the non-schooled graduate one. Investigation of their minimum scores, however, indicates that some learners have a deficient knowledge of the cloze procedure exercise. As shown in table 7.6 below, this skill deficiency is attained by 9 percent of the whole sample, 15 percent of the graduate non-schooled sample, 6 percent of the non-schooled post-graduates and 2 percent of the pre-schooled graduates.

**Table 7.6. Learning Levels for the Cloze Procedure by Grade Level and Pre-literacy Experience**

**Frequency Distribution for C/procedure L.L**
**Split By: PriorLitlevel, grade**

| | Deficient | Independent | Total |
|---|---|---|---|
| Total Percent | 9 | 91 | 100 |
| non-schooled, Graduate Percent | 15 | 85 | 100 |
| non-schooled, Post-Graduate Percent | 6 | 94 | 100 |
| pre-schooled, Graduate Percent | 2 | 98 | 100 |
| pre-schooled, Post-Graduate Percent | 0 | 100 | 100 |

(C/procedure L.L refers to the learners' learning levels in the cloze procedure exercise)

Qualitatively, no errors are reported when dealing with this the cloze-procedure exercise because the learners who did not know the answer simply avoided doing the exercise altogether. It is to be noted that avoidance is also considered as a simplification strategy.

## Summary

On the whole, the respondents performed well in the pre-reading exercises. When spilt by pre-literacy experience and grade level, the least performing group turned out to be the non-schooled graduate group and the most performing one is the pre-schooled post-graduate group. Investigation of the respondents' competence in the sub-components of the pre-reading test reveals that achievement is much higher in recognition skills (word picture matching, letter recognition and word order) than in productive skills (word completion, word production, sentence completion and sentence maze). The relevant question to ask at this juncture is: *To what extent do the learners master reading skills at the level of the text?*

## THE LEARNERS' PERFORMANCE IN THE BASIC COMPREHENSION EXERCISE

The analysis of the learners' achievement in the basic reading comprehension exercise shows that the most performing group is the pre-schooled post-graduate group with 7.3 as their score means and the least performing one is the target group with a score mean of 4.1. Note that this group scored below average and that the learners' total score means is 5.1, which is just above average. Investigation of the respondents' minimum and maximum scores reveals that while some learners scored above average, others did not. Hence, it would be interesting to investigate their basic reading comprehension ability in terms of learning levels and percentages as displayed in table 7.7 below. This table shows that the majority of the learners who scored under the weak and deficient learning levels belong to the target group. It is to be noted that only 13 percent of the learners from this group scored under the independent level. Note also that 13 percent of the pre-schooled graduate group and 24 percent of the non-schooled post-graduate group scored below the instructional level; none of the pre-schooled post-graduate learners scored below this level.

**Table 7.7. Learning levels for Basic Reading Comprehension by Grade and Pre-literacy Experience**

**Frequency Distribution for Basic Comprehension**
**Split By: grade, PriorLitlevel**

| | Deficient | Frustrational | Instructional | Independent | Total |
|---|---|---|---|---|---|
| Total Percent | 13 | 21 | 38 | 28 | 100 |
| Graduate, non-schooled Percent | 23 | 32 | 32 | 13 | 100 |
| Graduate, pre-schooled Percent | 2 | 11 | 62 | 26 | 100 |
| Post-Graduate, non-schooled Percent | 6 | 18 | 24 | 53 | 100 |
| Post-Graduate, pre-schooled Percent | 0 | 0 | 26 | 74 | 100 |

It follows, then, that basic reading comprehension is still challenging for an important sample of the certified graduates of adult literacy training. Based on this finding, it is predicted that the learners are not well equipped to handle every day literacy tasks. Before testing this prediction, it would be interesting to assess the impact of some predictor variables that are hypothesized to have an effect on the informants' basic attainments, namely, pre-reading skills and basic comprehension. The investigated variables are of three types: individual such as age and motivation, linguistic like the respondents mother tongue, and ecological or area related, in this case urban versus rural.

## THE EFFECT OF AGE AND MOTIVATION ON THE LEARNERS' BASIC LITERACY ATTAINMENT

As stated in chapter 5, the informant's age ranges from 12 to 60 years. Given this age disparity and based on the older respondents' feeling that acquiring literacy is *impossible* due to their advancement in age as they often compare themselves to "*an old monkey who is too old to learn*", it would be interesting to analyze the effect of age on their basic achievement. This is calculated by comparing the respondents' total basic score in terms of age groups to confirm or disconfirm part of the null hypothesis (a) stated at the beginning of this chapter. Analysis of Variance of the learners' score means by age group show that the effect of age is not significant (F=.95; df= 4–88; p>.05), which confirms the null hypothesis. When considering their score means, it is found that the most performing group is the oldest one (30.92) and the least performing group are the youngest (28.40).

It is noteworthy that the non-significant effect of the learners' age groups is also true for their performance in the individual components of the basic test. ANOVA results for the pre-reading exercises and basic reading comprehension are (F=1.66; df=4–88; p>.05) and (F=.212; df=4–88; p>.05) respectively. Furthermore, the learners' motivation does not have a significant impact on their basic literacy attainment (F=.09; df=1–91; p>.05). This is due to the fact that all the learners under study are highly motivated to acquire literacy. Thus, the null hypothesis (a) is maintained.

## THE EFFECT OF MOTHER TONGUE ON THE LEARNERS' BASIC LITERACY ATTAINMENT

The effect of mother tongue on children's acquisition of the language of literacy has been investigated by many studies, notably Moâtassime (1974), Skutnabb-Kansas and Toukomaa (1976), Ben-Zeev (1977), Ezzaki, Spratt and Wagner (1987), Aarssen, de Ruiter and Verhoeven (1992), cited in Saidi (2001), Wagner (1993) to name but a few. The general conclusion that can be drawn from these studies is that children whose language is different from the target language are outperformed by children whose mother tongue is not different from the language of literacy. This difference in attainment is either related to linguistic and cognitive abilities (Moâtassime, 1974; Skutnabb-Kansas and

Toukomaa, 1976) or concerns specific skills such as reading comprehension (Van de Wetering, 1990; Aarssen, de Ruiter and Verhoeven, 1992, cited in Saidi, 2001). Some studies found that reading differences between Arabophones and Amazighophones are maintained at least in the first three years of primary school (Ezzaki, et al. 1987; Wagner, 1993). Based on the foregoing results, the present section attempts to analyze the extent to which the mother tongue of the adult non-literate learner affects the learning of basic literacy. Such an analysis is done through an investigation of the target group's total score in the pre-reading exercises and basic reading comprehension questions.

ANOVA results show that the learners' mother tongue does not have a significant impact on their scores in the pre-reading exercises (F=2.38; df=1–91; p>.05). It is to be noted that the Arabophones scored slightly but not significantly higher (25.9) than the Amazighophones (24.9).

The non-significant difference between the Arabophones and the Amazighophones in the pre-reading exercises may be due to the respondents' comparatively higher performance in these exercises. Another explanation of the non-significant effect of the mother tongue at this level of learning is that both linguistic groups speak non-written languages, which means that both undergo the same stages of associating the sound with print and acquiring the grammatical system of Standard Arabic. It is hypothesized then that, once the Arabophones have mastered the pre-reading skills, they will outperform the Amazighophones in reading comprehension skills due to the relative similarity between Moroccan Arabic and Standard Arabic. As expected, the foregoing hypothesis is confirmed by the ANOVA results (F=36.77; df=1–91; p<.0001). These reveal that the Arabophone learners scored significantly higher in basic reading comprehension than the Amazighophones. Their score means being 4.9 and 3 respectively. It is noteworthy that the Amazighophones scored below average. In terms of percentage of correct answers, the Arabophones came out with 54 percent correct answers while the Amazighophones obtained only 33 percent correct responses.

The significant difference between Arabophones and Amazighophones is also maintained when the learners' total basic score is compared (F=10.89; df=1–91; p<.0001). The scores means are (30.8) and (27.9) respectively. Hence, the null hypothesis (b) stated in the introduction of this chapter is not confirmed, which means that the learners' mother tongue significantly affects basic literacy attainment.

It is worth mentioning here that the significant effect of the mother tongue on the non-schooled learners' attainment is no longer applicable at the post-literacy level for basic comprehension (F=.32; df=1–15; p>.05) where the Arabophones' score means is slightly superior (6.1) to that of the Amazighophones (5.6) and in overall basic literacy (F=.33; df=1–15; p>.05) where the score means for the Arabophones and the Amazighophones are (34.1) and (32.8) respectively.

## THE EFFECT OF AREA ON THE LEARNERS' BASIC LITERACY ATTAINMENT

The impact of area on the target group's basic literacy attainment is investigated to examine the relevance of the null hypothesis which states that the rural learners' and urban learners' performance in the basic test will not be significantly different. The ANOVA results disqualify this null hypothesis as they disclose highly significant differences (F=49.86; df=1–91; p<.0001) between rural (25.4) and urban learners (31.3) with respect to their overall performance in the basic test. When further split by mother tongue and area, the descriptive statistics displayed in table 7.8 below reveal that the most performing learners in the basic test and its components belong to the urban Arabophone group and the least performing learners are rural Amazighophones.

**Table 7.8. Means and Standard Deviations of the Basic Test and its Components (Pre-reading Exercises and Basic Reading Comprehension) by Area and Mother Tongue**

**Descriptive Statistics**
**Split By: Area, Mother Tongue**

| | Mean | Std. Dev. | Std. Error | Count | Minimum | Maximum | # Missing |
|---|---|---|---|---|---|---|---|
| Basic Reading Score, Total | 25,505 | 3,112 | ,323 | 93 | 19,000 | 30,000 | 0 |
| Basic Reading Score, urban, Arabic | 26,738 | 2,275 | ,351 | 42 | 21,000 | 30,000 | 0 |
| Basic Reading Score, urban, Berber | 26,625 | 2,551 | ,521 | 24 | 21,000 | 30,000 | 0 |
| Basic Reading Score, rural, Arabic | 23,083 | 2,937 | ,848 | 12 | 20,000 | 30,000 | 0 |
| Basic Reading Score, rural, Berber | 22,200 | 2,757 | ,712 | 15 | 19,000 | 27,000 | 0 |
| Basic Comprehension Score, Total | 4,140 | 1,815 | ,188 | 93 | 2,000 | 8,000 | 0 |
| Basic Comprehension Score, urban, Arabic | 5,476 | 1,383 | ,213 | 42 | 2,000 | 8,000 | 0 |
| Basic Comprehension Score, urban, Berber | 3,208 | 1,215 | ,248 | 24 | 2,000 | 7,000 | 0 |
| Basic Comprehension Score, rural, Arabic | 3,167 | 1,899 | ,548 | 12 | 2,000 | 8,000 | 0 |
| Basic Comprehension Score, rural, Berber | 2,667 | ,900 | ,232 | 15 | 2,000 | 5,000 | 0 |
| Total basic score, Total | 29,645 | 4,500 | ,467 | 93 | 22,000 | 38,000 | 0 |
| Total basic score, urban, Arabic | 32,214 | 3,468 | ,535 | 42 | 24,000 | 37,000 | 0 |
| Total basic score, urban, Berber | 29,833 | 3,158 | ,645 | 24 | 24,000 | 36,000 | 0 |
| Total basic score, rural, Arabic | 26,250 | 4,673 | 1,349 | 12 | 22,000 | 38,000 | 0 |
| Total basic score, rural, Berber | 24,867 | 3,182 | ,822 | 15 | 22,000 | 30,000 | 0 |

In view of the results displayed in table 7.8, three conclusions may be drawn:

1. The learners' age and motivation have no impact on their basic literacy attainment. . .
2. Reading comprehension ability is significantly affected by the learners' mother tongue as positive findings are associated with Arabophones and negative ones with Amazighophones.
3. The learners' area is an important predictor of reading comprehension with better results among the urban Arabophone sample.

### Summary

The analyses of the learners' pre-reading skills reveal that the informants of the present research have attained good pre-reading levels with the best results from the schooled post-graduate group. Qualitative investigation of the errors the respondents made shows that the learners under study follow the universal route of acquiring literacy in a second language. The overall basic reading comprehension is affected by linguistic and regional factors but not by individual differences such as age and motivation. Performance in reading comprehension which increases at the post-literacy level is still challenging for more than 50 percent of the target group. This raises the question of the efficiency of the literacy training process. Given this, one could only conjecture that these learners are not well equipped to handle everyday literacy skills. Verification of this hypothesis is done in the next section.

## THE LEARNERS' FUNCTIONAL LITERACY ATTAINMENT

The object of this section is to answer the research question which seeks to assess the extent to which the learners apply what they have learned to understand the skills they sought to learn at the onset of their training. In other words, it assesses the learners' proficiency in handling everyday document literacy. Before presenting the results, two details concerning the testing procedure need to be given here. First, the functional test is based on the kinds of texts the learners are likely to encounter in daily life. As explained in chapter four, it is constructed on the basis of the learners' real needs. As stated in chapter six, these needs are community based, consumer based and health related. Hence, the functional test consists of a kind of proficiency test as it is not linked to the learners' literacy course. During its administration, it displayed considerable motivation on the part of the learners and the teachers alike as it is comprises the authentic material that the learners sought to learn and their teachers would have liked to include in the syllabus. The respondents declared that it was the first time they were evaluated on their real *target skills* and estimated that it was a good opportunity for them to test their *real literacy competence.* Likewise, the teachers claimed that the contents of the test are very interesting and of high utility to the learners and wish that program designers should integrate them in adult literacy training. Second, before answering the questions, the respondents were asked to read the documents silently and then demonstrate comprehension by summarizing the information in either Moroccan Arabic or Amazigh, in cases they couldn't do so in Standard Arabic. After providing the answer, they were asked to locate loudly the passage, phrase or word that corresponds to the answer. Only the respondents who succeeded in scanning the right information and provided the correct evidence for it received credit for a correct answer.

The learners' score means in the functional test and all its components are given in table 7.9. below to get an insight into the respondents' overall and specific performance in the functional test while taking into consideration their grade level and pre-literacy levels.

In view of the score means that are displayed in table 7.9 above, the following statements can be made:

1. The learners' overall functional literacy attainment is moderate as the whole sample scored just above average. It is 10.1 out of 20.
2. The learners' overall proficiency in the CRE, community resources exercise, are just moderate (4.6) and are below average in CEE, consumer economics exercise (4), and HRQs, health related questions (1.3).
3. When split by pre-literacy experience and grade level, the most performing learners belong to the pre-schooled post graduate group with a score of 19.4. The least performing group is the non-schooled graduate group with very low scores in the whole test. Their total score is as low as 6.8.
4. The target group scored below average in the test and all its components
5. The minimum scores are obtained by the graduate group whether schooled or non-schooled
6. The maximum scores are attained by the post-graduate sample whether schooled or non-schooled
7. Functional proficiency increases with grade level and pre-literacy experience.

Interpretation of the learners' scores in terms of learning levels reveals that only 16.11 percent of the whole sample can be considered as functional independent readers, 44.44 percent are weak readers and 15 percent are deficient readers. When split by grade level and pre-literacy experience, none of the graduate sample, whether schooled or non-schooled, is revealed to be an independent reader. 68.81 percent of the non-schooled and 34 percent of the schooled are weak readers. In addition, 26.88 percent of the non-schooled graduates and 4.25 of the schooled ones are deficient readers. It is noteworthy that none of the post-graduate group scored under the weak or deficient levels and that 41.17

**Table 7.9. Means and Standard Deviations of the Learners' Scores in the Functional Test and its Components (Community-resources Exercise, Consumer-Economics Exercise, and Health-related Questions) by Grade Level and Pre-literacy Experience**

**Descriptive Statistics**
**Split By: PriorLitlevel, grade**

| | Mean | Std. Dev. | Std. Error | Count | Minimum | Maximum | # Missing |
|---|---|---|---|---|---|---|---|
| Total Functional Score, Total | 10,106 | 4,904 | ,366 | 180 | 3,000 | 20,000 | 0 |
| Total Functional Score, non-schooled, Graduate | 6,871 | 2,148 | ,223 | 93 | 3,000 | 10,000 | 0 |
| Total Functional Score, non-schooled, Post-Graduate | 15,824 | 2,963 | ,719 | 17 | 12,000 | 20,000 | 0 |
| Total Functional Score, pre-schooled, Graduate | 9,872 | 1,849 | ,270 | 47 | 4,000 | 13,000 | 0 |
| Total Functional Score, pre-schooled, Post-Graduate | 19,435 | 1,502 | ,313 | 23 | 13,000 | 20,000 | 0 |
| Community.res.score, Total | 4,694 | 1,997 | ,149 | 180 | 1,000 | 8,000 | 0 |
| Community.res.score, non-schooled, Graduate | 3,409 | 1,446 | ,150 | 93 | 1,000 | 6,000 | 0 |
| Community.res.score, non-schooled, Post-Graduate | 6,647 | 1,222 | ,296 | 17 | 4,000 | 8,000 | 0 |
| Community.res.score, pre-schooled, Graduate | 5,043 | 1,083 | ,158 | 47 | 1,000 | 7,000 | 0 |
| Community.res.score, pre-schooled, Post-Graduate | 7,739 | ,541 | ,113 | 23 | 6,000 | 8,000 | 0 |
| Consumer.eco. score, Total | 4,050 | 2,319 | ,173 | 180 | 2,000 | 9,000 | 0 |
| Consumer.eco. score, non-schooled, Graduate | 2,667 | ,518 | ,054 | 93 | 2,000 | 4,000 | 0 |
| Consumer.eco. score, non-schooled, Post-Graduate | 6,647 | 1,935 | ,469 | 17 | 3,000 | 9,000 | 0 |
| Consumer.eco. score, pre-schooled, Graduate | 3,532 | ,856 | ,125 | 47 | 2,000 | 6,000 | 0 |
| Consumer.eco. score, pre-schooled, Post-Graduate | 8,783 | 1,043 | ,217 | 23 | 4,000 | 9,000 | 0 |
| Health.score, Total | 1,361 | ,914 | ,068 | 180 | ,000 | 3,000 | 0 |
| Health.score, non-schooled, Graduate | ,796 | ,431 | ,045 | 93 | ,000 | 2,000 | 0 |
| Health.score, non-schooled, Post-Graduate | 2,529 | ,624 | ,151 | 17 | 1,000 | 3,000 | 0 |
| Health.score, pre-schooled, Graduate | 1,298 | ,548 | ,080 | 47 | ,000 | 3,000 | 0 |
| Health.score, pre-schooled, Post-Graduate | 2,913 | ,417 | ,087 | 23 | 1,000 | 3,000 | 0 |

percent of the non-schooled post-graduates are independent readers in comparison to 95.65 percent of the schooled ones.

In view of these results, which should be interpreted in terms of the investigated sample and the instruments used, only 16.11 percent of the tested learners have attained an independent learning level of everyday literacy. When further split by group and pre-literacy learning, it is revealed that the target group, which is normally composed of non-schooled graduates, is not well prepared to deal with everyday literacy. No learner from this group scored under the independent learning level and only 4 percent have attained the instructional learning level. This means that the *real needs* of these learners are not met by their training. Hence, the answer to the question whether the learners are able to deal with the everyday literacy tasks they sought to learn at the onset of their training is in the negative. Note, however, that significant positive results are attained at the post-literacy training level, especially with longer training periods ($r=.58$; $p<.0001$).

The qualitative analysis of the learners' interaction with the text reveals that they totally lack reading strategies that would ease comprehension. Such strategies involve the use of the context, main ideas versus details, using referents and linking words, scanning or skimming, and so on. Instead, the learners resort to other strategies that are socio-culturally based. For instance, most of the informants didn't succeed to answer the questions related to the money order exercise where they are asked to identify the sender and the receiver. In fact, the learners identified the correct answers. But when asked to locate in the text the information on which they based their answer, the respondents referred to explanations external to the text. Rather than giving textual answers, they gave culturally based explanation such as "*It's Rokayya who sent the money because she is on the right side*" or socio-economic ones such as "*well, it's because the money always comes from the North to the South, so it's the person who lives in Tangier who sent the money to the one who lives in Agadir*". Another example concerns the knowledge of the requested dosage of a medicine for a six month child. Rather than using the text, the learners supplied the appropriate answers based on prior knowledge as a medicine is usually taken during the daily three meals. Another prior-knowledge-based answer concerns the identification of the disease the medicine was prescribed for, namely diarrhoea in this case. Again, the learners supplied the correct answer not because they read the text but because the word *diarrhoea* was overused during their literacy training, as they explained when asked to locate the word in the text. It is to be noted that the medicine, used for their testing, was not familiar to them. Of course, familiarity was also used as a strategy, especially when dealing with the electricity and the water bill, particularly among the urban group.

Examples of mistakes made in the use of the text, relate to lexical knowledge, technical reading and reading ability. Lexical knowledge mistakes consist of a limited knowledge of some false cognates such as the Standard Arabic word **/ha̱dha:ri/** "be careful" and the Amazigh word **/ha̱dr/** "to save". Due to this confusion, the learners understood the message from the electricity consumption slogan which states "save energy". The written answer, however, was incorrect as it was "be careful" and not **/xaffiḏ/** "save".

The technical reading mistake concerns the confusion between the verb **/dhahabat/** "she went" and **/dhahabiyya/** "golden". This resulted in completely different understandings of the newspaper's publicity heading which reads: **/furs̱a dhahabiyya li-'imtila:ki sakani al-mustaqbali/** "a golden opportunity to own your house of the future". Confusing the word "golden" with the verb "she went", the learners came out with the following answer: "the opportunity to own your house of the future is gone".

Reading ability mistakes consist of the learner's inability to understand the text. To deal with the situation, the examinee does not give up but rather tries to locate the minimum possible information. One example in this respect concerns the message which consists of an invitation from a friend to another to meet at the hospital to have their children vaccinated. When dealing with this exercise, the readers scanned the common word "vaccination" and linked it to the context where they learned it in the classroom. They, therefore, understood the message as follows: "if you don't vaccinate your child, he will be sick" *or* "vaccination is good for your child's health".

Another example concerns the newspaper exercise where the learners were unable to scan the requested information due to language and comprehension deficiency. Thus, they looked for other textual clues, which were not text-based but numeracy-based, as a substitute. In this case, the respondents located the word ***/maRribiyya/*** "Moroccan" and linked it to their prior knowledge about a TV game, where the phrase **/xamsin dahram maRribiyya/** "Moroccan fifty dirhams" is frequently used. Based on these strategies, the concerned learners ended up saying that the document was about the TV game.

In addition to the lack of reading strategies and language difficulties, some learners have problems in arithmetic as well. These relate to their incapability to distinguish between the numbers "3" and "5", "6" and "9". They also had difficulty to read and write more than one digit number; in most cases they inverted the order of the numbers. At the same time, they couldn't use subtraction of three digit numbers. So, the majority failed to calculate the sale difference in the exercise dealing with the cooker's old and new price. Moreover, while most respondents identified the correct answer regarding the old versus new price of the cooker, an important proportion of them were unable to read the figures and gave the wrong denomination in riyal. It is to be noted that the respondents were not scored on the monetary conversions.

## THE LEARNERS' FUNCTIONAL LITERACY ATTAINMENT AND PREDICTOR VARIABLES

This section analyzes the impact of the learners' individual, linguistic and regional differences on their attainment in the functional test. The aim is to assess the validity of the null hypotheses stated in the beginning of this chapter and checked above for the learners' in-school literacy attainment. As already mentioned, only the target group's overall attainment in the functional test is computed to avoid any biased results from the impact of grade level and pre-literacy experience.

### The impact of age

As is the case with the basic literacy test, data from the functional test yielded no significant differences based on the learners' age groups (F=1.81; df=4–88; p>.05).

A consideration of the respondents' means, reveals that all the age groups scored below average and that the weakest performances are made by the youngest group whose score mean is (6.28). The highest scores are obtained by the 41–50 age group (8.09) and the fifty and up age group (7.53). One possible explanation for the non-significant impact of age is that all the age groups obtained weak scores. Similar results are found for motivation (F=.004; df=1–91; p>.05). This is due to the fact that all the investigated learners express high motivations for acquiring literacy.

### The impact of mother tongue and area

Despite the learners' equal weak performances in the functional test, their functional attainment is significantly affected by their mother tongue (F= 11.36; df=1–89; p<.001) and area (F=432; df=1–89; p<.0001). It is to be noted that the interaction between the learners' mother tongue and area is also highly significant (F=9.68; df=1–89; p<.01).

Investigation of the learners' scores reveals that the lowest means are obtained from rural Amazighophones (3.8).

### Conclusion

Overall, the learners' attainment in the functional test is very weak. Only 16 percent of the learners have attained the independent learning level. Investigation of the respondents' scores in the sub-components of the test reveals that the weakest results are obtained in the consumer-economics exercises which mostly deal with numeracy. The learners' weak functional performance is further affected by mother tongue and area but not by age or motivation.

## SUMMARY OF THE RESULTS AND DISCUSSION

The present chapter has addressed research questions pertaining to the extent to which course-based literacy and document literacy are mastered by a sample of female Moroccan adult literacy graduates.

In the light of the data analyzed above, course-based literacy is highly mastered in terms of pre-reading skills but not as a reading comprehension skill. Detailed analyses of the learners' pre-reading skills show that the learners' performance in recognition-based exercises is high, but it is low in production-based skills especially at the word and sentence level. Qualitative analyses of the respondents' errors reveal that these relate to case, agreement, definiteness, and spell. Similar mistakes are reported by other studies that have been carried out on the acquisition of Standard Arabic by Moroccan children. This similarity between adults and children may be due to the *natural development route* L2 learners undertake in the acquisition of the target language (Ellis, 1986). This is further confirmed by the reading strategies the subjects of the present study resort to when dealing with the assigned exercises. As explained above, these strategies are based on simplification techniques which consist of the omission of the preposition and the bound morpheme, reduction of the sentence and deletion of conjunctions. In fact, the use of these techniques is also specific to the early stages of both first and second language learning. This indicates that the learners under investigation follow the universal way of learning a second language. This in turn means that they have not yet progressed in the mastery of the target language. Some even still confuse the letters of the alphabet and others could not use letter appropriate configurations. Furthermore, reading a short text in Standard Arabic is still challenging for more than fifty percent of the target group and document literacy is attained by only 4.3 percent of learners from that group. Qualitative analyses of the interaction with the text show that the learners rarely resort to the text to provide answers. This reflects limited training in the use of reading strategies.

Literature on second language learning explains that reading in this language is not exclusively a linguistic problem (Alderson, 1984; Wagner, Spratt and Ezzaki, 1989). The authors claim that reading in a foreign language requires the transfer of old skills that have been developed in the acquisition of L1. These studies fit within Cummins' (1979) common underlying proficiency theory (CUP) of language learning acquisition which states that the cognitive academic language proficiency (CALP) is cross lingual. That is, once this language proficiency is mastered in L1 it will manifest itself in L2 if enough of the L2 code is available.

In the absence of L1 teaching, Moroccan Arabic or Amazigh, and given the fact that the learners have not been trained to use reading strategies in the acquisition of L2, which is Standard Arabic in this case, the target informants of the present research had no strategies to transfer or to apply; hence their poor proficiency in basic comprehension and the functional reading tests. Note, though, that the pre-schooled samples managed to obtain good reading levels. This is perhaps due to prior-training in such skills during formal schooling when a child. As Zahn (1980) explains, adults can relearn materials once learned and now forgotten with less effort than it took them in the first place.

Comparisons of the learners' basic and functional literacy attainments by age groups revealed two things. First, the learners' age is not a significant predictor of their performance. Second, older informants scored better than younger ones. The first finding may be attributable to the learners' *natural route of acquisition*, which as found by other studies, is the same for second language learners, irrespective of how old they are (Bailey, Madden and Crashen, 1974; Cazden, Cancino, Rosansky, and Shumann, 1975). The second result may be related to cognitive development, which, as Ellis (1986) explains, helps older learners to learn better than younger ones. Zahn (1980) contends that thanks to this cognitive capacity, which does not decrease with age, a sixty years old person can learn the same kinds of knowledge that s/he could learn at the age of twenty. The author adds that skill performance may be less not because of advancement in age but due to other variables such as lack of motivation, negative self-image, and decline in vision or hearing. While these psycho-physical factors may affect the speed of learning, they do not lessen the ability to learn.

The target learners' literacy attainments are not significantly affected by age and motivation but by mother tongue. The Arabophones did better in both tests than the Amazighophones. This difference is significant at the level of comprehension but not in the pre-reading skill achievement. These results give credence to Van de Wetering (1990) who found that *Berber-speaking* children had similar literacy attainments as Arab-speaking children with respect to mechanical reading but had lower scores in reading comprehension. As explained above, this attested difference in favor of the Arabophones may be attributable to the relative similarity between their mother tongue, in this case Moroccan Arabic, and Standard Arabic, especially at the vocabulary level. What gives further credence to this finding is the non-significant difference (F=2.68; df=1–91; p>.05) between the Arabophones (2.7) and the Amazighophones (2.5) with respect to their performance in the consumer-economics exercises which are mainly based on Arithmetic. This more or less equal competence between the Arabophones and the Amazighophones in numeracy can be explained by the fact that arithmetic is based on figures and not on letters or language. Therefore it is more related to cognitive skill than language knowledge.

The learners' lowest scores were obtained in numeracy-based exercises. This finding is in accordance with other studies which found that numeracy is the least acquired skill among adults (Boukous and Agnaou, 2001) and particularly among adult females (Carron, Mwiria, and Righa, 1989). Yet, daily experience requires non-adult literates to use numeracy and most of them are conversant with mental arithmetic. The respondents' poor performance in numeracy may be attributable to the difficulty to use the familiar in an unfamiliar way. Transferring numeracy as an oral skill into numeracy as a written one involves the use of new habits, skills, means and approaches. By doing so, the learners' past oral habits and experiences interfere with new ways of learning the familiar which becomes more difficult to grasp, especially when its learning is too different from the learners' old experience. Therefore, it is necessary to use authentic materials that are related to the learners' everyday life in the teaching of both literacy and numeracy.

Area significantly affects the respondents' basic and functional reading attainments with better results from urban learners. Many possible explanations may account for this difference. First, rural and urban women live in totally different ecologies. While urban areas are highly marked by literacy, rural ones are predominantly oral. In such different environments, literacy is obviously viewed, acquired and maintained differently. Urban women are more challenged by the power of literacy than rural ones. For a better integration in such a literate ecology where they are marginalized even inside their own family as they lose some control over their *literate* children (Wagner, 1993), urban women are highly motivated to acquire literacy. At the same time, while rural women are also highly motivated to learn literacy, the non-sustaining environment where they live has negative repercussions over their literacy attainments. The second explanation for the inferior attainment of rural women in comparison with urban ones with respect to reading may be related to rural women's involvement in various chores. In addition to domestic duties, rural women are involved in agricultural work, they fetch water and wood, breed and feed animals, and go to the market to sell or buy food for children who, in many cases, are abandoned by emigrant fathers. To make ends meet, these women take part in hand-made activities such as embroidery, wool spinning or carpet industry. In addition, they have to walk long distances to reach the literacy centers. This of course leaves little time and energy to concentrate fully on the lessons.

## CONCLUSION

In sum, the target informants of the present study have acquired only rudimentary basic reading skills. Therefore, they were not prepared to read the literacy material they sought to handle through participation in the literacy courses. The difficulty in attaining literacy is attributable to pedagogical, linguistic, and ecological factors, but not to individual differences such as age or motivation. This implies that conditions for fostering basic and functional literacy are inherent to the socio-cultural reality of non-literate women and to the literacy program's objectives, but not to the learners' themselves, especially that they are highly motivated to acquire literacy and do follow the *natural universal route* of acquiring a second language and use their own strategies to handle document literacy. This brings in the most critical challenge which designers of women's literacy are facing particularly as regards the satisfaction of *gender practical interests.* Now it would be interesting to see how this is applicable to *gender strategic interests.* This is the topic of the next chapter.

# 8
# Responding to Women's Strategic Needs

This chapter investigates the extent to which the textbooks designed for the teaching of non-literate adults in Morocco convey a culture of equity where women are represented in plural, balanced and non-discriminatory social roles. In so doing, it seeks to see whether the designed textbooks are free from gender discrimination and stereotyping, a necessary condition for promoting women's literacy and ensuring their effective participation in society at large. While not claiming reversal discrimination against men, the present chapter aims at supporting efforts to counter sexist prejudice and invites textbook designers to use literacy as a means to convey ideas that promote task-sharing between men and women both within and outside the home and to project images that highlight the status of non-literate women, assert their strategic needs and stress the importance of their participation in society. To this effect, the following general question is addressed:

*To what extent is the subscribed content consonant with a perspective that seeks women's empowerment?*

As explained in chapter 4, this question is investigated in terms of three sub-questions:

*How much space is given to women in the textbooks under study?*
*What functions do women occupy in such space?*
*What characteristics and traits are women assigned?*

To shed light on these issues, data are taken from the textbooks that are designed for the diverse literacy programs in which the informants of the present study are enrolled. As explained in chapter 4, the textbooks under study are the ones that were used by the informants during the fieldwork study. These are the two volumes, basic and graduate, of Literacy for All. Since the year 2000, these textbooks have gradually been replaced by "*Literacy and Basic Training for Adults*". Therefore, its analysis is also undertaken.

These textbooks are analyzed following Michel's checklist (1986) for the identification of sexism in school textbooks. As explained in chapter 4, this checklist comprises three quantitative analyses which seek to analyze the number of male versus female references, the number of conventional versus non-conventional activities attributed to males and females and the number of conventional versus non-conventional traits or characters that are used to portray males and females. Though it is difficult to delimit what is conventional and what is not, the present study considers conventional traits as those language items or pictures that are used to portray women as affectionate, weak, poor, submissive, helpless, self sacrificing, and the like. On the other hand, non-conventional traits are the ones which refer to women as being involved in family decision-making, problem solving, initiative taking, and being self-dependent, and so on. Male conventional traits refer to the well established stereotype of being strong, rich, brave, intelligent, authoritarian, and the like. Male non-conventional traits refer to men's willingness to encourage women's emancipation and empowerment through participation in paid work, literacy, family decision-making and sharing property.

The textbook areas that are subject to the analyses mentioned above are the titles, illustrations and texts. The analyzed textbook is judged sexist if it does not comprise a fair distribution of male and female occurrences. It is noteworthy that this distribution should not deviate by more than 10 to 20 percent from the equitable distribution of 50 percent as suggested by Michel and explained in chapter 4. Data are also analyzed qualitatively. The qualitative analysis presents and discusses the type of activities that have been assigned to women and men within a set of subsystems of the social life such as family, job, leisure and socio-political activities. It also analyzes the stereotypes that deal with citizenship, social fulfilment, resistance to pressure, moral and physical qualities and the linguistic bias, namely the exclusive use of masculine words in situations where feminine words can also be used, or avoidance of neutral words.

The foregoing issues are dealt with in the present chapter in four sections. The first three sections are respectively devoted to the analysis of the sub-research questions addressed above. The last section summarises and discusses the results in terms of the issue of gender, literacy, and empowerment.

## GENDER AND SPACE IN THE TEXTBOOKS

While gender refers to the social differences between men and women, equity refers to fairness governing such differences. Therefore, equity does not necessarily mean equality. Sexism is considered to go against equity between men and women. It refers to the way people are under-represented or stereotyped on the basis of belonging to the female or male sex. Equity is linked with language and the roles that are arbitrarily assigned to one or the other sex. The present section investigates gender and space in terms of equity by analyzing the number of male versus female references and representations in the textbooks. More specifically, it seeks to analyze the extent to which women are quantitatively visible in the textbooks under study. In so doing, it examines data under the first analysis that is provided in Michel's checklist which, as explained above, consists of counting the number of male versus female occurrences in the textbooks, particularly in the texts, titles, and illustrations.

### A non equitable space in the textbooks

The quantitative analysis of the number of male and female character featuring in the textbooks under study reveals that men occupy 65 percent of the allotted space while women occupy only 35 percent of that space. This under-representation of women is significantly maintained at the level of the text where men are allotted 68 percent of its space and women occupy only 32 percent of it as displayed in figure 8.1 below.

***Figure 8. 1. Male and Female Occurrences in the Text***

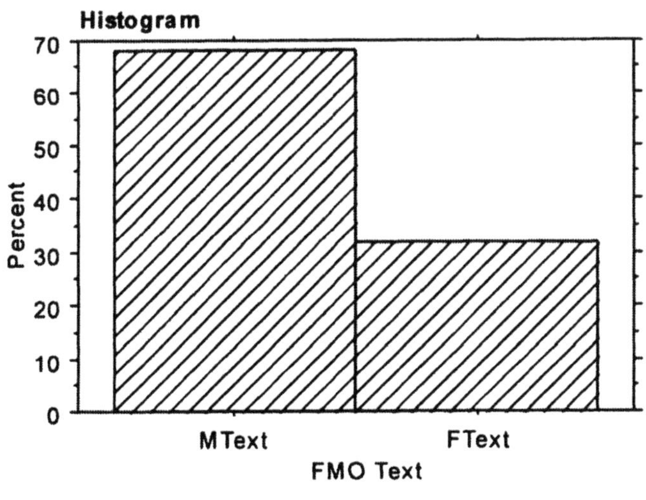

The precedence of men's space over that of women's, however, does not apply to the titles where there are twenty four male references in comparison to nineteen female ones. This may be explained by the fact that most of the titles do not evoke males or females as such but are rather thematic dealing with issues such as religion, good citizenship, agriculture, ecology, migration, drugs, health and family planning. Although the title references ratio is not significantly discriminatory, though the number of male occurrences is higher, the messages the titles convey are rather sexist as explained later in this chapter. Men's space in the illustration accounts for 54 percent in comparison to 47 percent for women.

In view of these results, the textbooks under study reveal a sense of sexism which is mostly significant at the level of the text. When split by textbook, it is found that women's under-representation is a feature of all analyzed textbooks. Males occupy 72 percent, 78 percent and 57 percent of the ascribed space while females occupy only 35 percent, 28 percent and 43 percent of it in volume one of Literacy for All, volume two of Literacy for All, and in Literacy and Basic Training for Adults" respectively. A consideration of these percentages shows that the second volume of Literacy for All is the most sexist textbook and Literacy and Basic Training for Adults is the least sexist one. As already stated, the limited space allotted to women in these textbooks is further affected by the linguistic bias.

Manifestations of the linguistic bias are numerous. Quantitatively, there is an unequal distribution of nouns and pronouns used to designate each sex in the texts as illustrated above. This marked preponderance of male occurrences over female ones involves the use of the verb as well. Its rate, however, changes from one textbook to the other. For example, a close consideration of the basic level of the textbook Literacy for All reveals that when dealing with instructional activities, the *Reading Comprehension Section* uses the Arabic neutral form of the first person singular in the simple present instead of the imperative masculine form. Examples of this rule are /*'aktubu*/ "I write", /*'ada3u*/ "I put", /*'arbitu*/ "I link", /*'amla'u*/ "I fill", /*'u3abbiru*/ "I express", /*'aqra'u*/ "I read", /*'ukawwinu*/ "I make", and /*'ulawwinu*/ "I colour". The arithmetic section, on the other hand, exclusively uses the masculine imperative forms such as /*la:hiz*/ "observe", /*fakkir*/ "think", /*'anjiz*/ "perform". This sexist grammatical form is maintained in the second volume in both the reading and maths sections. This can be considered as a sexist insinuation which attributes mathematical and cognitive skills to men as if such skills should not be accessible to women. This also means that graduation is programmed for men only. In addition, even in cases where neutral words are used as in Literacy and Basic Skills for Adults, the pictures associated with those verbs indicate that such actions are directed to men only.

With respect to the noun, there is a heavy use of masculine words to denote functions and occupations that are indiscriminately male or female in the Arabic language. For instance, the words /*zami:l*/ "colleague", /*mutarashshah*/ "candidate", /*muwa:tin*/ "citizen" and /*mudarris*/ "teacher" have female equivalent terms /*zami:la*/, /*mutarashshiha*/, /*muwa:tina*/ and /*mudarrisa*/. Yet, there is no reference to such words in the textbooks under study. Quantitatively, 75 percent of the illustrations associated with these terms are masculine, 12.5 percent are feminine and 12.5 percent are feminine and masculine. This linguistic discrimination assumes that the contents are made by men and addressed only to male readers. It is important to add here that this discrimination is present even when the text deals with *women's issues*.

## Gender roles in the textbooks

The present section deals with a description of the roles that women occupy within the limited space they are allocated in the textbooks under study. This is done through the application of the second analysis of Michel's checklist described above. This analysis consists of counting the type of activities attributed to males and females in terms of traditional versus non-traditional roles and functions. The quantitative analysis of data, illustrated in tables 8.1 and 8.2 below, show that the number of the conventional distribution of the gender roles in the textbooks is highly superior to the number of the non-conventional ones. Note that FCA, FNCA, MCA and MNCA refer respectively to female conventional activities, female non-conventional activities, male conventional activities and male non-conventional activities.

**Table 8.1. Conventional and Non-conventional Female Activities by Textbook**

**Frequency Distribution for FCA/FNCA**
**Split By: Textbook**

| | Total Percent | qiraa1 Percent | qiraa2 Percent | qiraiyya Percent |
|---|---|---|---|---|
| FCA | 96 | 100 | 100 | 89 |
| FNCA | 4 | 0 | 0 | 11 |
| Total | 100 | 100 | 100 | 100 |

(qiraa1, qiraa2, qiraiyya refer to *Literacy for All* volume 1, *Literacy for All* volume 2, and *Literacy Basic Training* for Adults respectively).

**Table 8.2 . Conventional and Non-conventional Male Activities by Textbook**

**Frequency Distribution for MCA/MNCA**
**Split By: Textbook**

| | Total Percent' | qiraa1 Percent | qiraa2 Percent | qiraiyya Percent |
|---|---|---|---|---|
| MCA | 99,333 | 100,000 | 100,000 | 98,000 |
| MNCA | ,667 | ,000 | ,000 | 2,000 |
| Total | 100,000 | 100,000 | 100,000 | 100,000 |

A close consideration of the figures displayed in both tables 1 and 2 above reveals that the distribution of the conventional and non-conventional activities attributed to males and females is not only unfair but it significantly deviates from the ideal distribution of 50 percent for all the analyzed textbooks.

Qualitatively, the activities that are portrayed in the textbooks fall into five types: domestic chores, child rearing and education, professional activities, socio-political activities and leisure activities. These are analyzed hereafter in terms of four domains: the family, work, society and leisure.

## Family activities

The distribution of family roles is highly conventional and sexist. The picture of a family composed of a mother and children predominates. Men are portrayed as fathers only occasionally. Housekeeping activities such as tidying up, cleaning, washing, cooking, sewing and related activities like child breeding, food shopping, water carrying, and cow milking are shown as being the exclusive domain of women and girls. While women are portrayed as performing material tasks such as domestic chores and child care, men are shown in roles of authority and performing spiritual tasks, and intellectual activities. In addition, women are denied any literacy activity in the family domain in opposition to men who are portrayed as reading the newspaper, responding to mail, signing checks, and reading for children. This insinuates that female literacy is less crucial than the everyday housework and family duties.

## Occupational activities

Women's occupational activities outside the family domain are also conventional but limited. They involve jobs which require little initiative and provide little money. In addition, they are an extension of women's traditional domestic roles where women are portrayed in dependent situations where they perform tasks instead of supervising or conceptualising them. These jobs involve occupations such as nurses, factory employers, carpet manufacturers, and assistant farmers. Other conventional occupations that are assigned to women in the textbook Literacy and Basic Training for Adults involve culturally and socially stigmatised roles where women are portrayed as beggars or involved in entertainment business as singers and dancers. The second volume of this textbook, however, is the only one where there is reference to very few non-conventional activities which the wives of the Prophet used to occupy as business women and religious scholars as shown on page 87 of that textbook. In this page there is also reference to the fact that a woman can hold many jobs including that of a minister. Still, this textbook is also considered as sexist as the number of the conventional occupations it portrays and describes is superior to that of the non-conventional ones.

## Social and political activities

In the preceding section, it was found that the social domains where women operate are home, the hospital, the market, the factory and the land, where they handle children and food. Women's social status is linked with marriage and children. Social reality, however, reveals that there are a significant number of women who assume the responsibility of single-parent families as divorced, widowed or separated women. Moreover, there are many women who successfully operate outside of motherhood and marriage and in other contexts than job or home. For instance, notwithstanding their marital status and jobs, Moroccan women are involved in responsibilities as presidents of non-governmental social, artistic, and cultural associations. They act as heads of university research groups, and responsible members of political parties. They are also leaders of cultural movements, militant writers, and literary critics. At the same time, non-literate women are involved in catering and textile industry, they attend feminist associations, and are even heads or members of agricultural cooperatives and village associations. In addition, they are prominent painters and engaged nationalist singers. Last but not least, they are excellent promoters of secular as well as religious education and about 10 percent of them participated in the *Green March* to the Moroccan Sahara in 1975. Unfortunately, though, none of the textbooks under study make reference to such socio-economic and political roles. The only political activity where women are involved beside men is the Election Day (see Literacy for All, volume 2, page 19).

### Leisure activities

The textbooks under study depict leisure activities as being exclusively masculine. Nowhere in the titles, texts, and illustrations are women presented as performing leisure tasks. It seems as if women do not have time for rest. In fact, women spend considerable time doing housework chores and, in many cases, perform job duties, educational tasks, and social activities. Yet, many non-literate women are involved in leisure activities such as reading, sport, painting, creative sewing, singing, music, and theatre. Avoidance of portraying women in these activities is an act of latent sexism where the portrayal of women is confined to motherhood and family life. Men, on the other hand, are portrayed as relaxing, doing weight lifting, sight-seeing, fishing, and reading. Regarding sport, only male professional figures are portrayed as football players and athlete champions. Yet, Morocco prides itself for having outstanding female athletes and Olympic medal winners. In sum, the investigated textbooks can be described as sexist with respect to leisure activities as well. In fact, they distort the real image of the society as they deliberately omit aspects of the reality where Moroccan women have achieved personal, professional, cultural and socio-political deeds.

## GENDER STEREOTYPING

Gender stereotyping reflects a society's perceptions, attitudes, value judgements towards men and women. This section analyzes the characteristics that are attributed to men and women in the textbooks under study. In so doing, it applies Michel's third quantitative analysis which consists of counting the number of the conventional versus non-conventional attributes that are used to portray men and women in the text, titles, and illustrations.

The comparative analysis of the conventional and non-conventional characters attributed to males and females in the titles, texts and illustrations of the investigated textbooks indicate that the number of the conventional traits is higher than the number of the non-conventional ones. The figures in tables 8.3 and 8.4 illustrate this non equitable distribution. The abbreviations FCT, FNCT, MCT and MNCT in the tables refer to female conventional traits, female non-conventional traits, male conventional traits and male non-conventional traits respectively.

Overall, female and male non-conventional characters account for only 12 percent and 7 percent respectively. When the distribution is split by textbook, the analysis shows that only Literacy and Basic Training for Adults contains non-conventional traits for both sexes. Notice, however, that the rate of the non-conventional ones is very low and significantly deviates from the ideal distribution of 50 percent.

**Table 8. 3. Conventional and Non-conventional Female Traits by Textbook**

**Frequency Distribution for FC/NC Traits**
**Split By: textbook**

| | Total Percent | qiraa1 Percent | qiraa2 Percent | qiraiyya Percent |
|---|---|---|---|---|
| FCT | 88 | 100 | 100 | 85 |
| FNCT | 12 | 0 | 0 | 15 |
| Total | 100 | 100 | 100 | 100 |

(qiraa1, qiraa2, qiraiyya refer to *Literacy for All* volume 1, *Literacy for All* volume 2, and *Literacy and Basic Training* for adults respectively).

**Table 8.4. Conventional and Non-conventional Male Traits by Textbook**

**Frequency Distribution for MC/NC Traits**
**Split By: textbook**

| | Total Percent | qiraa1 Percent | qiraa2 Percent | qiraiyya Percent |
|---|---|---|---|---|
| MCT | 93 | 100 | 100 | 84 |
| MNCT | 7 | 0 | 0 | 16 |
| Total | 100 | 100 | 100 | 100 |

Qualitatively, the traits attributed to men and women in the textbooks under study can be analyzed under four categories: citizenship, social fulfilment, resistance to social pressure, and moral and physical qualities

## Citizenship

The way the characters and traits are featured in the textbooks under investigation is in line with the conception of literacy adopted by adult literacy designers whose main objective is to teach the non-literate adults the dominant norms and social values of the society in terms of popular education and good citizenship. Unfortunately, these are transmitted through a sexist insinuation in favour of males, especially in the two volumes of Literacy for All. In these textbooks, good citizenship, for instance, is exclusively masculine. Only males are attributed positive qualities such as respect, dignity, seriousness and amiability as illustrated by the following statements:

> *Muhammadun muwa:tinun mustaqi:mun.*
> Mohammed is an honest citizen.
>
> *Muhammadun muwa:tinun mahbu:bun.*
> Mohammed is an amiable citizen.
>
> *Muhammadun muwa:tinun muhtaramun.*
> Mohammed is a respectful citizen.
>
> *Sa3i:dun muwa:tinun 3adi:mun.*
> Said is a great citizen.
>
> *za3i:mun muza :ri3un ma:hirun.*
> Zaim is a skilled farmer.

Good citizenship is portrayed in terms of participation in the Green March and the Olympic Games, and cultivating the land. By not including women in such activities in the analyzed materials, the textbook designers distort the image of reality where both men and women act as good citizens. This deliberate omission is a good example of latent sexism. Latent sexism involves featuring women in subordinate positions in relation to men and neglecting to suggest any alternative to improve or change such condition. It also consists of avoiding portraying all aspects of social reality where women operate not only as housewives, nurses and farmers but also in other occupations which are not yet prevalent as athletes, doctors, engineers and decision makers. Latent sexism is not associated with discriminatory judgements favouring one sex over the other, but conveyed by invisibility in socio-politically praised domains, in this case, participation in the *Green March*, representing Morocco in the Olympic Games and cultivating the land.

## Social fulfilment

The textbooks under study portray social success and wealth as being a characteristic of the male. The distribution of goods and professional opportunities is highly non-equitable. Men are portrayed as bank account holders involved in lucrative transactions. They possess land, houses, and specialized work places such as shops, offices and medical cabinets.

*yamliku 3alla:lun 3ima:ratan.*
Allal owns a building.

*ha:dha haqlu Ahmad.*
This is Ahmed's land.

*yu3linu adh-dhuktu:r 3abdu 'al-Raffa:r 3an'iftita:hi 3iyya:datihi.*
The doctor AdulRafar is opening his cabinet.

*'ishtara: as-sayyid Hami:d maxbazatan.*
Mr. Hamid bought a bakery.

Women, on the other hand, are featured as poor. Their only property is the house where they are portrayed as domestics. In addition they have no access to landownership, and when their husbands do have land; women are portrayed as assistants but not associates.

*ha:dha: manzilu Nuzha. Nuzha tunazzifu manzilaha:.*
This is Nouzha's house. Nouzha cleans her house

*yazra3u za3i:mun mazra3atahu. Zainabu tusa:3idu Za3i:man.*
Zaim is cultivating his land. Zainab helps Zaim.

Wealth as a masculine feature is also stressed when reference is made to the social institution of marriage.

*Tazawwaja ta:jirun fata:tan.*
A rich businessman married a girl.

**Resistance to social pressure**

The way men and women behave under pressure is portrayed differently in the textbooks under study. For example, men are portrayed as angry and women as tired.

*Al-'ummu mut3abatun.*
The mother is tired.

*Az-zawju qaliqun.*
The husband is angry.

In addition to being tired and overloaded with domestic duties, women are represented as insecure married women who attain legitimacy only when they become mothers especially of male off-springs.

> *TarRabu fi: 'an talida waladan xa:misan li tad̲mana ixla:s̲a al-'abi wa 'ilti-za:mahu ma3aha: fa la: yut̲alliquha:.*
> She wants to have a fifth child to ensure her husband's commitment so as not to repudiate her.

This feeling of insecurity and dependence changes into a feeling of helplessness and despair in the absence of the husband. For example, the only reference to the status of a woman as a widow features her as a helpless and a despaired person.

> *mund̲u 'an ma:ta zawjuha: 'as̲bah̲at tanz̲uru 'ila: 'al-h̲aya:ti naz̲rata 'al-ya'si.*
> Since her husband's death, she became helpless and pessimistic.

**Moral and physical qualities**

Strength of character and body as well as skill and talent are exclusively assigned to men.

> *Sa3i:dun s̲a:ni3un ma:hirun.*
> Said is a skilled manufacturer.

> *rah̲h̲a:lun muza:ri3un kabi:run.*
> Rahal is a great farmer.

> *Ah̲madu h̲arra:th̲un mujtahidun.*
> Ahmad is an industrious ploughman.

> *Muhammadu mithlu al-h̲is̲a:ni fi : al-quwwati.*
> Mohammed is as strong as a horse.

In view of these data, men are depicted as brave, skilled, competent, industrious and strong. Men's physical strength, however, is not always praised as they are portrayed, in a well established stereotype, as being aggressive. Morally, they are portrayed as cheaters and thieves. Females, on the other hand, are described as obedient, passive, affectionate and self-sacrificing.

To conclude, the role models that are portrayed and idealized are good citizenship and professional career for men and motherhood and household management for women. The character traits that are stereotyped are physical brutality, strength, skill and competence for men and emotional virtues, obedience and helplessness for women. Human potential involving intelligence, skill, competence, decision-making are shown to be exclusively masculine.

## SUMMARY OF THE RESULTS AND DISCUSSION

The male versus female occurrences analysis reveals a non equitable representation of male and females in the titles, texts and illustration. This is indeed a reflection of the sexist ecology where men and women operate. Reality, however, shows that the number of women in the Moroccan society is superior to that of men as they represent 52 percent of the total population. This under-representation of women in the textbooks under study is itself an indication of a sexist stereotype as it reflects the symbolic inferior position that women hold in society despite their significant statistical representation. Therefore, these teaching materials tend to solidify the established sexist social order.

Sexism and discrimination against women is deeply rooted in Moroccan social relations (El Attar, 1992; Sadiqi, 1995). This attested social feature inhibits women's development and eventually their daughters. Consequently, society deprives itself of its women' capital to which it denies full contribution in the process of sustainable development. Statistics to that regard are representative (*Femme Marocaine en Chiffres*, 1999). For example, the literacy rate for women over the age of 10 is only 40 percent compared to 67 percent for men. Such a deficit affects effective participation in the job market as well. Women's access to work in urban areas represents only 16.8 percent while it is 62 percent for men. In rural areas, the difference is less significant but the gender gap in literacy still persists. Only 37.2 percent women are involved in the active sector compared with 76.3 percent men. When it comes to decision making positions, the gap is even higher. In the current government, for instance, there are no female executive secretaries. Only 6.1 percent are departmental managers and 5 percent are executive managers. Women's participation in parliament in the nineties dropped from four women to three and the number of Secretaries of State decreased from four to none. For the first time in its history, the Moroccan government comprises a female Secretary of State since the last cabinet reshuffle which took place in September 2000 and which comprises more than thirty males. She, however, operates under delegation and her duty consists of an extension of a woman's traditional role which is handling women, family and children's affairs. In addition to that, while women's objective is parity with respect to the next elections, the quota is as low as 20 percent. With respect to education, where female participation is massive, only six women work at the university level as deans or directors of institutes and schools, compared to 119 males.

One of the main goals of adult literacy campaigns and programs is to incorporate women in development. The data analyzed in this book show that these women are not allotted sufficient space in the teaching materials. In addition, these textbooks do not recognize the current contributions made by women and worse they do not examine the conditions under which more effective contributions might be fulfilled.

For instance, the analysis of the male versus female activities reveals a non equitable representation of males and female within the family and the other sub-areas of society. Still, this limited representation is compatible with women's traditional domestic roles where they concentrate their energy to children and housework. On the other hand, men are shown as assuming economic and political responsibilities in public life. Such a distribution is commonly justified under the notion of the "complementarity" of the gender roles. Thus, the literacy courses' main objectives became to make women better wives, mothers and house managers. In so doing, these courses are described as providing functional literacy through drilling women on family planning and health. Such literacy however is conceived along the reproduction of the traditional and limited participation of women in society. In addition, while such functional training may, to some extent, satisfy women's target needs, it does not meet their learning needs nor does it answer their strategic needs.

The massive and exclusive representation of women in roles of married mothers performing domestic chores and the definition of men solely in terms of spiritual and respectful roles are indicators of sexism against women and reversal discrimination against men as well. In reality, both men and women perform their roles as parents and educators. Also, many families, especially in the urban areas and among the intellectual elite, operate in family systems other than the traditional one where both the mother and the father share responsibilities and decision making. Moreover, families other than those composed of a father, a mother and children exist. Many of these families are either headed by a widow or divorced male or female who, irrespective of their sex, get involved in domestic as well as educational responsibilities. Failure to portray such families in the textbooks is a reproduction of the dominant sexist reality and a rejection of the liberating values that are usually conveyed by the liberal elite whose role should partly consist in fighting oppression in society.

With respect to occupations, the qualitative data above reveals that men are featured as functioning in diverse socio-economic sectors. Women, on the other hand, are involved in household management and child care and very limited conventional occupations such as nursing, needlework and food handling. Men are portrayed in the workplace and outdoors. In comparison, women are valued only in their maternal and domestic roles. Other roles like professional and political ones are banned to them. The only textbook which values the importance of women in these roles is Literacy and Basic Training for All where, in addition to her conventional roles as a mother, a teacher, and a nurse, it is stated that a woman is also a Minister. The text also explains that women do contribute efficiently in many sectors of society such the family, the land, the factory, education, administration, and the government.

A*l-mar'atu 3unṣurun fa33a:lun wa musha:rikun fi al-mujtama3i.*
The woman is an efficient contributor in the society.

It is, however, important to state here that the pictures associated with this text limit women's potential to food handling in the family, the land and the factory. In addition to that, in the same page where reference is made to the diverse roles that a woman can occupy, reference is made to a well established stereotyped saying which praises the woman in her socio-culturally accepted role of wool spinning.

*al miRzalu bi yadi al-mar'ati 'aḇsanu mina ar-rumḇi bi yadi al-muja:hidi fi: sabi:li*
*al-lahi.*
A spindle in a woman's hand is better than a spear in the hands of a militant Moslem.

Women's contribution in the countryside is praised only in terms of their appreciated role in the family, where they are represented as fertile mothers, in the land, where they help their husbands, who are the only owners of the land, and in the market where they act as goods consumers (Literacy and Basic Training for adults, volume 2: 129). Yet, it is known that rural women participate in the market not only as consumers but as producers as well. Their contribution, however, takes place under oppressive conditions. Indeed, the literacy contents should be used as a means of reflecting on ways to change such conditions by providing information and knowledge on how to increase agricultural productivity, invest money, and attain a better socio-economic integration. In so doing, the literacy contents will provide access to written empowering knowledge and information.

Overall, the analyzed textbooks are explicitly sexist as they use sexist vocabulary and grammar. They portray women in typically female roles and men in typically male roles. They focus on outstanding male characters, ignoring female celebrities. Moreover, they show a marked preference of males over females as women are invisible and men are praised as good, skilled and competent citizens. As already explained, by reproducing women in stereotyped social roles with no attempt to criticise such stereotypes or portray women in roles where they prove that they are equal to men, the textbooks under study convey another type of sexism which is latent.

It's true that literacy programs should reflect the reality of women's lives but the power of such programs lies in providing women with the means of exercising control over those lives and changing them. In this respect, education and literacy are often regarded as agents of change in society. Indeed, among the fundamental functions of literacy is to unveil the realities of the non-literate and provide them with adequate cognitive and psychological means of changing what is oppressive in their lives. Hence, it is very important that the contents the learners read and hear not only reflect society, but show the ways to improve it. In many parts of the world, including Morocco, women require training in family planning, health and nutrition, they need sanitation and methods of facilitating housework and child education, and they lack access to credit, marketing and simple technology. Furthermore, they suffer from violence and social discrimination. In this case, literacy training directed to women should be drawn up in the light of both practical and gender interests and needs. Therefore, the literacy contents should teach women how to achieve better socio-economic integration within a new status where they act as equal partners with men in all fields of work, education, training and politics.

Actually, it is known that the causes behind the illiteracy of women are cultural and economic. It is to be noted, though, that none of the textbooks under study makes reference to women's illiteracy and ways of combating it. Yet, many Moroccan families still attach more importance to the education of male offspring than to the female one. Such male biased tradition, coupled with poverty, puts female education at risk as it is considered as a luxury and indeed a bad investment. As a result, many poor families make much effort and sacrifice to send their sons to school and are likely to keep their daughters indoor to help with household chores and increase their chances to get married. The feminization of illiteracy has itself led to the feminization of poverty which in turn significantly contributes to the impoverishment of society. In fact, when other variables are kept constant and when the same socio-economic conditions are offered, women suffer from poverty more than men do as quoted in Haider (1996:37):

> "When resources are stretched thin, it is women, the most marginalized in the first place, who suffer first and most. Women have the smallest share of the

resources pie of the world; when the pie shrinks, women's losses are greatest" (Seager and Olson, 1986)

The majority of non-literate women do not work and are, therefore, dependent on male guardians for the rest of their lives. As for working girls and women, some are ready to sacrifice job at marriage or child delivery and others are deprived by tradition from the money they gain in the informal sector where they operate as maids, cleaners or workers. Still, other women have no access or no control over their legal part of heritage. By excluding women from the workplace and limiting their potential to housework and child bearing, the textbooks under study reproduce women's dependence and marginalisation.

The reproduction of these gender relations is further emphasized by failing to promote female literacy in the textbooks. In these primers, all the literacy activities are exclusively carried out by men who are portrayed as filling out cheques, signing documents, responding to mail, and reading books and newspapers. By excluding women from such literacy domains, these literacy courses not only go against their main objective, which consists in eradicating female illiteracy, but indoctrinate men and women to accept current prevailing gender relations without questioning them. In so doing, adult literacy courses reinforce women's illiteracy and dependence.

## CONCLUSION

The object of this chapter was to find answers to how much space is given to women in the textbooks under study, what functions they occupy in such space and how they are represented. The aim was to find out whether the designed teaching materials convey a culture that seeks the empowerment of non-literate women by unveiling the structural inequalities that mark their daily life and suggesting practical ways of improving their condition and position. In view of the quantitative and the qualitative analyses given above, it is revealed that women occupy a limited space, where their main role consists of handling food and children, and where they are stereotyped as submissive, dependent, weak and poor. In this case, they are made literate through a content which legitimises and reproduces women's position of dependence, subordination and inequity in all domains and subsystems of society. Being victims of illiteracy, poverty and marginalisation, many of these women seek help and assistance in the literacy courses. Unfortunately, the findings of this research reveal that women are trained by absorbing messages which reproduce and perpetuate their symbolic under-representation, exclusion, and stereotyping. By emphasizing and reinforcing women's low status and role in society, these teaching materials might inhibit non-literate women's incentive for learning and lead to an internalisation of a low-self image and, eventually, "*dis-empowerment*". Concretely, drastic revisions of these teaching materials, with the aim of consciously empowering the learners, are highly needed. Hints to some ways of empowering women through the literacy contents are described in the next chapter.

# 9
# Toward New Perspectives of Women's Literacy

The original intent of this research was to investigate the relationship between gender, literacy, and empowerment in terms of the effectiveness of adult literacy instruction directed to non-literate women in Morocco. The investigation of such effectiveness could not be done without examining a set of issues that are centered on non-literate women as learners, especially as there is a wide gap between research and female literacy programming in Morocco. Eventually, the purposes of this book became to identify the profiles of these learners, investigate the causes of their illiteracy and obstacles to their effective participation in the literacy courses, assess their literacy needs, learning needs and literacy attainments, and analyze the contents through which they are made literate. These issues were investigated within a conceptual framework that regards female literacy as a necessary step to answer women's *practical needs*, by ensuring sufficient basic and functional literacy levels, and women's *strategic interests*, by designing empowering textbooks that are consonant with a perspective that seeks women's equal participation in the process of development and social change. The aim was to provide literacy policymakers, program managers, teachers, and researchers with findings that have pedagogical, theoretical, and policy implications for a better understanding of the triangular relationship between gender, literacy, and empowerment. Four related issues, which are necessary to be investigated when dealing with a gender-based needs analysis, made up the gist of this book: the profiles of the beneficiaries, the causes of illiteracy and dropping out of the literacy program, women's literacy needs and learning needs, women's literacy attainments, and women's empowerment.

This concluding chapter critically reviews the central issues that have been analyzed in the present book and considers them in perspective. In so doing, it summarizes the findings, investigates their implications, and suggests some related recommendations.

## THE BENEFICIARIES' PROFILES AND OBSTACLES TO THEIR LITERACY

The primary concern of the issue on the beneficiaries' characteristics and the causes of their illiteracy was to provide information on the learners' profiles and elucidate the causes of female illiteracy and the reasons of dropping out of the literacy courses. The investigation of the question dealing with the characteristics of the learners, which is an important issue to tackle when assessing the learners' needs and literacy attainments, revealed that the interviewed 204 current beneficiaries constitute a heterogeneous group divided up in terms of age, mother tongue, region, occupation and educational background. This heterogeneity, which has so far been neglected when designing adult literacy training, bears important policy implications especially since it was found to have a significant impact on the learners' literacy needs and literacy attainments. Some of these implications are discussed later in this chapter.

In addition to providing data on their characteristics, the same informants were asked to give reasons for their illiteracy as children and the causes of their irregular attendance in the literacy courses in adulthood. Analyses of data revealed that the most important obstacles to the learners' illiteracy as children relate to parents' opposition, distant or lack of schools, and school failure. Findings related to irregular attendance involve work, housework and socio-cultural events. To identify the causes of dropping out of the literacy course, a sample of 75 drop-outs were interviewed. The recurrent responses they came out with relate to domestic duty, program interruption, distance and husbands' opposition. In sum, the causes of female illiteracy and obstacles to their effective participation in adult literacy as reported by the informants of the present research are *situational* rather than *dispositional*. That is, they are external to the individual's control and are not based on personal attitude. Lack or no access to schools, poverty, school failure and lack of commitment on the part of some providers of the literacy courses go beyond the learner's control at both child and adult age. Likewise, gender roles, heavy demands of family life, and the weight of tradition relate to the dominant cultural pattern of the Moroccan society, which still does not value the education of girls in view of its limited returns especially in the villages where secondary school education is almost non existent, and because of the limited prestigious positions and horizons that are open to women in socio-economic and political domains.

These findings are suggestive and bear important policy implications for dealing with the scourge of illiteracy in Morocco, where illiteracy rates continue to soar among women, and where the absolute number of adult illiterates has been growing despite the government's efforts to combat illiteracy since Independence in 1956. The number of adult illiterates was 6,560,000 in the 1960's and has reached about 14 million in the twenty-first century. Hence, attacking illiteracy at its root by generalizing primary education and increasing its efficiency and providing non-formal education for the youth and adults as a solution to school failure and adult illiteracy still presents a challenge for Morocco.

Since the last decade, an increasing number of organizations, both governmental and non-governmental, have embarked upon the organization of nationwide literacy programs as explained in chapter 3. Likewise, the generalisation of primary education is now a top priority for the government. While the generalization of primary education seems to be feasible, the problem is how to ensure promotion from one grade to the other and retention of children at school. Repetition occurs most often in the first three grades of primary school. In most cases, this is due to the problem of granting literacy in a language that is different from the learners' mother tongue (Saib, 1995). In addition, children leave school without achieving minimum literacy skills for reasons of socio-economic and cultural nature. When adult, these school leavers fall in the category of adult illiterates looking for remedy. Still, obstacles to literacy continue to prevail at the adult age where limited training and inappropriate content go against the promotion of literacy as an enabling and empowering process.

While political will is working for better gains by building schools and literacy centers to attract girls and women, retaining them and sustaining their motivations for literacy becomes a difficult task as female literacy is highly embedded within cultural and socio-economic factors. Therefore, interest in culture and poverty should be taken into consideration before the launching of any educational or literacy project. In this respect, Mwiria (1993) claims that solutions to encouraging women to participate in adult literacy programs depend on how much society will change, particularly concerning gender inequality. Indeed, schools and literacy centers are condemned to failure and extinction unless they obtain support from the family and the community and unless they ensure the economic integration of their graduate beneficiaries. In this regard, many actions could be taken, For instance, to retain women in the classes, it would be advisable to create day care centers, use media to make families aware of the importance of female literacy, provide practical and relevant teaching to girls' and women's daily lives with an empowering focus, design practical education and training in marketable skills, and teach women how to earn money to improve their standard of living. All these activities can be achieved before or alongside the literacy classes to improve women's economic situation in the short-term future. Many testimonies from the present research, especially from rural women, evoke the problem of poverty as an obstacle to effective participation in the literacy courses. In fact, these cases represent an important population of poor rural women whose immediate concern is to earn a living. In fact, many rural girls and women migrate to towns looking for jobs in houses or in the informal sector. Hence, it would be recommended to use some income generating activities or micro-credit programs as a motivating measure to ensure effective participation in the literacy course. Actually, the Government has launched a campaign against rural women's poverty and some non-governmental organizations have already subscribed to this action. However, none of the visited regions implemented such training or facilities. So, perhaps, it would be advisable to generalize the experience all over the country especially since positive findings are reported from similar programs in Nepal where the beneficiaries of adult literacy programs in twenty eight districts gained an increase in self-confidence and economic autonomy by being involved in reproductive management and income-generating activities (USAID, 1998).

## IDENTIFYING WOMEN'S LITERACY NEEDS

The investigation of women's literacy needs and learning needs was carried out among the same informants that were interviewed on their profiles and the causes of their illiteracy (N=204). Its aim was to gain insight in women's perceived needs and real needs and the respondents' satisfaction with the ascribed course.

The learners' perceived needs, which refer to motivations in integrating the literacy course, fall into three types for the majority of the respondents: basic like learning to read, write and count, practical or functional such as using basic literacy to handle everyday and document literacy, and strategic or empowering like gaining self-confidence and social acceptance and developing autonomy and self-control. Additional needs pertaining to the learners' individual and sample differences have been reported. For instance, needs in terms of the Arabic language acquisition are mostly required by rural Amazigh respondents. Mothers seek to learn knowledge of matters related to child education. Wage earners who also wish to be literate in the French language want to learn how to deal with job matters. Re-integrating primary education is highly needed by pre-schooled informants and knowledge of cultural issues is a must for subjects who live or work in highly literate milieus. The respondents' real needs in terms of literacy acquisition include handling community-based and consumer-economics-based documents, and receiving health and religion related instruction.

While the program on offer aims at more or less the same target needs, it fails to deal with literacy as an empowering concept. In addition, it teaches functional literacy through a content that is of no practical relevance to the learners who express dissatisfaction with the ascribed topics and deplore the difficulty of the language of instruction. Last but not least, program designers do not consider the beneficiaries of adult literacy courses as a heterogenous group whose target literacy needs change as a function of age, occupation, mother tongue, marital status, region and educational background.

This discrepancy is the result of the way female literacy is conceived of in developing countries. With the emergence of women as agents of development, literacy provision for girls and women has been developed in many countries, including Morocco, as an investment that pays significant returns in economic growth, improved health and quality of life. Hence, literacy has been designed as a national program based on a deficit model, which regards women as incompatible with the requirements of socio-economic development. Within this perspective, women are regarded as retarding the country's development by ignoring family planning matters and popular education issues. Therefore, the courses targeted to non-literate women turn around issues that are linked to social, but not individual, development such as migration, ecology, and health in addition to religious, civic duties and ethical education.

Along with this traditional concept of literacy, illiteracy is regarded as a disease which has to be eradicated within a few months and among large populations. Hence emphasis is on quantity rather than quality. As a result, these literacy programs often evaluate success in terms of national enrolment rates with a focus on women and rural areas to justify their expenses and claim additional funds. Within this view of literacy, the learners' needs are not taken into consideration and literacy instruction is reduced to teaching non-literate adults rudimentary basic reading skills. Hence, many women are certified in public as literate after a maximum of eighteen months of instruction. The certified learners and their teachers receive honors, presents or symbolic gifts in the form of travelling tickets to do pilgrimage and are asked to express their feelings of contentment in front of the financing agencies. While such an action may empower women more than their limited training does, it should be taken with a lot of caution as many already schooled women register as totally illiterate only to be praised in public by important political figures and receive symbolic as well as material support. In addition, the satisfaction of the deserving non-schooled certified graduates could be only temporary as they have acquired only rudimentary reading skills that are liable to being lost, especially under conditions of non-use and no post-literacy training, which may result in a tragically missed opportunity.

The findings of the present research revealed that while the designed literacy course may bear some relevance for the learners, it is presented through a non-functional language and taught through inadequate methods by unprepared teachers and for non-sufficient periods of time. Hence, teaching relevant topics, developing learner-centered teaching methods, training teachers in andragogy, using functional language, involving the learners in the design of the programs, considering the beneficiaries' heterogeneity, providing post-literacy training and linking adult literacy to formal or vocational education and income generating resources are important measures to take in order to design literacy programs that are consonant with non-literate women's needs and expectations.

Lacking basic skills to handle everyday literacy, women enrol to learn to read. Suffering from problems inherent to underdevelopment such as big, poor and non-literate families, they also enrol to know how to solve the problems they face. Therefore, the literacy courses that are designed for non-literate women should be relevant to their reality and take the form of problem solving lessons rather than lecturing on how to prevent problems that have already marked the lives of these women. This necessitates a "down top" or "bottom up" strategy for a better understanding of the problems and the literacy situations women are likely to encounter in their daily lives.

In sum, investment in the potential of non-literate women could be achieved only through gender-based literacy programs that: link in-class literacy with the learners' daily lives and needs, afford pre-service and in-service training for the teachers, provide the necessary post-literacy work and continuing education for the learners, reflect on new methods and techniques for the teaching of the language of instruction, adopt new approaches to female literacy, associate the literacy work with income generating resources and micro-credits especially among the poor girls and women.

## RESPONDING TO WOMEN'S LITERACY NEEDS

The investigation of women's literacy attainments was meant to analyze the extent to which the certified learners master what they have learned and apply their school-based literacy to handle the tasks they sought to learn through their participation in the literacy course. It also aimed at identifying the individual and sample differences that would affect the learners' in-school and everyday literacy.

To elucidate the extent to which the learners master what they have learned in the literacy centers, an achievement test has been designed based on the learners' literacy courses. To gain insight into the extent to which the learners apply what they have learned to deal with everyday literacy, a proficiency test was constructed based on the respondents' real needs. The learners' scores in the literacy achievement and proficiency tests were analyzed as dependent variables and were subjected to analyses of variance where they were computed with as set of predictor variables such as the learners' age, mother tongue, motivation, educational background, and grade level. The aim was to value the effect of such variables on the learners' attainments in the assigned tests.

Investigation of the achievement test revealed that the respondents have attained high levels in pre-reading skills particularly in exercises that are based on recognition. Word and sentence production are only moderately mastered and basic reading comprehension is still challenging for more than half of the non-schooled graduate learners. Qualitative analyses of the learners' pre-reading mistakes showed that the respondents resort to simplification and L1 based strategies, which shows that they follow the universal development route of learning a second language. It is to be noted, though, that they are still at the beginning of the route as their inter-language is not well developed yet. In fact, it was found that while being certified as literate, some non-schooled graduate learners still confuse the letters of the alphabet and others were not able to use letter appropriate configurations. In addition, the majority could not understand a short written text. Analyses of the proficiency test showed that the graduate learners were not prepared enough to handle everyday and household literacy. Qualitative analyses of the graduate learners' interaction with the assigned documents revealed that reading difficulty pertains to limited linguistic ability and ignorance of reading strategies. Investigation of literacy and related predictor variables indicated that women's basic literacy and functional literacy attainment is related to area, grade level and mother tongue, but not to personal differences such as age and motivation.

Obviously, the findings related to the issues addressed above bear many policy implications. First, literacy training for women as evaluated by the present research revealed that it teaches only rudimentary reading skills that may dwindle in the absence of post literacy training. Hence, efforts to link basic literacy with the learners' every day lives, the use of a simple but functional language, and teaching the learners appropriate reading strategies to handle authentic written materials are necessary measures to take in the design of any future literacy programs. Second, it is important to consider the heterogeneity of the learners. For instance, the learners' formal educational background had a highly significant impact on their performance in both basic literacy and functional literacy. As stated in chapter seven, it was found that adults can re-learn more easily than they can learn new material (Zahn, 1980). Materials once learned as a child and forgotten as an adult could be relearned with less effort than it took at the first time of learning. These differences do have a negative effect on the non-schooled ones who reported that they could not keep up with their pre-schooled classmates. In this respect, the use of placement tests can be adopted as a solution to design classes that reflect the real literacy levels of the beneficiaries.

While age has no a significant effect on the learners' literacy attainment, it was revealed that the youngest sample was the least performing group. It was also found that the learners' needs change according to their age. Pedagogically this means that the learners' age is an important factor to be taken into consideration while designing adult literacy programs.

The learners' literacy attainment is highly sensitive to the learners' mother tongue and area; rural Amazighophones being the least performing group and the urban Arabophones being the most performing respondents, particularly at the level of basic and functional reading comprehension. This learning constraint should be taken into account during the learning process especially that similar syllabi and course durations are assigned to both linguistic communities and areas. In fact, language can constitute a barrier to literacy attainment. When learners speak unwritten languages and are expected to acquire literacy in languages they do not understand, becoming literate can be a tedious and frustrating enterprise. In addition to the age factor, adults become easily convinced that learning literacy in an unfamiliar language is beyond their grasp and leads them eventually to drop out.

Hence, it is recommended that before launching the same training for the learners, basic literacy programs should be built initially on the familiar language of the non-literate and remediation programs in the form of intensive courses should be designed for Amazighophones and rural beneficiaries. In addition, it would be wise to teach issues that are development and empowerment oriented in the learner's home language because information is thereby processed much more rapidly and without difficulty. In this way, literacy becomes a source of vigorous cultural diversity rather than mono-cultural hegemony and increases the chances of the Amazighophone women to catch up with their Arabophone classmates.

While evoking the language issue, it is worth mentioning here that the investigated women are highly motivated to learn Standard Arabic as it answers their literacy needs. In fact, Standard Arabic is the language that best meets the functional needs of the learners. Socially, it plays an important role in the learner's literate ecology, especially in the urban and semi-urban areas. Pedagogically, it has teaching materials and a teaching staff. Therefore, it could be taught effectively using the existing funds and materials. Linguistically, its learning yields a sort of additive relevant bilingualism. Psychologically, it is highly valued by the enrolees who would certainly maintain their effort to learn it provided that its teaching methods and techniques are based on communicative and authentic learning.

While Standard Arabic answers the target needs of the investigated women, it does not answer their learning needs as the majority regard it as difficult to learn. The difficulty of its learning is inherent to its status as a written language, and is also linked to the way it is taught. During the class observations that have been made for the present research, it was found out that an important proportion of the lesson is carried out in Moroccan Arabic, a fact that does not help the learners to acquire the language and puts the monolingual Amazighophones at a disadvantage. Thus, perhaps, the use of simple and functional language and the application of total immersion methods, after initial literacy training in the mother tongue of the learners, would give better results. It was also found that French answers the functional needs of an important proportion of the working learners. Therefore, it should be integrated in the literacy program at least at the graduate and post-literacy level as an optional subject.

Post-literate informants scored significantly higher than the graduate respondents in both basic and functional tests. This implies that while literacy programs provide their learners with rudimentary literacy skills, post-literacy training is a good predictor of basic and functional literacy. Considering the significant effect of pre-literacy experience and grade level, one may conclude that two years of literacy training, which is normally the programmed length of learning at the national level, is not enough to ensure satisfactory functional reading levels. Therefore, additional years in terms of literacy provision are needed to achieve better functional reading attainments. Unfortunately, such training was offered only by very few non-governmental associations and the best results were reported from at least four years of training.

This in turn implies that since post-literacy programs are not nationally designed, it is legitimate to conjecture that adult literacy graduates will eventually relapse into illiteracy. This is even more probable with the new literacy programs where the literacy training is reduced to nine months with no follow-up training. Thus, to attain satisfactory levels in basic and functional reading comprehension and to foster the learners' motivation which may dwindle, due to limited learning, and lead to dropping out, as attested by some informants of the present research, it is recommended to deal with adult literacy not as an end in itself but as an ongoing learning process. Such a learning process should aim at ensuring more than minimal learning and designing courses that are linked to the learners' needs and applicable in their practical lives. Furthermore, it should foster retention, integration and autonomy and consider the heterogeneity of its clientele.

## RESPONDING TO WOMEN'S STRATEGIC NEEDS

The analysis of women's empowerment through the literacy content sought to investigate the extent to which the learners' textbooks are consonant with a perspective that targets women's emancipation and empowerment. In so doing, it examined the space allotted to women in the textbooks, analyzed the functions they occupy in such space and identified the characteristics and traits they are attributed.

Analyses of the foregoing issues showed that women occupy one third of the allotted space where their main occupation is limited to conventional roles such as housework and child bearing and where they are represented as dependent, weak and poor. This limited visibility, further reinforced by dependence and helplessness, legitimises the reproduction of the symbolic inferior position women occupy in the society at large. Thus, women's literacy is far from being a quest for change and empowerment as it is based on a consolidation of the established conventional gender roles.

As stated in chapter 8, the problem with female literacy programs can be traced to their objectives, which stress the traditional roles of women as being limited to family health, child care, nutrition, and family planning. While such gender roles reflect the daily lives of non-literate women, the designed literacy programs do not provide these women with an instruction that would increase their socio-economic potential and value their effective visibility as responsible human beings and contributing members of their family and community.

As already stressed, female illiteracy is not only a socio-economic problem that can be resolved through the satisfaction of women's practical interests, but it is also a gender issue loaded with socio-cultural forces. This of course has many implications for female literacy programming whose objectives should also aim at women's autonomy and empowerment. In other words, the textbooks should not only unveil the subordinating condition of women, but give them a feeling that they can be active agents for improving such conditions. The textbook designers should address the problems inherent to women's illiteracy and present ways of dealing with such issues. In so doing, the textbooks' input can serve as catalyst for social changes. For instance, to attenuate the problem of dropping-out due to heavy housework duties, the textbook can provide women with information on how to save time, how to organize, or where to obtain day care facilities, and how to encourage husbands to help in household chores and child matters to allow their wives to participate in literacy courses. To value literacy, the textbook designers can, for instance, portray how a literacy graduate couple was able to help their children with the homework, and explain how literacy training helped both husband and wife to handle indoor and outdoor literacy and increase family income and welfare.

While stressing the importance of work for both men and women, the textbook should provide information on how to integrate or ameliorate productive work for couples with low levels of education. For instance, it should give indications on how to earn fair wages, work in better conditions, obtain loans, invest and earn money, create or integrate handicraft or agricultural cooperatives, deal with the problem of drought, food shortage and decent housing. In addition to this practical information, the literacy contents should convey messages that are related to the social and political roles of women and their civic rights as individual citizens and as a group. In addition, language should be reviewed to avoid giving precedence of one sex over the other. Traditional traits and sex roles should be stamped out. Equal rating of family, domestic activities, vocational, professional and political roles should be made explicit in the contents and illustrated in the pictures. In addition, female celebrities should appear beside the male ones.

Last but not least, women should be portrayed as effective responsible agents in the family and community. For example, instead of portraying women as passive assistants in their husbands' land, the text should raise women's potential in solving the problem of water shortage or poor crops and harvest products. In this regard, the texts should encourage women's participation in family decision-making. In addition, messages as to the importance of female literacy in joining income generating activities, agricultural cooperatives, and women's organizations should be stressed. Likewise the titles should convey messages against gender discrimination such as *Sons and daughters are equally valuable, Basic Education is important for both men and women, Advantages of educated mothers and fathers, Child Education is both Mothers' and Fathers' duty, Birth control: a man and a woman's responsibility, Men and women at work, Human rights, Protecting girls and women from ill-treatment and sexual abuse, Encouraging girls' and women's literacy, Increasing family income, How to gain access to both material and informational resources for a better functioning of the family* and the like. The idea is to invite both men and women to develop critical thinking on their traditional gender roles and at the same time reflect on ways of changing them. In so doing, female literacy will be a means through which both men and women question the pre-established discriminatory cultural norms and work towards changing them for a better functioning of their families and community.

## METHODOLOGICAL AND THEORETICAL IMPLICATIONS

The present book attempted to elucidate as many issues underlying female literacy in Morocco as possible due to the paucity of research in this area. In so doing, it provided the profiles of a selected sample of beneficiaries from governmental and non-governmental adult literacy centers in rural and urban areas; and it investigated the causes of women's illiteracy and obstacles to their effective participation in the literacy courses. It also assessed their literacy needs and learning needs, evaluated their basic and functional attainments and analyzed the content through which they are made literate.

In fact, this needs' analysis comprehensive research can be considered as an impetus for future studies on female literacy in Morocco. For instance, further research may limit itself to one of the four issues that have been analyzed in the present research with a focus on one area and a specific institution. Future investigations in adult literacy can, through a longitudinal sample, examine how non-literate learners progress from technical reading to basic and to functional reading comprehension. But great attention should be paid to the problem of absenteeism, dropping-out and discontinuity, which are the very common features of the non-formal education sector, a fact that may make the undertaking of such studies very tedious and frustrating. Additional research may investigate the empowering effect of literacy through the beneficiaries' testimonies. This would require a longitudinal study and methodological designs that draw from anthropology and sociology. Future contributions may deal with post-literacy effects such as retention/attrition or functional literacy in the workplace.

In addition to triggering further research, the present book came out with findings that bear implications for female literacy theorizing in particular and adult literacy in general. Such theorizing is discussed in terms of the adopted theoretical framework, which regards literacy as basic, functional and empowering.

In adult literacy, basic education refers to the acquisition of the three R's namely reading, writing, and arithmetic in accordance with UNESCO's 1958 definition of literacy. Within this traditional view of literacy, people are considered literate if they can sign, write their names, or read a short text. In the mid sixties, adult literacy was no longer defined as a skill to be acquired, but is considered in the light of its functional dimension as a task, and the role it plays in the social integration and participation of the functionally illiterate, who while possessing basic literacy cannot use it to function appropriately in their environment. Literacy as a task rather than a skill becomes then related to life contexts and is defined as the ability to use the acquired skills to function productively and effectively in society at large. In other words, literacy is seen as the ability to "understand and use the printed material one normally encounters in work, leisure and citizenship" (Stedman and Kaestle, 1991:92). Functional illiteracy, on the other hand is comparable to dependence, underdevelopment and difficulty in socio-economic integration. To increase productivity and ensure socio-economic integration of the functionally illiterate, the EWLP, the Experimental World Literacy Program was launched. This, however, has led to an excessive exploitation of the working human resources. In addition, it was revealed that poverty, low productivity, poor health, cultural deprivation or injustice are associated with illiteracy, but not caused by it. Thus, the empowerment of the human potential came into focus with the theoretical definition of literacy as a critical reflection. Interest in the acquisition of literacy as a critical consciousness of one's social condition and position and as a process towards transforming what is oppressive about it came into use in the seventies with the publications of Paulo Freire's works as explained in chapter 1.

This emancipatory concept of literacy as a critical reflection considers illiteracy as a symptom of poverty, injustice, submission and resignation and regards literacy as a means to understand how the structuring of society oppresses people and their struggle to overcome this oppression. Literacy as a liberating and empowering factor has also been adopted as a revolution against the prevailing traditional patriarchal systems. As a result, emancipatory theorizing of female literacy marked the beginning of the eighties. Drawing upon this theoretical evolution of literacy the present book deals with female literacy teaching as a basic, functional and empowering process whose aim is to answer women's practical and strategic needs. Such a theoretical construct was used as a research design to elucidate the relationship between gender, literacy and empowerment in the designing of women's literacy in Morocco.

Findings of the present work, which should be interpreted in terms of the data it used and the period it examined, revealed that more than forty years after the launching of its first literacy campaigns, Morocco still subscribes to the traditional definition of adult literacy. This conception of literacy does not go beyond the teaching of rudimentary literacy skills that may eventually be subject to attrition and even loss, especially that almost no post-literacy training is programmed. Therefore, the graduates of these programs, which limit the teaching of literacy to the acquisition of elementary reading skills, will shortly fall again in the category of illiterates and their training will become an effort in vain. But, as Jones (1990) claims, such wastage and errors in adult literacy programming can be avoided if greater attention is paid to the fundamental view of literacy.

It has been explained that decision makers in developing countries promote literacy in circumstances where they want to promote change in society. The societal issues that gain priority in such societies include health, family planning and environment protection as pre-requisites for sustainable development. As these subjects can be transmitted through other channels and in the learners' mother tongues, and given their inappropriate teaching, such topics did not appeal to the informants under study who seek information not on how to prevent underdevelopment but how to deal with it.

Unable to use in-school literacy for everyday functional purposes and being trained through content which emphasizes the teaching of ideal social conducts and traditional cultural norms, women under study will do little with their literacy. From their testimonies many refer to a feeling of exclusion because of their illiteracy. To remedy this situation, they enrolled in the literacy courses. In view of their low competence in the functional test, these women do certainly still feel excluded not because they are completely illiterate but because they have not been sufficiently trained to apply what they have learned in everyday circumstances despite their motivation and conscious awareness of the stakes associated with literacy. Handling daily functional literacy skills which they sought to learn and which in fact constitutes the boundary between literacy and illiteracy is not yet within their reach despite their being certified as literate. In addition, their socialization is carried out through content that partially answers their literacy needs and learning needs and reinforces their inferior position in the family and society.

One salient theoretical implication of these findings is to demonstrate that there is a need to go beyond traditional literacy theorizing by providing appropriate literacy courses that will serve the immediate practical needs of women to improve their condition and answer their strategic interests to ameliorate their position. This, of course, can be done only by designing gender-based literacy programs. Gender-based literacy programming is recommended not because women learn differently from men or because they have lower cognitive abilities, but because the so far existing literacy programs continue to relegate women to inferior positions in society by reproducing the dominant patriarchal relations. Results from the present research reveal that non-literate adult women, like any other learners, do follow the universal route of development of language learning. Gender programming is, thus, needed to fill the gap in the fundamental view of literacy as practical and empowering. Defining literacy simply as a discrete skill inevitably leads to a training that is unlikely to answer needs beyond those related to deciphering words and sentences. Women's illiteracy is not only a problem of not knowing how to read and write, nor is it simply linked to the inability to be functional in family, society, and work, but it is also a gender issue which draws its origins from sexist and patriarchal societies. Hence, women's literacy should be a quest for a better socio-economic integration as well as liberation from the weight of tradition. In so doing, literacy training will facilitate women's empowerment from 'within' first, which is a prerequisite for mobilizing for 'collective empowerment'.

## RECOMMENDATIONS

In view of the findings of this book, it is revealed that the relationship between gender, literacy, and empowerment is far from being attained. Neither women's practical needs nor their strategic needs are answered by the analyzed literacy programs. Therefore, redefinition of literacy as task-based and gender-based still represents an enormous challenge to the designers of adult literacy in Morocco.

In fact, female literacy could be achieved only if its political, human and cultural dimensions are taken into consideration and if it aims at skill development, socio-economic integration and consciousness-raising. Theoreticians of gender-based literacy studies claim that such a conception could be achieved only if women are involved in decision-making positions and in the designing of female literacy programs and teaching materials. Still, female intervention should stress the importance of *transformative* rather than *integrative* approaches to development. With the increasing participation of Moroccan liberal feminists in public policy and with the ongoing interest of researchers in gender studies, there is evidence for some hope toward the re-conceptualisation of literacy as an enabling and empowering process that targets sustainable development of the society as a whole.

What call for such an optimistic conclusion are the recent events that have marked the Moroccan political scene as regards women's increased participation in decision-making positions. Recently, the number of Moroccan women in the parliament, though still low, has risen from three to thirty five in the legislative elections of September, 2002. Their participation in the government consists of three Secretaries of State with one of them at the head of adult literacy issues. These well-timed changes together with the new educational reform, which as dictated by the Charter of Education and Training subscribes to the principles of human rights and centers teaching on the learners' self-esteem, self-reliance and personality development, will hopefully contribute to the creation of a literate nation where the relations between men and women are based on justice and equity. Still, it is wise to bear in mind that it is only when democratic, decentralized and gender-based approaches to literacy are adopted that female literacy could be an investment that pays.

# References


Abu Nasr, J. et al. *Identification and Elimination of Sex Stereotypes in and from School Textbooks: Some Suggestions for Action in the Arab World.* Paris : UNESCO, 1983.

Agnaou, F. "The Strategic Gender Movement in Morocco: Sexism as an Obstacle." A Discussion Paper Presented at The Second Mediterranean Social and Political Research Meeting. Florence, March 21–25, 2001.

Agnaou, F. "EFL Attrition : Features and Compensatory Strategies". *Languages and Linguistics* 3 (1999): 123–43.

Agnaou, F. "Adult Literacy in Morocco: A Language Needs Analysis". *Plurilinguismes* 16 (1998): 89–117.

Akinnaso, F.N. "Policy and Experiment in Mother Tongue Literacy in Nigeria." *International Review of Education* 39, 4 (1993): 255–85.

Alderson, J. C. "Reading in a Foreign Language: A Reading Problem or a Language Problem?" In *Reading in a Foreign Language,* ed. J. C. Alderson, and A.H. Uquhart. New York: Longman, (1984): 1–24.

Alisjahbana, S.T. "The Problem of Minority Languages in the Overall Linguistic Problems of our Time". In *Linguistic Minorities and Literacy,* ed. F. Coulmas. New York: Mouton Publishers (1984): 47–55.

Al-mamlaka al-maRribiyya. Wiza:rat at-tashRi:l wa al-shu'u:n al-ijtima:3iyya. Al-qira:'a li al-jami:3. qira:'a wa h̲isa:b. marh̲alat al-asa:s. kita:b al-da:ris, 1995.

Al-mamlaka al-maRribiyya. Wiza:rat al-tashRi:l wa al-shu'u:n al-ijtima:3iyya. Al-qira:'a li al-jami:3. qira:'a wa hisa:b. marhalat at-takmi:l. kita:b al-da:ris, 1994.

Al-mamlaka al-maRribiyya. Wiza:rat al-tanmiyya al-ijtima:3iyya wa al-tada:mun wa al-tashRi:l wa al-takwi:n al-mihani:. Mudi:riyyat mahw al-ummiya. Al-qira:'iyya wa at-takwi:n al-'asa:si li al-kiba:r. al-juz'u al-awwal, 1998.

Al-mamlaka al-maRribiyya. Wiza:rat al-tanmiyya al-ijtima:3iyya wa al-tada:mun wa al-tashRi:l wa al-takwi:n al-mihani:. Mudi:riyyat mahw al-ummiya. Al-qira:'iyya wa at-takwi:n al-'asa:si li al-kiba:r. al-juz'u al-'ath-tha:ni, 1998.

Al-mamlaka al-maRribiyya. Wiza:rat al-tanmiyya al-ijtima:3iyya wa al-tada:mun wa al-tashRi:l wa al-takwi:n al-mihani: Mudi:riyyat mahw al-ummiya. Al-qira:'iyya wa al-takwi:n al-asa:si li al-kiba:r. al-juz'u al-tha:lith, 1998.

Al-Saadat, K.E. *Adult Vocational Needs in Saudi Arabian Adult Education as* Perceived by Saudi Students in the United States and Educators and Trainers in Saudi Arabia. Unpublished Ph.D. Dissertation. Nebraska: University of Nebraska, 1993.

Arnove, R. L. "Community-based Literacy Educators: Experts and Catalysts for Change." *New Directions for Continuing Education* 42 (1989): 35–42.

Arnove, R.F., and H.J. Graff. *National Literacy Campaigns. Historical and Comparative Perspectives.* New York: Plenum Press, 1987.

Auerbach, E.R. "Literacy and Ideology". *Annual Review of Applied Linguistics* 12 (1992): 71–85.

Auerbach, E. R., and N. Wallerstein. *ESL for Action: Problem-posing at Work.* Reading, MA: Addison-Wesley. 1987.

Bailey, N.et al. "Is There a Natural Sequence in Adult Second Language Learning." *Language Learning* 24, (1974): 235–44.

Bamgbose, A. "Minority Language and Literacy". In *Linguistic Minorities and Literacy,* ed. F.Coulmas. New York: Mouton Publishers, (1984): 21–28.

Bamgbose, A. *Mother Tongue Education: The West African Experience.* London: Holder and Stoughton, 1976.

Beauvoir, S. de. *The Second Sex.* New York: Modern Library, 1949.

Beder, H. "The Stigma of Illiteracy". *Adult Education Quarterly*1, 2 (1991): 67–77.

Belarbi, A. *Situation de la petite fille au Maroc.* Association Marocaine de Soutien à l'Unicef. Unicef. Casablanca: Najah El Jadida, 1991.

Bentolila, F. ed. *Devinettes Berbères.* Paris : CILF, 1986.

Ben-Zeev, S. "The Effect of Spanish-English Bilingualism in Children from Less Privileged Neighborhoods on Cognitive Development and Cognitive Strategy". *Working Papers on Bilingualism* 14 (1977): 38–122.

Bhola, H.S. Adult Literacy for Development in India: An analysis of Policy and Performance. In *National Literacy Campaigns: Historical and Comparative Perspectives,* ed. R.F. Arnove and H.G. Graff. New York: Plenum Press (1987): 245–268.

Bhola, H.S. *Campaigning for Literacy: Eight National Experiences of the Twentieth Century, with a Memorandum to Decision Makers.* Paris: UNESCO, 1984.

Bokamba, E.G. "Language and Literacy in West Africa". In *Prospects Quarterly Review of Education* 28 (1992): 40–74.

Bordia, A., and A. Kaul. "Literacy Efforts in India". In *World Literacy in the Year 2000, Annals, AAPSS* 520 (1992): 151–62.

Bormuth, J.R. "Reading Literacy: Its Definition and Assessment". In *Toward a Literate Society,* ed. J.B. Carroll, and J. Chall. New York: McGraw-Hill, 1975.

Boukhris, F. Danses et Chorégraphies. In *Civilisation Marocaine : Arts et cultures,* ed. M.Sijelmassi, A, Khatibi, E.H. Elmoujahid. Casablanca : Editions Oum Actes Sud/Sindbad. (1996) : 234–37.

Boukous, A., and F. Agnaou. *Alphabétisation et développement durable au Maroc: Réalité et Perspectives.* Rabat : Publications de la Faculté des Lettres et des Sciences Humaines, 2001.

Boukous, A. *Société, langues et cultures au Maroc: Enjeux symboliques,* Rabat: Publications de la Faculté des Lettres et des Sciences Humaines, 1995.

Boukous, A. *Langage et culture populaires au Maroc.* Casablanca: Dar Al-Kitab, 1977.

Bourqia, R., et al. *Femmes, culture et société* au Maghreb: Culture, femmes et famille. Casablanca: Afrique-Orient, 1996.

Bowers, J. "Language Problems and Literacy". In *Language Problems of Developing Nations,* ed. J. Fishman, et al. New York: Wiley (1968): 381–401.

Bowren, F.R., and M.V. Zintz. *Teaching Reading in Adult Basic Education.* Dubuque, Iowa: William C. Brown Company Publishers, 1977.

Brackhaus, B. "Needs Assessment in Adult Education: Its Problems and Prospects". *Adult Education Quarterly* 34 (1984): 233–239.

British Council. *English Language Teaching Profile: the Gambia.* London: English Teaching Information Centre, 1978.

Calvet, L-J. *Linguistique et Colonialisme.* Paris: Payot, 1974.

Carmack, N.A. "Women and Illiteracy: The Need for Gender Specific Programming in Literacy Education". *Adult Basic Education* 2, 3 (1992):176–94.

Carron, G., K et al. *The Functioning and Effects of the Kenya Literacy Program.* IIEP Research Report, 76. Paris: UNESCO, 1989.

Cazden, C. H. et al., *Second Language Acquisition Sequences in Children, Adolescents, and Adults.* Final Report, US Department of Health Education, and Welfare, 1975.

Chacoff, A. "(Bi)literacy and Empowerment: Education for Indigenous Groups in Brazil". *Working Papers in Educational Linguistics,* Philadelphia: Language Education Division of the University of Pennsylvania, (1989): 43–62.

Chambers, F. "A Re-evaluation of Needs Analysis in ESP". *The ESP Journal* 1,1 (1980): 25–33.

Chlebowska, K. *Knowing and Doing. Literacy for Women.* Paris: UNESCO, 1992.

Coombs, P. *The World Crisis in Education: The View from the Eighties.* New York: Oxford University Press, 1985.

Coulmas, F. *Linguistic Minorities and Literacy.* New York: Mouton Publishers, 1984.

Couvert, R. *The Evaluation of Literacy Programmes: A Practical Guide.* Paris: UNESCO, 1979.

Cowan, J.R. *Evaluation of the Local Languages Literacy Project in the Southern Sudan: Third Impact Evaluation Report.* Whashington, DC: Center for Applied Linguistics, 1983.

Cummins, J. "Linguistic Interdependence and the Educational Development of Bilingual Children." *Review of Educational Research* 49 (1979): 222–51.

Dave, R.H. "Designing a System of Evaluation for Literacy and Post-literacy Programs." In *Issues in Planning and Implementing National Literacy Programs,* ed. G. Carron, and A. Bordia. Paris: UNESCO. International Institute for Educational Planning, (1985): 283–303.

De Clerck, M. *Alphabétismes et alphabétisations (Au Pluriel).* Hambourg : Institut de L'UNESCO pour L'Education, 1993.

Dumont, B. *Functional Literacy in Mali: Training for Development*, Paris: UNESCO, 1973.

Ehringhaus, Ch. "Functional Literacy Assessment: Issues of Interpretation". *Adult Education Quarterly* 40, 4 (1990): 87–196.

El Anzoule, A. *Mesure du niveau d'alphabétisation: Comparaison entre la méthode classique et la méthode directe.* Mémoire de Troisième Cycle. Rabat : Institut National des Statistiques et de l'Economie appliquée, 1997.

El Attar, B. *Les Proverbes marocains.* Casablanca : Najah El-Jadida,1992.

El Bindari, A.H. and C. Mulholland "Functional Literacy, Health, and Quality of Life". *World Literacy in The Year 2000. The Annals AAPSS* 520 (1992): 103–20.

El Joundi, M., et al. Nahwa wad3i xutta muwahhada li mahwi al-'ummiya da:xila bulda:ni al-maRrib al-3arabi. Rabat. al-ma3had al-malaki: li al-takwi:ni al-'utur wa al-'in3a:sh al-niswi: wa riyyad al-atfa:l,1998.

Ellis, R. *Understanding Second Language Acquisition.* Oxford: Oxford University Press, 1986.

El-Saadawi, N. "Growing up Female in Egypt". In *Women and the Family in the Middle East*, ed. E. W. Fernea. Austin: University of Texas Press, 1985.

El-Sanbary, N. "Middle East and North Africa." In *Women's Education in Developing Countries: Barriers, Benefits, and Policies*, ed. M. King and M.A. Hill. London: The Johns Hopkins University Press, (1993): 136–74.

Essaknaoui, M. Siyya:sa:t mahw al-'ummiya wa ta3li:m al-kiba:r fi al-'aqta:r as-sa'ira fi: tari:qi an-numuw. Namu:dhaj al-maRrib. Rabat : Kulliyat al-3ulu :m al-qa :nu :niya wa al-iqtisa :diyya wa al-ijtima :3iyya, 1998.

Ezzaki, A. et al. "Language Differences, Preschool Experience, and Literacy Acquisition among Children in Rural Morocco". In *The Future of Literacy in a Changing World*, ed. D.A. Wagner. London: Pergamon (1987):159–73.

Ferguson, Ch. "Contrasting Patterns of Literacy Acquisition in a Multilingual Nation". In *Language Use and Social Change*, ed. W.H. Whitely. London: Oxford University Press, 1971.

Fingeret, A. "The Social and Historical Context of Participatory Literacy Education". *New Directions for Continuing Education* 42 (1989): 5–16.

Freire, P. *Education for Critical Consciousness.* New York: The Seabury Press, 1973.

Freire, P. "The Adult Literacy Process as a Cultural Action for Freedom". *Harvard Educational Review* 40, 2 (1970): 205–25.

Freire, P. *Pedagogy of the Oppressed.* New York: Herder and Herder, 1970.

Galal, S. "Women and Development in the Maghreb Countries". In *Gender and Development in the Arab World, Women's Economic Participation: Patterns and Policies*, ed. London: Zed Books Ltd. (1995): 49–70.

Goody, J. *Literacy in Traditional Societies.* Cambridge: Cambridge University Press, 1968.

Gray, W.S. *The Teaching of Reading and Writing.* Paris: UNESCO, 1956.

Haidar, R. *Gender and Development.* Cairo: The American University Press, 1996.

Hamadache, A., and D. Martin. *Theory and Practice of Literacy Work, Policies, Strategies and Examples.* Paris: UNESCO, 1986.

Heath, S. B. *Ways with Words.* New York: Cambridge University Press, 1983.

Hicks, N.L. *A Note on the Linkage Between Basic Needs and Growth.* Washington, D.C.: World Bank, 1979.

Hill, M.A., and M. King "Education in Developing Countries: An Overview". In *Women's Education in Developing Countries: Barriers, Benefits, and Policies*, ed. M. King, and M. A. Hill. London: The Johns Hopkins University Press (1993): 1–49.

Hoben, S. *The Socio-linguistic Context of Literacy Programs: A review of Non-Formal Adult Literacy Programs.* Report for Agency for International Development, 1980.

Hunter, C., and D. Harman. *Adult Illiteracy in the United States*, New York: McGraw-Hill, 1979.

Hutchinson, T., and A.Waters. *English for Specific Purposes: A Learning Centered Approach.* Cambridge: Cambridge University Press, 1987.

Ibaaquil, L. L'école marocaine et la compétition sociale : Stratégies, aspirations. Rabat: Edition Babil, 1996.

Isenman, P. *The Relationship of Basic Needs to Growth, Income Distribution and Employment: The Case of Sri Lanka.* Washington, D.C.: World Bank, 1978.

Jones, Ph. *Literacy and Basic Education for Adults and Young People: Review of Experience.* Paris: UNESCO, 1990.

Jones, P.W. *International Policies of Third World Education : UNESCO, Literacy Development.* London: Routledge, 1988.

Jouad, H. *Le Calcul inconscient de l'improvisation : Poésie berbère, rythme, nombre et sens.* Paris, Louvain : Peeters. 1995.

Jurmo, P. *Learner Participation Practices in Adult Literacy in the United States.* Unpublished. Doctoral Dissertation. Amherst: University of Massachusetts, 1987.

Kabbaj, M.M. *Al-'ummiya fi al-maRrib: hal min 3ila:j?* al-ma3rifa li al-jami:3, 2. Rabat. Manshura:t Ramsis, 1998.

Kassam, Y. "Who Benefits from Illiteracy ? Literacy and Empowerment". *Prospects*19, 4 (1989): 531–535.

Kazemek, F.E. "Adult Literacy Education: Heading into the 1990s". *Adult Education Quarterly* 41, 1 (1990): 53–62

Kazemek, F. "Women and Adult Literacy: Considering the Other Half of the House".*Lifelong Learning* 11, 4 (1988): 23–25.

Kirsh, I., and A. Jungleblut. *Literacy Profiles of America's Young Adults. Final report of the National Assessment of Educational Progress.* NJ: Princeton, ETS, 1986.

Kirsh, I., and J.T. Guthrie. "The Concept and Measurement of Functional Literacy." *Reading Research Quarterly* 4 (1977): 485–507.

Knowles, M.S. *The Modern Practice of Adult Education.* Chicago: Association Press, 1982.

Kowalski, T.J. *The Organization and Planning of Adult Education.* New York: State University of New York Press, 1988.

Lavy, V., and J. Spratt. Patterns of Incidence and Change in Moroccan Literacy. *Comparative Education* Review 41, 2 (1997): 120–41.

Lavy, V., Spratt, J., and N. Leboutcher. Changing Patterns of Illiteracy in Morocco: Assessment Methods Compared. LSMS Paper 115. Washington, DC: The World Bank, 1995.

Lind, A., and A. Johnston. *Adult Literacy in the Third World: a Review of Objectives and Strategies.* Stockholm: Swedish International Development Agency, 1990.

Lourié, S. "World literacy: Where We Stand Today". *One* Billion Illiterates. A Challenge for our Time. *The UNESCO Courier.* Paris: UNESCO (1990):13–14.

Lytle, S. M. Wolfe. "Contrasting Perspectives on Adult Literacy Education." *Adult Literacy Education: Program Evaluation and Assessment.* Columbus, Ohio: ERIC (1989): 5–17.

Maamouri, M. "Arabic Diglossia and its Impact on the Quality of Education in the Arab Region." A Discussion Paper Prepared for the World Bank at The Mediterranean Development Forum, Marrakesh, 1998.

Maddi, L. *Ta3li:m al-kiba:r wa maḇw al-'ummiya. Muqa:raba di:da:kti:kiyya.* Rabat: manshu:ra:t majallat 3ulu:m al-tarbiyya, 2000.

Manzoor, A. "Literacy in a Larger Context". In *World Literacy in The Year 2000. The Annals of AASS* 520 (1992): 32–35.

M'Bow, A. *A Moral Imperative.* UNESCO Courier 37, 2 (1984): 4–5.

Mekyassi, L. *Contribution à l'évaluation des actions d'alphabétisation : Cas de l'ORMVA du Tadla.* Thèse de Troisième Cycle non publiée. Meknès : Ecole Nationale d'Agriculture, 1999.

Mernissi, F. *Beyond the Veil: Male-female Dynamics in Modern Muslim Society.* Bloomington: Indiana University Press, 1987.

Mernissi, F. et al. *Femmes et violences.* Rabat: El Maarif Al Jadida, 1993.

Mezirow, J. "Perspective Transformation. " *Adult Education* 28, 2 (1978): 100–10.

Michel. A. *Down with Stereotypes! Eliminating Sexism from Children's Literature and School Textbooks.* Paris: UNESCO, 1986.

Mikulecky, L. "Job literacy: the Relationship between School Preparation and Workplace Actuality". *Reading Research Quarterly*17 (1982): 400–19.

Moâtassime, A. "Le Bilinguisme sauvage: Blocage linguistique, sous-développement et coopération hypothétique. L'exemple maghrébin. Cas du Maroc". *Tiers-Monde, Education et Développement*15 (1974) : 619–70.

Molyneux, M. "Mobilization without Emancipation? Women's Interests, the State and Revolution in Nicaragua," *Feminist Studies* 11, 2 (1987).

Mouhcine, Kh. *Le conte berbère marocain.* Thèse pour le Doctorat d'Etat, non publiée. Toulouse : Université Toulouse-le-Mirail, 1992.

Munby, J. *Communicative Syllabus Design.* Cambridge: Cambridge University Press, 1978.

Mwiria,K. "Kenyan Women Adult Literacy Learners: Why Their Motivation is Difficult to sustain". *International Review of Education* 39, 3 (1993): 183–192.

Naamane-Guessous, S. *Au-delà de toute pudeur.* Casablanca : Eddif, 1988.

Newman, A. and Beverstock, C. *Adult Literacy: Contexts and Challenges.* Bloomington, Indiana: International Reading Association, 1990.

Okedara, J.T., and C.A.Okedara. "Mother Tongue Literacy in Nigeria". *World Literacy in The Year 2000. The Annals, AAPSS* 520 (1992): 91–102.

Okezie, J.A. "Language Planning and Literacy Development". In *Patterns in Language, Culture and Society: Sub-Saharian Africa,* ed. R. Herbert *Working Papers in Linguistics* 19 (1975): 27–36.

Ouane, A. "Functional Literacy: North-South Perspectives". In *World Literacy in The Year 2000, The Annals, AAPS* 520 (1992): 66–75.

Oxenham, J. *Literacy: Writing, Reading and Social Organization.* London: Routledge, 1980.

Packwood, T, and T. Whitaker. *Needs Assessment in Post-16 Education.* Philadelphia: The Falmer Press, 1988.

Ramdas, L. "Women and Literacy: A Quest for Justice." *Prospects* XIX, 4 (1989): 519–30.

Reder, S.M. "Comparative Aspects of Functional Literacy Development: Three Ethnic American Communities." In *The Future of Literacy in a Changing World,* ed. D.A. Wagner. New York: Pergamon, (1987): 250–269.

Royaume du Maroc. Commission Spéciale Education-Formation. *Charte Nationale de l'Education et Formation.* Rabat, 1999.

Royaume du Maroc. Direction de la Lutte Contre l'Analphabétisme. *Bilan des Programmes d'Alphabétisation. Exercice 1998/1999.* Rabat: Direction de la Lutte Contre l'Analphabétisme, 1999.

Royaume du Maroc. Direction de la Lutte Contre l'Analphabétisme. *Séminaire de Formation au Profit des Coordonnateurs d'Alphabétisation.* Rabat: Direction de la Lutte contre l'Analphabétisme, 1997.

Royaume du Maroc. Direction de la Statistique. *Résultats de l'Enquête Nationale sur le Budget-Temps des Femmes. (Période : Juin 1997–Juin 1998).* Rabat : Direction de la Statistique, 1998.

Royaume du Maroc. Secrétariat d'Etat Chargé de la Protection Sociale, de la Famille et de l'Enfance. *Femme Marocaine en Chiffres.* Rabat : Ministère de la Santé, 1999.

Ruiter, J.J. de. " Position of Moroccan Berberophone and Arabophone Pupils between Arabic and French." *Cahiers du Centre d'Etudes sur les Mouvements Migratoires Maghrébins* 5, Oujda: Université Mohammed 1er, (1997) : 139–62.

Ruiter, J.J. de. " Quelle(s) langue(s) enseigner dans l'enseignement de la langue d'origine (ELO) aux enfants marocains aux Pays-Bas? " In *Langues du Maroc : Aspects linguistiques dans un contexte minoritaire,* ed. P.Bos. Tilburg : Tilburg University Press. 1995

Ruiter, J.J. de. "Enseignement de la langue maternelle." In *L'Annuaire de l'Emigration Marocaine,* ed. K. Basfao, and H. Taarji. Rabat: Ministère des Marocains à l'étranger. (1994): 514–18

Ruiter, J.J. de. "La langue berbère aux Pays-Bas et la deuxième génération." In *Le Maroc et la Hollande. Actes de la Deuxième Rencontre Universitaire.* Rabat : Publications de la Faculté des Lettres (1990) : 307–15.

Ryan, J. "Literacy Research, Policy and Practice: The Elusive Triangle." In *World Literacy in The Year 2000. The Annals, AAPSS* 520 (1993): 36–41.

Sadiqi, F. "Aspects of Moroccan Feminism." In *Feminist Movements : Origins and Orientations,* ed. F. Sadiqi, et al. Fès: Publications de la Faculté des Lettres. Dahr El Mehraz (2000): 195–214.

Sadiqi, F. "The Language of Women in the City of Fès, Morocco." *International Journal of the Sociology of the Language* 112 (1995): 63–79.

Saib, J. "Apprentissage dans une langue non maternelle et réussite scolaire: le cas d'élèves berbères en milieu rural. " *Awal* 12 (1995): 67–87.

Saidi, R. *The Teaching of Modern Standard Arabic to Moroccan Pupils in Elementary Schools in the Netherlands: A Study on Proficiency , Status and Input.* A published Ph.D. Dissertation. Tilburg: Katholieke Universiteit Brabant, 2001.

Scribner, S. "Literacy in Three Metaphors." In *Perspectives on Literacy,* ed. E. Kintgen, et al. Carbondale and Edwardsville: Southern Illinois University Press, (1988): 57–70.

Scribner, S., and M. Cole. *The Psychology of Literacy.* Cambridge: Harvard University Press, 1981.

Shaw, W.D. *The Choice of a Language for Adult Literacy Programs: A Guide for Decision Makers.* Unpublished Ph.D. Dissertation. Amherst: U Mass University, 1983.

Shrivastava, O. "What Language for Literacy?" . *Development Communication Report* 30(1980): 7–11.

Sjostrom, R, and M. Sjostrom. *Literacy Schools in a Rural Society: A Study of Yemissrach Dimts Literacy Campaign in Ethiopia.* Uppsala: Scandinavian Institute of African Studies, 1977.

Skutnabb-Kangas, T., and P. Toukomaa. *Teaching Migrant Children's Mother Tongue and Learning the Language of Host Country in the Context of the Socio-Cultural Situation of the Migrant Family.* Helsinki: Finnish National Commission for UNESCO, 1976.

Spencer, J. "Language and Independence." In *Language in Africa,* ed. J. Spencer. London: Cambridge University Press (1963): 25–39.

Spratt, J.E. "Women and Literacy in Morocco." In *World Literacy in The Year 2000. The Annals, AAPSS* 520 (1992): 121–132.

Stedman, L., and C. Kaestle. "Literacy and Reading Performance in the United States from 1880 to the Present." In *Literacy in the United States: Readers and Reading since 1880,* ed. C. Kaestle et al. New Haven: Yale University Press (1991): 75–128.

Stercq, C. *Literacy, Socialisation and Employment.* UNESCO Institute for Education. London: Jessica Kingsley Publishers Ltd.,1993.

Stitch, T.G. *Reading for Working: a Functional Literacy Anthology.* Alexandria, VA: Human Resources Research Organization, 1975.

Srivastava, R.N. "Consequences of Initiating Literacy in a Second Language." In *Linguistic Minorities and Literacy,* ed. F. Coulmas. New York: Mouton Publishers (1984): 29–38.

Street, B.V. *Literacy in Theory and Practice.* London: Cambridge University Press,1985.

Stromquist, N.P. *The Theoretical and Practical Bases for Empowerment.* UNESCO Institute for Education. International Seminar on Women's Education and Empowerment, 1995.

Stromquist, N.P. "Women and Literacy: Promises and Constraints." In *World Literacy in The Year 2000. The Annals, AAPSS* 520 (1992): 54–65.

Stromquist, N.P. "Women and Illiteracy : the Interplay of Gendered Subordination and Poverty". *Comparative Education Review* 34 (1990): 95–111.

Stromquist, N.P. "Empowering Women through Education: Lessons from International Cooperation". Adult Education and Development, N°28. 1987.

Tomori, S.H.O., and J.T. Okedara. *A Comparative Study of the Learning of English as a Second Language by Literate and Illiterate Tobacco Farmers of Oyo North District, Western State, Nigeria.* Ibadan: University of Ibadan, 1971.

UNESCO. *World Education Report.* Paris: UNESCO, 1998.

UNESCO. *World Education Report.* Paris: UNESCO, 1993.

UNESCO *A Literate World.* Paris: International Bureau of Education. UNESCO, 1991.

UNESCO *Final Report on the World Conference on Education for All: Meeting Basic Learning Needs. Jomtien, Thailand.* Paris: UNESCO, 1990.

UNESCO. (1976). *Seminar on the Problems of Teaching the Mother Tongue in Africa.* Dakar: BREDA.

UNESCO. *The Use of Vernacular Languages in Education.* Paris: UNESCO, 1953.

UNITED NATIONS. *National Household Survey Capabilities Program: Measuring Literacy Through Household Surveys.* New York: United Nations, 1989.

USAID. *Promoting Education for Girls in Nepal.* CDIE Impact Evolution 5. Washington, D.C: USAID, 1998.

Vygotsky, L. *Thought and Language.* Boston: M.L.T. Press, 1962.

Wagner, D.A. *Literacy, Culture, and Development: Becoming Literate in Morocco.* New York: Cambridge University Press, 1993.

Wagner, D.A. "World Literacy: Research and Policy in the EFA Decade." In *World Literacy in The Year 2000. The Annals, AAPSS* 520 (1992): 12–26.

Wagner, D.A. et al. "Does Learning to Read in a Second Language Always Put the Child at a Disadvantage? Some Counter-Evidence from Morocco." *Applied Psycholinguistics* 10 (1989): 31–48.

Wagner, D.A., and J.E. Spratt. "Cognitive Consequences of Contrasting Pedagogies: The Effect of Quranic preschooling in Morocco." *Child Development* 58, 5 (1987):1207–19.

Walsh, C. *Literacy as Praxis: Culture, Language and Pedagogy.* Norwood, New Jersey: Ablex, 1991.

Widdowson, H.G.. *Learning Purpose and Language Use.* Oxford: Oxford University Press, 1983.

Zahn, J. C. "Differences Between Adults and Youth Affecting Learning." In *Issues and Trends in Adult Basic Education: Focus on Reading,* ed. F. Karnes et al. University Press of Mississippi (1980): 22–34.

Ziegahn, L. "The Formation of Literacy perspective." In *Adult learning in the Community,* ed. R. Fellenz, and G. Conti. Bozeman, Montana: Center for Adult Learning Research (1990): 1–31.

# Index

For Product Safety Concerns and Information please contact our EU representative GPSR@taylorandfrancis.com
Taylor & Francis Verlag GmbH, Kaufingerstraße 24, 80331 München, Germany

www.ingramcontent.com/pod-product-compliance
Ingram Content Group UK Ltd.
Pitfield, Milton Keynes, MK11 3LW, UK
UKHW021959180926
475701UK00003B/104
* 9 7 8 0 4 1 5 6 4 7 9 3 9 *